The Victorian Ghost Hunter's Casebook

The Victorian Ghost Hunter's Casebook

Edited by
TIM PRASIL

BROM BONES BOOKS

The front cover illustration, captioned "Haunted," is from James John Hissey's *A Holiday on the Road: An Artist's Wanderings in Kent, Sussex, and Surrey* (Richard Bentley & Son, 1887).

ISBN-10: 1-948084-07-4
ISBN-13: 978-1-948084-07-9

DEDICATION

This book is dedicated to the kind spirits
in the Big Séance parlor.
As Catherine Crowe says in Case 2:
"I should not object to seeing a ghost
in such agreeable society."

CONTENTS

INTRODUCTION

Tim Prasil

What makes ghosts and the Victorian era (1837-1901) such fitting companions? It might be the elegant architecture of the houses—those fancy cornices and cupolas—that make them seem especially suitable for haunting. It might be that some of the greatest supernatural stories ever written—from Charles Dickens' *A Christmas Carol* (1843) to Bram Stoker's *Dracula* (1897)—are steeped in Victorian customs, costumes, and cultural concerns. Is it because photography arose during this period and those often-expressionless faces have crept into our twenty-first century consciousness as spectral visages of people long dead? Or was it all simply the mental effects of gas leaking from the lights?[1]

There's probably a mixture of reasons why a haze of ghostliness lingers around the Victorians, but among that blend is their revitalization of the debate over whether or not ghosts are real. The 1800s *began* with widespread agreement among intellectuals and the press that belief in spectral visitations was disappearing as humanity progressed into the new century. Medical men seemed to be at the frontline. In 1805, Dr. John Alderson presented a paper clarifying how ghostly encounters "owe their origin entirely to a disordered state of bodily organs" and how "great mental anxiety, inordinate ambition, and guilt, may produce similar effects." In 1813, Dr. John Ferriar wrote a book to explain how historic accounts of ghosts and related phenomena can be explained "from the known laws of animal economy, independent of supernatural causes." In another book, published in 1825, Dr. Samuel Hibbert turned away from physiology and toward psychology and sociology, arguing that "apparitions are nothing more than ideas, or recollected images of the mind, which have been rendered more vivid than actual impressions" and that these false impressions are rooted in "the

---

[1] Ghosts are traced to furnace gas in Franz Schneider, Jr.'s "An Investigation of 'Haunted' House," *Science,* 37.958 (May 9, 1913), pp. 711-712.

various systems of superstition, which for ages have possessed the minds of the vulgar."[2]

But medical science wasn't alone in its efforts to launch the nineteenth century without the heavy burden of earlier centuries' superstitions. Joseph Taylor compiled an anthology of tales that tantalized readers with spooky scenes but then corrected their false assumptions by unveiling the *natural* explanations behind events that had seemed otherworldly. The title page of this 1814 volume says it all: "*APPARITIONS; or, The Mystery of Ghosts, Hobgoblins, and Haunted Houses, Developed.* Being a Collection of ENTERTAINING STORIES, Founded on Fact; And selected for the purpose of ERADICATING THOSE RIDICULOUS FEARS, Which The Ignorant, the Weak, and the Superstitious, Are but too apt to encourage, FOR WANT OF PROPERLY EXAMINING INTO THE CAUSES OF SUCH ABSURD IMPOSITIONS." Taylor includes a tale told by the Mareschal de Saxe, and since it involves a ghost hunter of sorts, it's among the most relevant to the book now in your hands. While returning to Dresden, the Mareschal came upon a small village in the chilly shadow of a haunted castle. The villagers insisted that a phantom had been heard and seen at the castle, and the brave Mareschal announced he would spend the night there to confront the ghost. That night, the Mareschal was awoken by a tall figure in armor. Upon being threatened by the Mareschal's pistols and sword, the figure was then joined by *others!* But they turned out to be living men, who confessed that they were a band of counterfeiters and were ensuring their privacy at the castle by pretending to be ghosts. The coiners gave the Marseschal the option of keeping their secret—or being killed. He opted for the former.[3]

---

[2] John Alderson's speech was published in *The Edinburgh Medical and Surgical Journal* 6.23 (July, 1810) pp. 287-96. Alderson then revised the paper for *An Essay on Apparitions, in which Their Appearance Is Accounted for by Causes Wholly Independent of Preternatural Agency* (Longman, et al., 1823). John Ferriar, *An Essay towards a Theory of Apparitions* (Printed for Cadell and Davies by J. and J. Haddock, 1813) p. 14. Samuel Hibbert, *Sketches of the Philosophy of Apparitions; or, An Attempt to Trace Such Illusions to Their Physical Causes* (Oliver & Boyd/Geo. B. Whittaker, 1825) p. v.

[3] Joseph Taylor, *Apparitions; or, The Mystery of Ghost, Hobgoblins, and Haunted Houses Developed* (Printed for Lackington, Allen, and Co., 1815) pp. 103-12. The tales follow the same pattern of some key Gothic novels, from Ann Radcliffe's *The Mysteries of Udolpho* (1794) to Charlotte Brontë's *Jane Eyre* (1847), in concluding with a natural explanation for what had seemed to be ghostly events.

The tale's lesson is obvious: ghosts can be as phony as counterfeit money.

Despite this general movement to abolish the belief in ghosts, it's nearly impossible to keep people from sharing ghost stories. Writers wanting to do so in print prefaced their tales with comments on the pervasive skepticism of the era. In an 1824 essay titled "On Ghosts," for example, Mary Shelley, author of *Frankenstein* (1818), notes the passing of romantic and fantastical beliefs, ending with a nod to Shakespeare:

> What has become of enchantresses with their palaces of crystal and dungeons of palpable darkness? What of fairies and their wands? What of witches and their familiars? and, last, what of ghosts, with beckoning hands and fleeting shapes, which quelled the soldier's brave heart, and made the murderer disclose to the astonished noon the veiled work of midnight? These which were realities to our fore-fathers, in our wiser age—
>
> —Characterless are grated
> To dusty nothing.

Shelley was not alone. The sentiment is echoed by a writer identified only as "Anslem" in "A Chapter on Ghosts," published in 1830: "The belief in ghosts and hobgoblins, in fact, is the basis and key-stone of all superstition; and though 'the march of intellect' has of late years done away a good deal with the prejudices of the 'times of old,' yet it still lurks, and, probably, will ever continue to do so, with the ignorant and vulgar of all countries."[4] Curiously, both of these pre-Victorian writers use these comments on outmoded beliefs to then recount allegedly true ghostly encounters, prompting readers to retain an open mind and maybe even a sense of wonder when it comes to the reality of ghosts.

Around 1840, the tide began to turn back toward—if not *believing* in ghosts—then, at least, considering the *possibility* that they might be real, and for some reason, Cambridge University rode the crest of the first waves. In the *Cambridge University Magazine*,

---

[4] Mary Shelley, "On Ghosts," *London Magazine* 9 (March, 1824) p. 253. The Shakespeare quotation is from *Troilus and Cressida* (1602). Anslem, "A Chapter on Ghosts," *The Pocket* 2.1 (July, 1830) p. 29. This article is continued in "Another Chapter on Ghosts," *The Pocket* 2.2 (Aug., 1830) pp. 132-38.

an article written by someone identified only as "ΨYXH" argues in *favor* of the reality of ghosts. Like Shelley and "Anslem," the writer opens by acknowledging how resistant readers will be to such a thesis "in these days of universal incredulity and skepticism." Over the course of the essay, he supports his case by citing Scripture, the ancient philosophers, and the power that a "good ghost story" has to inspire the "most incredulous" to rethink their convictions. The primary argument, though, comes in the form of inductive reasoning, specifically testing two premises: 1) there is no proof *against* the reality of supernatural visitation and 2) "incontrovertible human testimony" is in *favor* of that reality. This is accompanied by rebuttal of the primary arguments against ghosts. For instance, as if implying Taylor's book of rationalized ghost stories, the writer contends that

> though ninety-nine stories may be resolved into cases of false perception, mere imagination, or imposture—and we have no doubt that the great majority of them may—still, if the hundredth should be absolutely incapable of any such solution, it is sufficient to prove the existence of apparitions; and, consequently, that the attempt to explain away some stories only, without disproving all, must ever be unsatisfactory.[5]

Given the academic associations of the journal in which it appears and the staunch opposition the writer admits to facing, the article is historically significant in its boldness.

It's conceivable that this article might have some relation with a development at Cambridge University occurring about a decade later. In 1851, fellows at that institution's Trinity College met to discuss and investigate ghosts and similar phenomena. The group was known as the Ghostlie Guild—or, perhaps, the Cambridge Association for Spiritual Inquiry—but it is remembered as the Ghost Club, and by 1862, it had become a formal organization. According to a circular describing the club and its goals, the focus was on accumulating "an extensive collection of authenticated cases of supposed 'supernatural' agency." Beyond the experiences of members themselves, the club would seek "written communi-

---

[5] "A Chapter on Ghosts," *Cambridge University Magazine* 1.2 (May, 1839) pp. 145, 146, 148.

cations, with full details of persons, times, and places."[6] There is no mention in this document of performing any field work, but even as "armchair ghost hunters," the Ghost Club set a precedent for paranormal research organizations to come.

Probably the best-known organization to follow in the path of the Ghost Club is the Society for Psychical Research (SPR), founded in 1882. Both groups were spurred by a curiosity about traditional hauntings along with spiritualist séances, mesmerism/hypnotism, and clairvoyance. However, there was a fundamental difference between the Ghost Club and the SPR. The name at the end of that circular issued by the former is Brooke Foss Westcott (1825-1901), a theologian who would go on to become Cambridge's Regius Professorship of Divinity and, later, the Bishop of Durham. Other founding Ghost Club members included Fenton J. A. Hort (1828-1892), another Biblical scholar and minister; and Edward White Benson (1829-1896), who became the Archbishop of Canterbury. Though the SPR looked again to Cambridge University to find its first President, that man was Henry Sidgwick, known primarily for his work in economics. Other prominent members brought a distinctively scientific, not religious, view to the table: William F. Barrett and Oliver Lodge were physicists, William Crookes was a chemist, and Edmund Gurney and William James came from Psychology. Both groups included members with perspectives other than strictly religious or scientific, of course—Charles Dickens was a member of the Ghost Club, for example, and Arthur Conan Doyle joined SPR—but one senses that the conversations at the two organizations' meetings would have reflected those fundamental differences.

We can use this distinction as a rough guide to the evolution of the chronicles presented in this book. Case 1 is taken from the Reverend Frederick George Lee's *Glimpses in the Twilight: Being Various Notes, Records, and Examples of the Supernatural* (1885), which opens with a lament about the sorry condition of England's

---

[6] Arthur Wescott uses the name "Ghostlie Guild" in a biography of his father, *Life and Letters of Brooke Foss Wescott* (Vol. 1, Macmillan, 1903) p. 117, and Epes Sargent uses both "The Cambridge Association for Spiritual Inquiry" and "The Ghost Club" in *Planchette; or, The Despair of Science* (Roberts Brothers, 1869) p. 203. "Circular of a Society Instituted by the Members of the University of Cambridge, England, for the Purpose of Investigating Phenomena Popularly Called Supernatural" is reprinted in Appendix A of Robert Dale Owen's *Footfalls on the Boundary of Another World* (J.B. Lippincott, 1860) pp. 514-16.

soul: "Of late years it cannot but have been noted by the thoughtful and observant, that the Christian Religion has been too commonly and too generally disregarded." He goes on to explain how things have become so irreligious, and generous shares of the blame go to "what some American pointedly termed 'a firm faith in the almighty dollar'" as well as to certain ideas propounded by Charles Darwin regarding the origin of the humans species.[7] Lee, it becomes clear, is presenting his collected accounts of supernatural interventions into the natural world to counteract this trend toward secularization. Ghost hunters, then, were seeking empirical evidence—not just of ghosts—but of an entire spirit existence.

Nonetheless, as the Victorian era proceeded, science gradually took over ghost hunting. No doubt, some scientists were also looking for confirmation of their spiritual faith, but others were testing the boundaries of observable existence or, at least, looking for a reason why ghosts have such a recurrent place in human history. Regardless of their motives, this new generation of scientists no longer echoed the sweeping skepticism of Drs. Alderson, Ferrier, and Hibbert. In its place, they brought a cautious, if not clinical, curiosity to the topic. This book's best representative of this movement is Frank Podmore, whose name appears in Cases 7, 8, and 9.

These scientists were rising to a challenge made around mid-century, and the chief instigator was popular novelist Catherine Crowe. Her compilation of "true" supernatural events, *The Night-Side of Nature* (1848) is a book that would have had a prized place on the bookshelf of any proper Victorian ghost hunter and by almost anyone else interested in the supernatural. In her Introduction, Crowe presents ghosts as more a concern of science than religion by first praising German intellectuals for "thinking independently and courageously" and for "promulgating the opinions they have been led to form, however new, strange, heterodox, or even absurd, they may appear to others." She then asserts: "But here, in Britain, our critics and colleges are in such haste to strangle and put down every new discovery that does not emanate from themselves, or which is not a fulfilling of the ideas of the day. . . ." British intellectuals routinely reject new ideas, Crowe contends, adding:

---

[7] Frederick George Lee, *Glimpses in the Twilight* (William Blackwood and Sons, 1885) pp. 3, 14-19.

And one of the evils of this hasty and precipitate opposition is, that the passions and interests of the opposers become involved in the dispute: instead of investigators, they become partisans; having declared against it at the outset, it is important to their petty interests that the thing shall not be true; and they determine that it *shall* not, if they can help it.

For many traditional Victorian readers, these strong words from a "woman novelist" might have been easily shrugged off if they hadn't been stated in a book that garnered such extensive popularity.[8]

A few pages later, Crowe positions ghosts firmly within the realm of science. She explains that the subjects covered in her book—prophetic dreams, presentiments, and second-sight along with apparitions—will *not* be treated as supernatural phenomena. Crowe says that, "on the contrary, I am persuaded that the time will come, when they will be reduced strictly within the bounds of science. It was the tendency of the last age to reject and *deny* everything they did not understand; I hope it is the growing tendency of the present one to *examine* what we do not understand."[9] Here, then, was Crowe's challenge: that scientists boldly go into new fields, new disciplines and, at least, *explore* those widespread human experiences with what had traditionally been deemed "supernatural."

Crowe's book relies quite a bit on work done by those German scientists she had praised. She knew the language well enough to have earlier translated *The Seeress of Provorst*, by Justinus Kerner. The first part of this book is Dr. Kerner's chronicle of his treatment of a "ghost-seer" and clairvoyant named Frederica Hauffe. The second part reviews ghosts more generally. In addition to Kerner's writings, *Night-Side* includes references to similar work done by Johann Heinrich Jung-Stilling, Karl August von Eschenmayer, and others. Presumably, these were the scientists Edwin Paxton Hood had in mind when declaring that, after its strong skepticism at the

---

[8] Catherine Crowe's *The Night-Side of Nature; or, Ghosts and Ghost Seers* (T.C. Newby, 1848) pp. 8-9. In the Victorian era, subsequent editions of this popular book are: T.C. Newby, 1849; G. Routledge, 1852; a "New Edition" from G. Routledge, 1857; G. Routledge, 1866; and G. Routledge, 1882. Meanwhile, American editions are: J.S. Redfield, 1850; Redfield, 1853; W.J. Widdleton, 1868; and another "New Edition" from Henry T. Coates, 1901. These are just the editions I've confirmed with online scans. More may certainly exist.

[9] Crowe, p. 17-18.

start of the century, science was leading us back to ghosts: "Who could have thought that these men of the electric rod and the battery, the magnet and the retort, would have kindled for humanity a new torch of belief, and thrown a light from a new lamp into the world of spirits? We wait in anxiety and in awe for the results of future investigations."[10] Here, along with a call for action aimed at Victorian scientists, we see the roots of 21st-century ghost hunters with their EMF meters, EVP recorders, and night-vision equipment.

While some British scientists rose to the challenge issued by the likes of Crowe and Hood, this book illustrates how Victorian ghost hunting was not limited to those on a specifically scientific mission—*or* those on a specifically religious one. Authors renowned for their fiction, travel writers, journalists, and even a few self-proclaimed psychics chronicled their investigations of haunted sites. They were part of a wave of ghost hunters, but they were hardly the first. In fact, some Victorians would have known about Athenodorus, a philosopher from ancient Rome. According to legend, Athenodorus learned of a house with a reputation for being haunted and rented the place to investigate it. Pretty quickly, he observed the ghost, followed it to where it disappeared into the ground, marked the spot, and afterwards led an effort to dig there. A buried skeleton in chains was discovered, and when the bones were re-interred elsewhere with far greater respect and ceremony, the house was cleansed of its ghost.[11]

Perhaps the next notable pre-Victorian ghost hunter is Joseph Glanvill, who investigated ghostly manifestations at the house of John Mompesson sometime around the 1660s. The case, as he describes it in *Saducismus Triumphatus,* bore signs of possible witchcraft—or maybe poltergeist activity—and the culprit behind it became known as "The Drummer of Tedworth" once it became a

---

[10] Edwin Paxton Hood, *Dream Land and Ghost Land: Visits and Wanderings There in the Nineteenth Century* (Partridge and Oakley, 1852) p. 30. Crowe's translation of Kerner's book is titled *The Seeress of Prevorst* (J.C. Moore, 1845).

[11] Victorian readers might have become familiar with the story from its original source, Pliny the Younger, translated by Alfred Church and W.J. Brodribb for *Pliny's Letters* (William Blackwood and Sons, 1872) pp. 163-64—or from articles about specters, such as Edwin Sharpe Grew's "Famous Ghosts," *Ludgate Monthly* 4 (July, 1897) pp. 257-58.

standard piece of ghostlore in Victorian publications. Roughly contemporary with Glanvill were two Cornish vicars, whose legendary exploits appeared in Victorian print. The Reverend John Rudall was able to put to rest the suffering spirit of Dorothy Dingley, a.k.a. the Botathen ghost, while the Reverend Richard Dodge exerted his ghost-busting skill in Talland to expel a vengeful phantom who appeared dressed in black and driving a carriage pulled by headless horses.[12]

Yet another contemporary of Glanvill had a very different reputation as a ghost hunter. This is Antoinette du Ligier de la Garde Deshoulières, a fearless woman who—upon hearing that the castle in which she was guest had a haunted room—insisted on sleeping in it. That night, she discovered the horrible manifestations could all be attributed to a large, affectionate dog. The woman was real, but her ghost hunt is probably a fable, one often ending with a lesson about the folly of superstition. Not surprisingly, many of the print sources of it appear in those early decades of the 1800s. However, the tale did survive long enough to appear in Sarah Josepha Hale's *Woman's Record; or, Sketches of All Distinguished Women,* published in 1853.[13]

Two more pre-Victorian ghost hunters—both debunkers like Deshoulières—would have been familiar enough to serve as

---

[12] Glanvill's own account of his investigation can be found in the second part of *Saducismus Triumphatus: or, Full and Plain Evidence Concerning Witches and Apparitions* (third edition, printed for A.L. and sold by Roger Tuckyr, at the Golden Leg, 1700) pp. 49-62. Victorian retellings of this ghost hunt are many, but include J.E. Smith's "The Drummer of Tedworth," *Legends and Miracles and Other Curious Stories of Human Nature* (B.D. Cousins, 1837) pp. 41-47 and the anonymous "A Third Evening with the Witchfinders," *Dublin University Magazine* 31.184 (April, 1848) pp. 440-44. The legends of Rudall and Dodge can also be found in various sources, but most readers probably would have learned about the former from Robert Stephen Hawker's "The Botathen Ghost," *All the Year Round* 17.421 (May 18, 1867) pp. 501-04, and the latter from Thomas Q. Couch's "The Spectral Coach," which first appeared in Robert Hunt's *Popular Romances of the West of England; or, The Drolls, Traditions, and Superstitions of Old Cornwall* (John Camden Hotten, 1865) pp. 252-60.

[13] The pre-Victorian sources are the anonymous "Madame Deshoulieres, the French Poetess," *The Literary Gazette* 1.46 (Dec. 6, 1817) pp. 363-64; the anonymous "The Ghost Discovered," *The Repository of Arts, Literature, Fashions, Manufactures, &c.* 5.25 (Jan. 1, 1818) pp. 38-40; and Joseph Clinton Robertson and Thomas Byerley (as Shoto and Reuben Percy), *The Percy Anecdotes* (printed for T. Boys, 1820) pp. 136-40. The Victorian source is the "Deshoulières, Antoinette du Ligier de la Garde" article in Sarah Josepha Hale's *Woman's Record; or, Sketches of All Distinguished Women* (Sampson Low, Son, 1853) pp. 288-89.

cautionary examples during Victoria's reign. The first was author and lexicographer Samuel Johnson, who joined a team of ghost hunters to investigate the famous Cock Lane haunting of 1762. The case is too complicated to detail here, but it involved twelve-year-old Elizabeth Parsons, who claimed to have encountered a ghost. Her father discovered that, with Elizabeth acting as a medium, the ghost could communicate through knocking. In this way, the spirit's business became clear: she had returned from the Great Beyond to accuse William Kent of *poisoning* her. News of these posthumous accusations spread quickly, and Johnson got involved. The assembled ghost hunters' probe led to the conclusion that, first, Elizabeth's father had a grudge against Kent and, second, the girl had "some art of making or counterfeiting particular noise, and that there is no agency of any higher cause."[14] One would think, then, that Johnson leaned toward skepticism when it came to ghosts, wouldn't one?

Unfortunately, some would remember him differently. A character named Imlac in Johnson's novel *Rasselas* (1756) argues:

> There is no people, rude or learned, among whom apparitions of the dead are not related and believed. This opinion, which perhaps prevails as far as human nature is diffused, could become universal only by its truth; those that never heard of one another would not have agreed in a tale which nothing but experience can make credible.

In his authoritative *The Life of Samuel Johnson, LL.D.* (1791), James Boswell quotes this passage as evidence of how well the author could feign an argument in favor of ghosts, but he cautions that "it is a mistake to suppose that he himself ever positively held" the same view. Nonetheless, many subsequent writers have taken Imlac's statement to mirror the author's own view. In *Accredited Ghost Stories* (1823), for instance, T.M. Jarvis quotes this passage and declares that it should be seen "as conveying as the opinions of Johnson." Even Herman Melville's *Moby Dick* (1851) includes the line: "There are other ghosts than the Cock-Lane one, and far

---

[14] Samuel Johnson, *Gentlemen's Magazine* 32 (Feb., 1762) p. 81. Johnson's authorship is confirmed in James Boswell, *Life of Johnson*, Vol. 1 (printed by Henry Baldwin for Charles Dilly, 1791) p. 220.

deeper men than Doctor Johnson who believe in them." Returning to Boswell's biography, we find that—though Johnson *did* retell ghost stories he had heard from people he trusted—the closest pronouncement he made regarding the subject was noncommittal: "All argument is against it; but all belief is for it."[15] The lesson here is that even a debunker might be pegged as a *believer* by simply daring to go ghost hunting.

Shortly after the 1700s became the 1800s, another debunker appeared, and he illustrated a far more dangerous side of ghost hunting. In the final months of 1803, the Hammersmith district of London was plagued by a ghost—or someone dressed up like one. One incident involved Thomas Groom, who had been passing through the churchyard and, in his words, "some person came from behind a tomb-stone . . . and caught me fast by the throat with both hands, and held me fast." Thanks to a nearby companion, Groom escaped. He had seen nothing, but had hit what felt to him like "a great coat."[16] Other frightening encounters were reported by the newspapers, and after several weeks of this, the braver locals decided to take action.

Among these ghost hunters looking to pull the sheet off the cruel prankster was Francis Smith. With a pistol at the ready, he conducted surveillance in Black Lion Lane. Suddenly, he spotted a figure dressed in white. He shouted, "Damn you, who or what are you?" And his gun fired! The white figure was not a ghost, though. It wasn't even someone masquerading as a ghost. Instead, it was Thomas Millford, a tradesman whose work with plaster accounted for his white, smock-like apparel. Tragically, Smith's bullet penetrated Millford's jaw and fatally shattered his spine. Smith quickly confessed his terrible mistake, was sentenced to death for willful murder, but was pardoned and served only one year. The 1800s began on a dark note for ghost hunting.

Interestingly, sprinkled among the earliest press reports on the Hammersmith ghost incident are the earliest uses of the term

---

[15] Samuel Johnson, *Rasselas* (Willis P. Hazard, 1856) p. 58. Boswell, Vol. 1, p. 186. T.M. Jarvis, *Accredited Ghost Stories* (printed for J. Andrews, 1823) p. 2. Herman Melville, *Moby Dick* (Harper & Brothers, 1851) p. 345. Boswell, Vol. 2, p. 190.

[16] Old Bailey Proceedings Online (www.oldbaileyonline.org, version 8.0, 13 October 2019), January 1804, trial of FRANCIS SMITH (t18040111-79).

"ghost-hunter" that I've found after several years of searching.[17] Perhaps this was a cryptic sign that the new century would experience a curious surge of ghost hunters, especially after an 18-year-old named Victoria took the throne. And it's high time I let some of those who chronicled their investigations take the stage. I have done little to alter their language other than correct obvious errors or touch up a few confusing spots. I retained the nuances of nineteenth-century English, including the hyphens in words such as "to-night" and "bed-room," two-word phrases that have *become* single words such as "any one" and "some one," and the plentitude of commas. In this way, the Victorian ghost hunters can narrate their own chapter of history with much greater charm and distinctiveness than the quick pre-Victorian history I provide above.

And, as I mentioned, theirs was a distinctively *ghostly* period of history to narrate.

---

[17] Smith and the others lying in wait for the Hammersmith ghost are referred to as "ghost-hunters" in an anonymous recap of current events called "Domestic Incidents," *Universal Magazine of Knowledge and Pleasure* 1.1 (Jan., 1804) p. 63. It also appears in "Affairs in England," *Scots Magazine and Edinburgh Literary Miscellany* 66 (Jan., 1804) p. 68. The Hammersmith/Smith tragedy joined the Cock Lane/Johnson as popular British ghostlore, and Victorian readers would have had an easy time either reading or hearing about them.

Case 1: A Chamber of Deathly Light

Investigation: conducted by two unnamed ghost hunters at a house in Taunton, England. The year of the investigation is unknown but the secondhand chronicle of it was written in 1840. Therefore, while this is an example of a ghost hunt *recounted* during the Victorian era, the investigation itself occurred beforehand.

Manifestations: a dim light in a single room of a deserted house; a feeling of being drained of life experienced by those who enter.

Pertinent Facts: The Reverend Frederick George Lee (1832-1902) compiled letters, articles, and other chronicles of supernatural events occurring in the physical world. He presented them in a book titled *Glimpses in the Twilight*. The first line below, which comes from a chapter called "Apparitions and Haunted Localities," makes Lee's purpose for the book very clear: he shared these documents to counteract the skepticism of his age. That chapter also presents a chronicle written by someone who had met a ghost hunter with a story worth telling.

From *Glimpses in the Twilight*

Frederick George Lee[1]

In the present age of unbelief and scepticism, when universal traditions regarding things spiritual are being flung aside as useless, and when so many persons profess to reject the doctrine of the immortality of the soul as well as that of the resurrection of the

---

[1] This is extracted from *Glimpses in the Twilight: Being Various Notes, Records, and Examples of the Supernatural* (William Blackwood and Sons, 1885) pp. 48-51.

body, it may not be out of place to gather together and set forth various records of remarkable facts and well-authenticated traditions in support of the Supernatural. These examples, gathered from various sources, of varying interest and of different kinds, are—the large majority of them, at all events—now published for the first time, and have been intrusted to the author for publication with the direct and excellent intention of duly preserving such instances of supernatural intervention, and in future life are of no moment whatsoever in comparison with the pressing need of vaccination, or a knowledge by telephone or electricity of the exact state of the Funds. In fact, the supremely confident and over-dogmatic "great thinkers," maintaining that scepticism is a duty,[2] are succeeding in completely demolishing some of our most sacred ideas, and in reducing the ordinary British mind to the dry and dead level of a rationalistic and utilitarian philosophy.

Yet, as John Wesley so acutely and reasonably remarked, "If but one account of the intercourse of men with separate spirits be admitted, the whole castle-in-the-air (Deism, Atheism, and Materialism) falls to the ground."

Let the following records therefore be carefully studied. The sneers of the cynical, be it remembered, and the scoffs of the unbelieving, most certainly cannot alter facts. . . .[3]

In the year 1840 I was detained for several months in the sleepy old town of Taunton. My chief associate during that time was a foxhunting squire—a bluff, hearty, genial type of his order, with just sufficient intellectuality to temper his animal exuberance. Many were our merry rides among the thorpes and hamlets of pleasant Somersetshire; and it was in one of these excursions, while the

---

[2] "Scepticism is the highest of duties; blind faith the one unpardonable sin."—'Lay Sermons,' by T. H. Huxley, p. 21. London. "Five-sixths of the public are taught Adamitic monogenism—i.e., of Adam and Eve being the parents of all mankind—as if it were an established truth, and believe it. I do not, and I am not acquainted with any man of science or duly instructed person who does."—T. H. Huxley in the 'Fortnightly Review,' "On the Methods and Results of Ethnology." [Lee's footnote.]

[3] Lee next presents two firsthand accounts of ghostly encounters. He attributes the first to "a Buckinghamshire friend" but leaves the second source unidentified. However, it comes from an article titled "Ghosts and Haunted Houses," published in *Notes and Queries* 11.275 (April 5, 1873) pp. 273-74, where it is credited to T[homas] Westwood (1814–1888). This is the same source for Lee's third record, the secondhand chronicle of a ghost hunt that follows.

evening sky was like molten copper, and a fiery March wind coursed, like a race-horse, over the open downs, that he related to me the story of what he called his "luminous chamber."

Coming back from the hunt after dark, he said he had frequently observed a central window, in an old hall not far from the roadside, illuminated. All the other windows were dark, but from this one a wan, dreary light was visible; and as the owners had deserted the place, and he knew it had no occupant, the lighted window became a puzzle to him.

On one occasion, having a brother squire with him, and both carrying good store of port wine under their girdles, they declared they would solve the mystery of the luminous chamber then and there. The lodge was still tenanted by an aged porter; him they roused up, and after some delay, having obtained a lantern and the keys of the hall, they proceeded to make their entry. Before opening the great door, however, my squire averred he had made careful inspection of the front of the house from the lawn. Sure enough, the central window *was* illuminated: an eerie, forlorn-looking light made it stand out in contrast to the rest—a dismal light, that seemed to have nothing in common with the world, or the life that is. The two squires visited all the other rooms, leaving the luminous one till the last. There was nothing noticeable in any of them; they were totally obscure. But on entering the luminous room, a marked change was perceptible. The light in it was not full, but sufficiently so beneath them to distinguish its various articles of furniture, which were common and scanty enough. What struck them most was the uniform diffusion of the light: it was as strong *under* the table as *on* the table, so that no single object projected any shadow on the floor, nor did they themselves project any shadow. Looking into a great mirror over the mantelpiece, nothing could be weirder, the squire declared, than the reflection in it of the dim, wan-lighted chamber, and of the two awe-stricken faces that glared on them from the midst—his own and his companion's. He told me, too, that he had not been many seconds in the room before a sick faintness stole over him; a feeling—such was his expression, I remember—as if his life *were being sucked out of him.* His friend owned afterwards to a similar sensation. The upshot of it was, that both squires decamped, crestfallen, and made no further attempt at solving the mystery.

It had always been the same, the old porter grumbled: the family had never occupied the room; but there were no ghosts—the room had *a light of its own.*

A less sceptical spirit might have opined that the room was full of ghosts,—an awful conclave, viewless, inscrutable, but from whom emanated that deathly and deadly luminousness. My squires must have gone the way of all squires ere this. "After life's fitful fever," do they "sleep well"?[4] Or have they both been "sucked" into the luminous medium, as a penalty for the intrusion?

4 In Shakespeare's *Mabeth,* the title character says: "Duncan is in his grave. / After life's fitful fever he sleeps well" (3.2.25-26).

4

Case 2: A Haunted Room with Two Views

Investigation: conducted by Edward Drury and Thomas Hudson at Willington, England, in 1840.

Manifestations: footsteps, whisperings, laughter, and other untraceable noises; a female apparition; a clerical male apparition; a disembodied face.

Pertinent Facts: The Willington haunting is one of the most famous in Britain. Probably the most detailed account of it was written by Edmund Procter, son of the house's owner, Joseph. Combining quotations from his father's papers with his own memories, Procter says the haunting began in 1835 with disembodied footsteps. Soon, a variety of untraceable noises were heard by several people. A hazy female figure dressed in bluish-gray and without eyes, and a luminous apparition in priestly apparel were spotted. Those sleeping in the house felt themselves inexplicably lifted. Screams, moans, whistles, and bells were heard. In 1840, a ghost hunt was conducted, and the two investigators recorded individual views of the ghost hunt they had shared: one in the letters Edward Drury sent to the homeowner, published just a couple of years after the investigation, and the second in Thomas Hudson's recollections, which didn't appear until 1884. A follow-up investigation was conducted by William Howett, and key passages of his report are included in the same article that made Hudson's recollections public. These ghost hunts did nothing to stop the haunting, though, and Edmund Procter points out that his family finally left the house in 1847, explaining that it was "no longer tolerable."[1]

---

[1] Edmund Procter, "The Haunted House at Willington," *Journal of the Society for Psychical Research* 5.95 (Dec., 1892) pp. 331-52.

AUTHENTIC ACCOUNT OF A VISIT TO
THE HAUNTED HOUSE AT WILLINGTON

M.A. Richardson[2]

Were we to draw an inference from the number of cases of reported visitation from the invisible world that have been made public of late, we might be led to imagine that the days of supernatural agency were about to recommence, and that ghosts and hobgoblins were about to resume their sway over the fears of mankind. Did we, however, indulge such an apprehension, a glance at the current tone of the literature and philosophy of the day, when treating of these subjects would shew a measure of unbelief regarding them as scornful and uncompromising, as the veriest atheist or materialist could desire. Notwithstanding the prevalence of this feeling amongst the educated classes, there is a curiosity and interest manifested in every occurrence of this nature, that indicates a lurking faith at bottom, which an affected scepticism fails entirely to conceal. We feel, therefore, that we need not apologize to our readers for introducing the following particulars of a visit to a house in this immediate neighbourhood, which had become notorious for some years previous, as being "haunted," and several of the reputed deeds or misdeeds of its supernatural visitant had been published far and wide by rumour's thousand tongues. We deem it as worthy to be chronicled as the doings of its contemporary *genii* at Windsor, Dublin, Liverpool, Carlisle, and Sunderland, and which have all likewise hitherto failed, after public investigation, to receive a solution consistent with a rejection of spiritual agency.

We have visited the house in question which is well known to many of our readers as being near a large steam corn-mill in full view of the Willington viaduct on the Newcastle and Shields railway; and it may not be irrelevant to mention that it is quite detached from the mill or any other premises, and has no cellaring under it. The proprietor of the house, who lives in it, declines to make public the particulars of the disturbance to which he has been subjected, and it must be understood that the account of the visit we are about to lay before our readers is derived from a friend, to

---

[2] This appeared in Richardson's *The Local Historian's Table Book* (Vol. I, M.A. Richardson, 1842) pp. 299-304.

whom Dr. Drury presented a copy of his correspondence on the subject, with power to make such use of it as he thought proper. We learnt that the house had been reputed, or at least one room in it, to have been haunted forty years ago, and had afterwards been undisturbed for a long period, during some years of which quietude the present occupant lived in it unmolested. We are also informed that about the time the premises were building, viz. in 1800 or 1801, there were reports of some deed of darkness having been committed by someone employed about them. We should extend this account beyond the limits we have set to ourselves, did we now enter upon a full account of the strange things which have been seen and heard about the place by several of the neighbours, as well as those which are reported to have been at various times seen, heard and felt, by the inmates, whose servants have been changed, on that account, many times. We proceed therefore to give the following letters which have passed between individuals of undoubted veracity, leaving the reader to draw his own conclusions on the subject.

(Copy—No. 1.)

To Mr. Procter.
17 June, 1840.

Sir,

Having heard from indisputable authority, viz. that of my excellent friend Mr. Davison, of Low Willington, farmer, that you and your family are disturbed by most unaccountable noises at night, I beg leave to tell you that I have read, attentively, Wesley's account of such things,[3] but with, I must confess, no great belief: but an account of this report coming from one of your sect, which I admire for candour and simplicity, my curiosity is excited to a high pitch, which I would fain satisfy. My desire is to remain alone in the house all night with no companion but my own watchdog, in which, as far as courage and fidelity are concerned, I place much more reliance than upon any three young gentlemen I know of. And it is also my hope that if I have a fair trial I shall be enabled to unravel this mystery.

---

[3] John Wesley (1703-1791) was a prominent cleric of the Church of England. His influence on a revival of Methodism is still felt today. In his memoir "An Account of the Disturbances in My Father's House," he lists encounters with a poltergeist-like ghost, nicknamed "Old Jeffrey," that he and other members of the household experienced. The essay is reprinted in Volume 13 of *The Works of Rev. John Wesley, A.M.* (John Mason, 1831), pp. 459-64. Curiously, William Howitt reports that the male ghost in this case is also dubbed "Old Jeffrey."

Mr. Davison will give you every satisfaction if you take the trouble to enquire of him concerning me.

I am, Sir,
Yours most respectfully,
Edw. Drury.

At
C.C. Embleton's, Surgeon,
No. 10, Church Street,
Sunderland.

(Copy—No. 2.)

Joseph Procter's respects to Edwd. Drury, whose note he received a few days ago, expressing a wish to pass a night in his house at Willington. As the family is going from home on the 23rd inst., and one of Unthank and Procter's men will sleep in the house, if E.D. incline to come, on or after the 24th, to spend a night in it, he is at liberty so to do, with or without his faithful dog, which, by the bye, can be of no possible use, except as company. At the same time J.P. thinks it best to inform him that particular disturbances are far from frequent at present, being only occasional and quite uncertain, and therefore the satisfaction of E.D.'s curiosity must be considered as problematical. The best chance would be afforded by his sitting up alone in the third story, till it be fairly daylight—say two or three a.m.

Willington, 6 Mo. 21st, 1840.

J.P. will leave word with T. Maun, foreman, to admit E.D.

[Mr. Procter left home with his family on the 23rd of June, and got an old servant, who was then out of place in consequence of ill health, to take charge of the house during their absence. Mr. P. returned alone, on account of business, on the 3rd of July, on the evening of which day, Mr. Drury and his companion also unexpectedly arrived. After the house had been locked up, every corner of it was minutely examined. The room out of which the apparition proceeded, as well as the adjoining rooms, was unfurnished, and the closet out of which it issued, is too shallow to contain any person. Mr. Drury and his friend had two lights by them, and are satisfied that there was no one in the house besides Mr. P., the servant, and themselves.][4]

---

[4] These are Richardson's bracketed comments. Drury's friend is Thomas Hudson.

(Copy—No. 3.)

Monday morning, July 6th, 1840.
To Mr. Procter.

Dear Sir,

I am sorry I was not at home to receive you when you kindly called yesterday to enquire for me. I am happy to state that I am really surprised that I have been so little affected as I am, after that horrid and most awful affair, the only bad effect I feel is a heavy dullness in one of my ears, the right one; I call it heavy dullness because, I not only do not hear distinctly, but feel in it a constant noise; this I was never affected with heretofore, but I doubt not it will go off. I am persuaded that no one went to your house at any time more disbelieving in respect to seeing anything peculiar—now, no one can be more satisfied than myself. I will in the course of a few days send you a full detail of all I saw and heard. Mr. Spence and two other gentlemen came down to my house in the afternoon to hear my detail; but sir, could I account for these noises from natural causes, yet so firmly am I persuaded of the horrid apparition, that I would affirm, that what I saw with my eyes, was a punishment to me for my scoffing and unbelief; that I am assured, as far as the horror is concerned, they are happy that believe, and have not seen. Let me trouble you, Sir, to give me the address of your sister (from Cumberland), who was so alarmed, and also of your brother. I would feel a satisfaction in having a line from them, and above all things it will be a great cause of joy to me if you never allow your young family to be in that horrid house again. Hoping you will write a few lines at your leisure,

I remain,
Dear Sir,
Yours very truly,
Edward Drury.

(Copy—No.4.)

Respected Friend,
Willington,
7 mo. 9, 1840.
E. Drury,

Having been at Sunderland, I did not receive thine of the 6th till yesterday morning. I am glad to hear thou art getting well over the effects of thy unlooked-for visitation. I hold in respect thy bold and manly assertion of the truth in the face of that ridicule and ignorant conceit with which that which is called the supernatural, in the present day, is usually assailed.

I shall be glad to receive thy detail, in which it will be needful to be very particular in shewing that thou couldst not be asleep, or attacked by nightmare, or mistake a reflection of the candle, as some sagaciously suppose.

I remain, respectfully,

Thy Friend,
Josh. Procter.

P.S. I have about 30 witnesses to various things which cannot be satisfactorily accounted for, on any other principle than spiritual agency.

(Copy—No.5.)

Sunderland,
July 13th. 1840.

Dear Sir,

I hereby, according to promise in my last letter, forward you a true account of what I heard and *saw* at your house, in which I was led to pass the night, from various rumours circulated by most respectable parties, particularly from an account by my esteemed friend Mr. Davison, whose name I mentioned to you in a former letter. Having received your sanction to visit your mysterious dwelling, I went on the third of July, accompanied by a friend of mine named T. Hudson. This was not according to promise, nor in accordance with my first intent, as I wrote you I would come alone, but I felt gratified at your kindness in not alluding to the liberty I had taken, as it ultimately proved for the best. I must here mention that not expecting you at home I had in my pocket a brace of pistols, determining in my mind to let one of them drop, as if by accident, before the miller, for fear he should presume to play tricks upon me—but after my interview with you I felt there was no occasion for weapons, and did not load them, after you had allowed us to inspect as minutely as we pleased every portion of the house. I sat down on the third story landing, fully expecting to account for any noises I might hear, in a philosophical manner—this was about eleven o'clock P.M. About ten minutes to twelve we both heard a noise, as if a number of people was pattering with their bare feet upon the floor; and yet so singular was the noise that I could not minutely determine from whence it proceeded. A few minutes afterwards we heard a noise, as if someone was knocking with his knuckles among our feet; this was immediately followed by a hollow cough from the very room, from which the apparition proceeded. The only noise after this was, as if a person was rustling against the wall in coming upstairs. At a quarter to one, I told my friend that feeling a little cold, I would like to go to bed as we might hear the noises equally well there; he replied that he would not go to bed till daylight. I took up a note, which I had accidentally dropped, and began to read it—after which I took out my watch to ascertain the time, and found that it wanted ten minutes to one. In taking my eyes from the watch they became riveted upon a closet door, which I distinctly saw open, and also saw the figure of a female attired in greyish garments, with the head inclined downwards, and one hand pressed upon the chest as if in pain, and the other, viz. the right hand, extended towards the floor, with the index finger pointing downwards. It advanced with an apparently cautious step across the floor towards me; immediately as it approached my friend who was slumbering, its right hand was extended toward him; I then rushed at it, giving at the time, as Mr. Procter states, a most awful yell, but instead of grasping it I fell upon my friend—and I recollected nothing distinctly for nearly three hours afterwards. I have since learnt that I was carried downstairs, in an agony of fear and terror.

I hereby certify that the above account is strictly true and correct in every respect.

Edw. Drury,
North Shields.

The following more recent case of an apparition seen in the window of the same house from the outside, by four credible witnesses, who had the opportunity of scrutinizing it, for more than ten minutes, is given on most unquestionable authority. One of these witnesses is a young lady, a near connection of the family (who for obvious reasons did not sleep in the house), another, a highly respectable man who has been many years employed in, and is foreman of the manufactory, his daughter, aged about seventeen, and his wife, who first saw the object and called out the others to view it. The appearance presented was that of a bareheaded man, in a flowing robe like a surplice, which glided backwards and forwards about three feet from the floor, or level with the bottom of the second story window, seeming to enter the wall on each side and thus present a side view in passing; it then stood still in the window, and a part of the body came through both the blind (which was close down), and the window, as its luminous body intercepted the view of the framework of the window. It was semi-transparent, and as bright as a star, diffusing a radiance all around. As it grew more dim it assumed a blue tinge, and gradually faded away from the head downwards. The foreman passed twice close to the house under the window, and also went to inform the family, but found the house locked up. There was no moonlight, nor a ray of light visible anywhere about, and no person near. Had any magic lantern been used it could not possibly have escaped detection, and it is obvious nothing of that kind could have been employed in the inside, as in that case the light could only have been thrown upon the blind, and not so as to intercept the view both of the blind and window from without.[5] The owner of the house slept in that room, and must have entered it shortly after this figure had disappeared.

✤

The Willington Ghost

Anonymous[6]

WILLINGTON MILL, near North Shields, was the scene of one of the most popular ghost stories in the North of England, though many years have elapsed since anything uncanny has been seen or heard in the neighbourhood.

It was about 1840 and the four or five succeeding years that the ghostly visitations attracted the greatest amount of public notice. At that time the house adjoining the mill was occupied by Mr. Joseph Procter, whose relatives appear to have bought the building in 1806. The mill itself was used then for grinding flour by Messrs. Unthank and Procter but is now occupied as a store for oilcake. The Procter family lived in the house till 1847, prior to which the "visitations" had become much less frequent. A rumour that the house was haunted gained some currency previous to the time of its purchase by Mr. Procter's relatives, although it is stated that nothing of the kind was noticed during the first twelve years of Mr. Procter's own residence there. At last, both the people outside and the family inside began to hear sounds often, and to see apparitions frequently, for which there was no visible cause. The house was built in 1800, and there were reports of a deed of darkness having been committed by someone engaged in the work. Mr. William Howitt, whose narrative we shall presently quote, also mentions that Mr. Procter had discovered a book which made it appear that the same

---

[5] Magic lanterns were optical projectors that combined a strong light source, a lens, and painted—later photographed—slides. By the late 1700s, the devices were used in "Phantasmagoria," theatrical shows designed to thrill audiences by projecting a variety of scary images, including ghosts that seemed to move.

[6] This appeared in *North Country Lore and Legend* 1.4 (June, 1887) pp. 177-81.

kind of thing went on in a house on the same spot about two hundred years before. . . .[7]

Mr. Howitt, who visited Willington about 1840 or 1841, tells the following story in his "Visits to Remarkable Places":

One of Mrs. Procter's brothers, a gentleman in middle life, and of a peculiarly sensible, sedate, and candid disposition, a person apparently most unlikely to be imposed on by fictitious alarm or tricks, assured me that he had himself, on a visit there, been disturbed by the strangest noises; that he had resolved, before going, that if any such noises occurred he would speak, and demand of the invisible actor who he was, and why he came thither. But the occasion came, and he found himself unable to fulfil his intention. As he lay in bed one night, he heard a heavy step ascend the stairs towards his room, and some one striking, as it were, with a thick stick on the banisters as he went along. It came to his door and he essayed to call, but his voice died in his throat. He then sprang from his bed, and, opening the door, found no one there, but now heard the same heavy steps deliberately descending, though perfectly invisibly, the steps before his face, and accompanying the descent with the same loud blows on the banisters.

My informant now proceeded to the room door of Mr. Procter, who he found had also heard the sounds, and who now also arose, and with a light they made a speedy descent below, and made a thorough search there, but without discovering anything that could account for the occurrence.

The two young ladies who, on a visit there, had also been annoyed by this invisible agent, gave me this account of it. The first night, as they were sleeping in the same bed, they felt the bed lifted up beneath them. Of course they were much alarmed. They feared lest some one had concealed himself there for the purpose of robbery. They gave an alarm, search was made, but nothing was found. On another night their bed was violently shaken, and the curtains suddenly hoisted up all round to the very tester, as if pulled up by cords, and as rapidly let down again, several times. Search again produced no evidence of the cause. The next day they had the curtains totally removed from the bed, resolving to sleep without them, as they felt as though evil eyes were lurking behind them. The consequences of this, however, were still more striking and terrific. The following night, as they happened to awake, and the chamber was light enough for it was summer to see everything in it, they both saw a female figure of a misty

---

[7] Here, the anonymous writer describes the mill and its surroundings; summarizes the Richardson article, quoting at length Drury's letter about his ghostly vigil; and then retells Richardson's anecdote about the four witnesses and the apparition of the bareheaded, robed man.

substance, and bluish grey hue, come out of the wall at the bed's head and through the head-board, in a horizontal position, and lean over them. They saw it most distinctly. They saw it as a female figure come out of, and again pass into, the wall. Their terror became intense, and one of the sisters from that night refused to sleep any more in the house, but took refuge in the house of the foreman during her stay, the other shifting her quarters to another part of the house. It was the young lady who slept at the foreman's who saw, as above related, the singular apparition of the luminous figure in the window, along with the foreman and his wife.

It would be too long to relate all the forms in which this nocturnal disturbance is said by the family to present itself. When a figure appears, it is sometimes that of a man, as already described, which is often very luminous, and passes through the walls as though they were nothing. This male figure is well known to the neighbours by the name of "Old Jeffery." At other times it is the figure of a lady, also in grey costume, and as described by Mr. Drury. She is sometimes seen sitting wrapt in a sort of mantle, with her head depressed, and her hands crossed on her lap. The most terrible fact is that she is without eyes.

To hear such sober and superior people gravely relate to you such things gives you a very odd feeling. They say that the noise made is often like that of a pavior with his rammer thumping on the floor.[8] At other times it is coming down the stairs, making a similar loud sound. At others it coughs, sighs, and groans like a person in distress; and, again, there is the sound of a number of little feet pattering on the floor of the upper chamber, where the apparition has more particularly exhibited itself, and which for that reason is solely used as a lumber room. Here these little footsteps may be often heard as if careering a child's carriage about, which in bad weather is kept up there. Sometimes, again, it makes the most horrible laughs. Nor does it always confine itself to the night. On one occasion, a young lady, as she assured me herself, opened the door in answer to a knock, the housemaid being absent, and a lady in fawn-coloured silk entered, and proceeded upstairs. As the young lady, of course, supposed it a neighbour come to make a morning call on Mrs. Procter, she followed her up to the drawing-room, where, however, to her astonishment, she did not find her, nor was anything more seen of her.

Such are a few of the questionable shapes in which this troublesome guest comes. As may be expected, the terror of it is felt by the neighbouring cottagers, though it seems to confine its malicious disturbance almost solely to the occupants of this one house.[9]

---

[8] A pavior is a person who paves streets.

[9] The full account is in William Howitt, "The Haunted House at Willington, Near Newcastle-on-Tyne," *Howitt's Journal* 1.21 (May 22, 1847) pp. 289-93.

Mr. Drury's version of the adventure in the haunted house had been before the public for more than forty years ere Mr. Hudson consented to give his. The latter gentleman's narrative, reprinted further on, was first published in the *Newcastle Weekly Chronicle* on December 20, 1884. How it happened that Mr. Hudson so long remained silent on the subject was thus explained: When the permission of Mr. Procter was given to the visit in 1840, he requested the visitors not to make known their experiences, because of the difficulty he found in retaining domestic servants, who were naturally terrified at the idea of residing in a house that was reputed to be haunted. Mr. Hudson scrupulously observed Mr. Procter's injunctions. But the reason for silence had disappeared in 1884. Mr. Procter was dead, his family had removed from Willington, and the premises had been converted to other uses. There was, therefore, no longer any reason for reticence. So it happened that we have now Mr. Hudson's narrative of the incidents of the memorable night he spent in the haunted house nearly half-a-century ago.

Mr. Hudson's Story

One Midsummer afternoon, in 1840, my young "governor," Mr. J. Ogilvie, jun., chemist, North Shields, said to me in an offhand way, "Tom, the doctor (Drury) is going tonight to make the acquaintance of the ghost at the haunted house at Willington. How would you like to go with him, and see that he doesn't come back with a cock-and-bull story about it?" To give the "powdered aloes" the "go-by," even for one afternoon, was a prospect too tempting to give up, especially after having had for many hours the acute aroma of that dust in my nostrils. "Most willingly," was my ready reply. And not many minutes afterwards I bade the great mortar a joyful "good-bye," and set off for the mysterious mansion.

That was before the days of railways, and as the Newcastle omnibuses, which then ran hourly to and beyond Willington, charged two shillings for the journey, we elected to tramp it. It was a beautiful evening. Golden clouds shone in the sky, the air was rich with the scent of wild flowers, the trees and hedges seemed clothed in gold, and the peaceful hum of the industrious bee in the green fields around us fell like dreamy music on the ear. These were the "delightful days of old," before "buzzers" were born; when old Father Tyne kept sand beds right up the river for sleepy steamers to get stranded upon for hours daily at low tide; and when fiddlers were always part of the crew, for the amusement of the company on board. Palmer had not then built his palaces of labour nor his plantations of iron ships at Jarrow on the opposite shore. Even Willington had not heard the ghost of a whisper that the *Weekly Chronicle* had become the eighth wonder of the world! Quietude reigned everywhere. There was nothing ghostly about except the memory of the many tales told of the headless old lady whom it was our vaunted ambition to accost on her nocturnal excursion from the other world.

We arrived at the mansion by the mill at the appointed time—eight p.m.—and were most kindly entertained to supper by the genial and worthy miller, whose memory will long be revered on Tyneside. Mr. Procter told us he had never seen the apparition himself, but he had heard many utterly unaccountable sounds on several remarkable occasions. However, from the accounts given to him by his children (who felt not at all alarmed at the "old lady's" appearance by night or day)—accounts which, he told us, agreed in every detail—he was quite satisfied that the story of the supernatural appearance in his house was founded on fact. "Moreover," said he, "the testimony of most trustworthy witnesses, such as friends, neighbours, and people on the premises, seem proof enough for the most sceptical." "If," continued our interesting and respected informant, "if you feel inclined to stay all night on the chance of seeing *it* [as the visits, it seemed, were ever erratic], you are welcome to do so, or to return upon any future occasion when curiosity may call you here again." Having enjoyed a salubrious but anti-stimulative supper, we listened to the story of all that was known concerning the ghost for about two hours. Mr. Procter related incidents so unmistakable and circumstantial as to be almost enough to forbid even a syllable of controversy afterwards. We were then taken through every part of the premises, so as to assure ourselves of the impossibility of any intrusion or hoax-playing.

At ten o'clock, Mr. Procter and his housekeeper retired to rest. We had been previously led to the upper stairhead, where the "old lady" had been so distinctly seen by the children and others on many occasions. Here two chairs, a small table, two wax candles lighted, and two silk night-caps were kindly left for our use, as we intended to watch diligently till daylight. Four bedroom doors stood open around us. All the bedrooms were furnished, but none of them was occupied on the night in question, Mr. Procter's family being away from home at the time. Dr. Drury, being my senior, took the choice of seats, and sat upon one nearest the stairs, without, of course, any intention of beating an ignominious retreat at the advance of the ghost. So brave was he, indeed, that at my request he left his pocket pistol downstairs, being now assured that whatever might appear would be skinless, and not susceptible to shot. I occupied a central position, two rooms being to the right of me and two to the left, while the stairs were at a right angle. Both of us looked as profoundly philosophical as possible in the light of the two stately wax candles, and there was not a sound save the occasional creech of the old-fashioned snuffers. Two hours crept slowly by in this solemn silence. The clock struck the ghostly hour of twelve without a single incident having occurred worthy of a word of comment. Fifteen minutes afterwards, however, a most unearthly, hollow sound broke upon our ears. Knowing that coming events often cast their shadows before, we awaited breathlessly in the anticipation that these sounds might be the prelude to sights. But we waited in vain. Later on, sounds came in a sort of rumbling and unequal fashion, such as might have been caused by wagon wheels travelling over the skeleton of the Willington Bridge, then in course of construction. Anon my friend was a little excited by a vibrating noise which he said sounded "like the fluttering of an angel's wing!" My answer was that it was more likely to be the echo of a steamer's paddle wheels on the adjoining river. Then there came another awfully perplexing sound, as if something was trying to squeeze itself through the floor at our feet. This was simple as a matter of fact, yet it produced in us a great degree of nervous uneasiness. Not, however, to an alarming extent, as we knew that the house was built upon piles, and was, therefore, more sensitive to sounds than other buildings resting on more substantial foundations. This thought calmed our feelings. About a quarter to one the most unaccountable disturbance we had yet heard occurred in one of the rooms close by the room to my right hand. It was as if someone were really there, walking on his (or her) bare feet, and approaching us. But nothing met our vision.

We had both been up from six a.m. the previous morning, and now at last tired nature was weighing my eyelids down. Drury suggested that we should go to bed and keep watch from there. But to this I would not agree until daylight should appear. I suggested, however, that he might go to bed, and leave me as "captain of the watch." He refused somewhat testily, and not only so, but in a bad temper refused all further conversation, nursing his "pet" to keep it warm. To retaliate, lad-like, I took out a cigar in a strong spirit of independence, and jocosely remarked that I would take his white hat for a spittoon. This annoyed him, and he reminded me that we were engaged on too serious a matter for levity or laughter. Thus, after sitting there nearly three hours, without a book to read or a friend to chat with—the doctor refusing to speak—I naturally became exceedingly drowsy, yet I was awake enough for any emergency. I saw my friend reading a note which he had taken from his waistcoat pocket, and I closed my eyes for a few seconds only. I was quickly startled, however, by a hideous yell from Drury, who sprang up with his hair standing on end, the picture of horror. He fainted and fell into my arms, like a lifeless piece of humanity. His horrible shouts made me shout in sympathy, and I instantly laid him down and went into the room from whence the last noise was heard. But nothing was there, and the window had not been opened. So loud was his scream that two or three neighbours were awakened by it, so they afterwards told me. Mr. Procter and the housekeeper came quickly to our assistance, and found the young doctor trembling in acute mental agony. Indeed, he was so much excited that he wanted to jump out of the window. Coffee was kindly given to us, and we shortly afterwards left for North Shields.

Drury declared his unbounded belief in the ghost. He said he had seen the grey old lady in a grey gown proceed from the room at my right hand side, and slowly approach me from behind. She was, he said, just about to place her hand on my slumbering head, while he was strongly endeavouring to touch my foot with his, but though our feet were only a few inches apart, he had not power to do so. Instead, he shouted with all his might, and then swooned. My opinion, however, is that Drury saw the appearance of the mysterious lady, as others had seen her, in much the same way as Macbeth saw the ghost of Banquo and the dagger; but whether it was or was not a spirit in form will remain a mystery to some, a fact to a few, and simply a mental delusion to many. The latter will be the more prevalent opinion in this age of materialism, when the question is asked: How can there be a shadow without substance, or mind without matter, except in our dreaming eyes and foolish fancies?

Thomas Hudson.

Case 3: A Ghost Expert Goes Hunting

Investigation: conducted by Catherine Crowe and unnamed others, including a clairvoyant. The location is unknown, but the year was between 1848 and 1859.

Manifestations: metallic, clanging noises; white lights of various types.

Pertinent Facts: Along with novels including *The Adventures of Susan Hopley* and *The Story of Lily Dawson,* Catherine Crowe (1803-1876) is responsible for one of the most popular and important compilations of allegedly true ghost stories: *The Night-Side of Nature*, first published in 1848 and frequently reprinted. Her subsequent book, *Ghosts and Family Legends,* also relates spooky stories, all framed as having been told by a fire over several evenings at a yuletide gathering. On the eighth evening, Crowe narrates her own adventure.

EIGHTH EVENING

Catherine Crowe[1]

As this was our last evening, I was called upon for a story; but I pleaded that I had told all mine in the 'Night Side of Nature,' and of personal experience I had very little to tell; but I said I will give you the history of a visit I made several years ago to a haunted house although it resulted in almost nothing.

After the publication of the 'Night Side,' I received many valuable communications—I wish I had kept a note of them all, but I never expected to publish again on the same subject. Amongst

---

[1] This appeared in Crowe's *Ghosts and Family Legends* (Thomas Cautley Newby, 1859) pp. 135-47.

others, I received a letter from a gentleman called Mc. N., and as it contained several interesting particulars, I requested him to call on me. I remember, in the letter, he told me that a few years previously, he had been on an excursion from home, and that while stopping at an inn, one morning, about five o'clock, the door opened and his father entered; he came to the bedside, looked at him, and then went out again. The young man sprang from his bed, and followed him downstairs, where he lost sight of him. He returned home, and found his father had died on that morning.

He was employed in a lawyer's office, and, amongst other things, he mentioned to me that there was not very far off a house said to be haunted, of which they had the charge, but that it was impossible to do anything with it. 'We offer it at a mere nominal rent, but no one will stay there.'

I was often absent from home at this time, but for the next two or three years sometimes met him and inquired about the house. The report was always the same; till, at length, no one would go into it; it was shut up—the shutters were closed, and the boys of the neighbourhood threw stones at the windows and broke the glass. Yet it was situated in a street where every other house was inhabited, and which had not been built many years.

It was as much as six or seven years after I had first heard of this house, that I happened to mention the circumstance to some gentlemen of my acquaintance—very eminent men, with honest, inquiring minds; truth seekers, who, if she were in the bottom of a well, would have thought it right to go after her. As they had humility enough to feel that they could not pronounce upon a question that they had never studied or investigated, they expressed a wish to visit the house. Accordingly, I applied to Mr. Mc. N., who had the keys in his office, and he obligingly consented to accompany us. Our expedition was to be kept a profound secret; and it was so, till sometime afterwards, when, like most other secrets, it got wind and it spread abroad.

We started in a carriage, between eleven and twelve o'clock at night, taking with us a young girl who was easily mesmerised, and when in that state a good clairvoyante. She was not told the object of our journey, and had no means whatever of learning it. We said we were going to look at a house, and that that was the most convenient time for the gentleman to show it us. We did not drive to the door, but Mr. Mc. N. met us in the next street, where we alighted, lest we should attract observation. We walked to our destination, and Mr. Mc. N. explained to the policeman on duty who he was and where we were going, lest he should suspect mischief, and interrupt us. He then unlocked the door with the aid of the policeman's lantern, for it was a dark winter's night; and on entering, we found ourselves in a narrow passage.

It was a small house, in no respect different from the others in the street. They seemed all of the same description. A narrow frontage, with one window and the door, on the ground floor and two windows above; two rooms on a floor, three stories in height; and a kitchen, scullery, and cellars underground.

As soon as the door closed on us, we were in utter darkness, but we had provided ourselves with candles and matches, and when we had lighted them, we entered the back parlour, which Mr. Mc. N. had heard from the different inhabitants was the room in which they had met with most annoyance.

The clairvoyante was then put to sleep, and asked if she liked the house, and would recommend us to take it. She shuddered and said, 'No; two people had been murdered there, and we should be *troubled.'* We asked in which room; she answered, 'it was before this house was built—that another house stood there then—a very old house.' This was not exactly on the same ground, but the room we were in was on part of it. She said that it was these murdered people who would trouble us. We asked if she could see them, and she answered 'no.'

We then waited in silence to see if anything occurred; but nothing did, except a metallic sound at the door, which was ajar, like the striking of two pieces of iron. We all heard it, but could not say what occasioned it.

After a little time, someone suggested that we should extinguish the lights. We did so, and were then in absolute darkness. There was but one window in the room, and that was coated with dust, and the shutter was shut; besides, as I have said, it was a very dark night, and this room, being at the back, looked into a yard, I believe; at all events, not into a street.

Presently, the clairvoyante started, and exclaimed, 'Look there!' We saw nothing, and asked what it was.

'There!' she said. 'There again! don't you see it?'

'What?' we asked.

'The lights!' she said. 'There! Now!' These exclamations were made at intervals of two or three seconds.

We all said we saw nothing whatever.

'If Mrs. Crowe would take hold of my hand, I think she would see them,' she suggested.

I did so; and then at intervals of a few seconds, I saw thrown up, apparently from the floor, waves of white light, faint, but perfectly distinct and visible. In order that I might know whether our perceptions of this phenomenon were simultaneous, I desired her, without speaking, to press my hand each time she saw it, which she did; and each time I distinctly saw the wave of white light. I saw it, at these intervals, as long as I held her hand and we were in the dark. Nobody saw it but she and myself; and we did not follow up the experiment by the others taking her hand, which we should have done.

During this interval, another light suddenly appeared in the middle of the room, away from where we were standing, I saw a bright diamond of light, like an extremely vivid spark—only not the colour of fire; it was white, brilliant, and quiescent, but shed no rays. I did not mention this, because I wished to learn if it was visible to anybody else—but nobody spoke of it; not even the clairvoyante. Whether she saw it or not, I cannot say. When the candles were relighted these lights were no longer visible, and one of the gentlemen went over the house above and below, but saw nothing but the dust and desolation of a long uninhabited dwelling.

When we came away, and Mr. Mc. N. had locked the door, we walked to the carriage. I said, 'then none of you saw the waves of light.'

'No,' said they.

'Well,' said I, 'I certainly did, and I never saw anything like it before. Moreover, I saw another sort of light.'

'Did you,' said Mr. Mc. N., interrupting me; 'was it a bright spark of light like the oxy-hydrogen light?'

'Exactly,' said I. 'I could not think what to compare it to; but that was it.'

I thus was certain that he had seen the same thing as myself; he had not spoken of it from a similar motive; he waited to have his impression confirmed by further testimony.

You see our results were not great, but the visit was not wholly barren to me. Of course, many wise people will say, I did not see the lights, but that they were the offspring of my excited imagination. But I beg to say that my imagination was by no means excited. If I had been there *alone,* it would have been a different affair; for though I never saw a ghost nor ever fancied I did, I am afraid I should have been very nervous. But I was in exceedingly good company, with two very clever men, besides the lawyer, a lady, and the clairvoyante; so that my nerves were perfectly composed, as I should not object to seeing any ghost in such agreeable society. Moreover, I did not *expect* any result; because, there is very seldom any on these occasions, as ghosts appear we know not why; but certainly not because people wish to see them. They generally come when least expected and least thought of.

Mr. Mc. N., on inquiry, learnt that unaccountable lights were amongst the things complained of. What occasioned them and the other phenomena, it had certainly been the proprietor's interest for many years to discover; it had also been the interest of numerous tenants, who having taken the house for a term, found themselves obliged to leave it at a sacrifice. Yet, for all those years, no explanation could be found for the annoyances but that the house was haunted. No tradition seems extant to account for its evil reputation. If what the clairvoyante said was true, the murders must have occurred long ago.

A gentleman, an inhabitant of the same city, once mentioned to me that a friend of his, many years previously, when quite a young man, had one Sunday evening been walking alone in the fields outside this town; and that he met a young woman, a perfect stranger, who, on some pretense asked him to see her safe home. He did so; she led him to a lone farmhouse, and then inviting him to walk in, shewed him into a room and left him. Whilst waiting for her return, idly looking about, he found hidden under the table, which was covered with a cloth, a dead body. On this discovery, he rushed to the door; it was locked; but the window was not very high from the ground, and by it he escaped; terrified to such a degree, that he not only left the city that very evening, but hastened out of the country, apprehensive that he had been enticed to the house and shut up with the murdered man, for the purpose of throwing the guilt on him; and as justice was not so clear sighted, and much more inexorable than in these days, he feared the circumstantial evidence might go against him. He settled in a foreign country and finally died there.

Where this locality was, I don't know, except that it was in the environs of the city—environs which have since been covered with buildings; what if the house that we visited should have been erected on the site of that lone farm!

It may be so; at all events, this story shews how possible it is that some similar event might have occurred on the spot where the haunted house stands.

In conclusion, let me once more recall to my readers that one, whose insight none will dispute, reminds us, in relation to this very subject, that "our philosophy" does not comprehend all wisdom and all truth. Philosophy is a good guide when she opens her eyes, but where she obstinately shuts them to one class of facts because she has previously made up her mind they cannot be genuine, she is a bad one.

Professor A. told me that when he was at Gottingen, as great favour, and through the interest of an influential professor there, he was allowed to see a book that had belonged to Faust, or Faustus, as we call him.[2] It was a large volume, and the leaves were stiff and hard like wood. They contained his magic rites and formulas, but on the last page was inscribed a solemn injunction to all men, as they loved their own souls, not to follow in his path or practice the teaching that volume contained.

There appears to be a mystery out of the domain—I mean the present domain of science—within the region of the hyper-psychical, regarding our relations, while in this world, with those who have past the gates, a belief in which is, I think, innate in human nature. This belief, in certain periods and places, grows rank and mischievous; at others, it is almost extinguished by reaction and education; but it never wholly dies; because, everywhere and in all times, circumstances have occurred to keep it alive, amongst individuals, which never reach the public ear. Now, the truth is always worth ascertaining on any subject; even this despised subject of ghosts, and those who have an inherent conviction that they themselves are spirits, temporarily clothed in flesh, feel that they have an especial interest in the question. We are fully aware

---

[2] Johann Georg Faust (c. 1480 or 1466 –c. 1541) was a German alchemist who quickly became a legend and who allegedly penned several grimoires (or books of magical spells). His legend inspired Christopher Marlowe's play *The Tragical History of Doctor Faustus* (c. 1592) and Johann Wolfgang von Goethe's two-play sequence *Faust* (completed in 1831) along with symphonies and more.

that the investigation presents all sorts of difficulties, and that the belief is opposed to all sorts of accepted opinions; but we desire to ascertain the grounds of a persuasion, so nearly concerning ourselves which in all ages and all countries has prevailed in a greater or less degree, and which appears to be sustained by a vast amount of facts, which, however, we admit are not in a condition to be received as anything beyond presumptive evidence. These facts are chiefly valuable, as furnishing cumulative testimony of the frequent recurrence of phenomena explicable by no known theory, and therefore as open to the spiritual hypothesis as any other. When a better is offered, supported by something more convincing than pointless ridicule and dogmatic assertion, I for one, shall be ready to entertain it. In the meanwhile, hoping that time may, at length, in some degree, rend the veil that encompasses this department of psychology, we record such experiences as come under our obser- vation and are content to await their interpretation.

Case 4: When Ghosts Are Something Else

Investigation: reconnaissance by William Howitt in the spring of 1859 and surveillance by Captain D— in Thorpe, Derbyshire, the following winter. Emma Hardinge Britten conducted a follow-up investigation at a nearby site, date unknown.

Manifestations: knockings, roaming lights, dark figures observed within those lights.

Pertinent Facts: As suggested in Case 2, William Howitt (1792-1879) was a major figure among Victorian ghost hunters. He was an author, not a clergyman, but he had an evangelical devotion to spiritualism and the belief that the supernatural was accessible to those in the physical realm. His conviction—and ambition—is apparent in the title one of his books: *The History of the Supernatural in All Ages and Nations and in All Churches, Christian and Pagan, demonstrating a Universal Faith.*[1] Howitt's vision of the supernatural realm extended to spirits that had never existed in physical form on Earth—beings that were something *other* than ghosts—evident in his investigation of a house called Clamps-in-the-Wood. He was unable to witness these curious spirits himself, though, and passed that task to a man he refers to as Captain D—. Is this military man the anonymous author of the second document in this case? Some clues suggest so, but it remains inconclusive. More certainly, Emma Hardinge Britten (1823–1899) knew of Howitt's report and agreed with his conclusions, which guided her own subsequent investigation of the same otherworldly beings in the area of Clamps-in-the-Wood.

---

[1] William Howitt, *The History of the Supernatural in All Ages and Nations and in All Churches, Christian and Pagan, demonstrating a Universal Faith* (Longman, Green, Roberts, Longman, Green, 1863).

BERG-GEISTER—CLAMPS-IN-THE-WOOD

William Howitt[2]

It is a curious question to what extent variety of spirits reaches in the invisible world. The variety of animated life in this world is infinite, measuring from the elephant to the animalcule which requires vast microscopic power to perceive it. May we not then suppose that some such analogy prevails in the spiritual world; and that such spirits as are but a little lower than the grade of men and angels may have almost identity with them, and may be distinguished only by lesser stature, by different hue, or by peculiarity of habits? We know that classical antiquity peoples air, earth, wood and water with such varied beings. The Naiad, the Dryad, the Hamadryad, the Nereid, enlivened mountain, forest, and ocean, to their imaginations, and have added a whole world of creation in their poetry to the natural one. The middle ages abounded with imps, incubi, brownies, necks, pixies and fairies, and even yet there are those who maintain that these are more than poetic entities. We know that the miners of Germany and the North have always asserted and do still assert the existence of Kobolds and other Berg-Geister, or spirits of the mountains and the mines, and that they assist or thwart their exertions in quest of ore, according as they are irritated or placated. They describe them as short and black, and declare that when they are attached to certain mines they go before them in the solid subterranean rock, knocking with their hammers, and thus indicating the presence of metal and the devious course of the vein. If it is lost by a break in the strata, or a fault as they call it, the sound of the Berg-Geist's hammer directs where again to seek for it; and when there in a busy and energetic thumping of many hammers, it is the certain announcement of abundant ore.

I might quote whole chapters of relations of this kind from German writers, but these things are too well known to need that. I was lately reading somewhere of three or four of these spirits of the mines making occasional visits to a house in the vicinity of mines in Germany or Norway. They were described as about four feet in height, perfectly black, and seeming to enjoy the approach to the

---

[2] This appeared in *The Spiritual Magazine* 3.10 (Oct., 1862) pp. 450-59.

fire and the society of the inmates. I have repeatedly sought for this account, not having made a note of it at the time, but in vain. My reason for this was to quote it, with time and place, as a curious coincidence of what I am now going to relate. It was but the other day, too, that I met with a mechanic in Wales who has been led to the discovery of a vein of copper ore by the knocking of the spirits of the mine.

In the spring of 1859, we spent a few pleasant months at Thorpe, in my native county of Derby, near the entrance to the charming glen, Dovedale. Whilst here a poor woman from the hills at a few miles distance came to a neighbouring clergyman to beg that he would go to her cottage and exorcise some spirits which haunted it, and which she said she was afraid might frighten the children. She described them as coming enveloped in a peculiar light, which sometimes illuminated the whole house. The clergyman, a young and clever Oxfordman, told the woman that there were no such things as ghosts, that all such notions were now exploded as silly and superstitious, and that the best proof was that such things never appeared to the enlightened and well-educated. He assured her that at the same time he perfectly believed her story, and did not doubt the annoyance to which she was subjected, but that she might depend upon it that it proceeded from some of her neighbours in the flesh, who probably wanted to get her cottage if they could frighten her out of it; and that the light, he had as little doubt, was thrown into her house by a magic-lantern.[3] He advised her to keep a sharp look-out, and try to discover her disturbers. The poor woman shook her head and returned, nothing assured by this learned lecture.

Hearing of this from the clergyman himself, I asked him, much to his astonishment, whether he was quite so sure that these were not spirits? He looked hard at me to see whether I were not quizzing him; but being told that I was quite serious, he grew more astonished. He was prepared for superstition in an old peasant-woman, but not amongst the "book-larned," as they are styled up there. I added, for his further astonishment, that the visits of spirits in London, as well as all over America, were now things of daily occurrence; that I, myself had seen their amazing doings, had received many communications from them, and had repeatedly

---

[3] See footnote 5 on page 12 regarding magic lanterns.

shaken hands with them.[4] It was a proof of my friend's firmness of mind that he did not at once advise my family to have me well looked after. Perhaps he did not do that because he found them all asserting the same experiences.

Naturally desirous to ascertain the amount of truth in the old woman's story, I asked the person whose cottage I occupied whether he had ever heard of a place called Clamps-in-the-Wood being haunted. "Oh," said he, "that is a very old story. Clamps, a labourer, lived there fifty years, and he always talked of the lights which every few evenings lit up his house. He was grown very fond of them, and called them his 'glorious lights.' When he was out anywhere, and it was growing late, he used to say, 'Well, I must go home, I want to see my glorious lights.'" "Does he live there now?" I asked. "No, sir," said my informant, a dry, clear-headed unimaginative carpenter; "no, sir, old Clamps left the cottage four years ago, and went to the next village, where he died. He was then above eighty years of age, and wanted caring for." "And did anyone else ever see these lights?" I asked. "Oh, bless you, sir, yes, plenty of people. They were no ways healer (shy). They would come when neighbours were in." "But were they only lights? Did Clamps and his friends never see any figures, ghosts, or anything of that sort?" "Not as I ever heard of. They were lights as came and went."

Finding that this was an old affair, and that it was well known all over the neighbourhood, there was an end of the magic-lantern. Very improbable as it was that any magic lantern was to be found up there, even if such a thing had been heard of, it was still more improbable that some wag or generation of wags had been playing it off on Clamps and his successors for half a century. But what these lights were I determined to know. According to the old woman's story, there were now visible not only lights but spirits.

On a fine afternoon in June, I therefore set out for Clamps-in-the-Wood. My way led me past the charming Ilam Hall, the seat of Jesse Watts Russell, Esq.,[5] and along the banks of the Manifold, that pleasant and careering trout stream, and so up into the hills beyond.

---

[4] By the time this article appeared, the spiritualism movement had a firm following in the U.S., the U.K., and elsewhere.

[5] Jesse Watts-Russell (1786-1875) was a wealthy industrialist who served as Sheriff of Staffordshire and a Member of Parliament, and became a Fellow of the Royal Society. In the 1820s, he had Ilam Hall rebuilt in keeping with the Gothic Revival movement.

It was drawing towards evening when the footpath, into which I had been directed by a cottage girl sitting sewing in the moorland valley below, led me directly in front of a good country mansion, with a garden enclosed by a stonewall before it, and a pair of tall, ornamental gates admitting a view of this pleasant and flowery area. There were some children at play in this garden, and of them I enquired the way to Clamps-in-the-Wood. "Oh," said they, "you must keep along the outside of the garden wall to the right, past the farmyard, and then you will see the road leading over the hills." Thanking my young informants, I was turning away, when I saw a gentleman rushing swiftly from the house, and beckoning me to stop. I waited, and found that he knew me by having seen me at Ilam, and would insist that I should go in and take tea with them. "We have just returned," he said, "from picnic in Dovedale, and are having a tea-dinner."

I went in, where I was introduced to the lady of the house, and to two other ladies, visitors. Tea over, I excused my leaving them by stating my intention of proceeding to Clamps. There was a curious expression passed over the faces of the ladies, but no remark was made. My host walked out with me, saying, "The man who now lives at Clamps is my labourer; he is just going home, and will shew you the way." He called—"David," and a young, intelligent fellow appeared from the cow-house, and his master bade him shew me the way to Clamps. He himself continued to walk with us some distance, and then saying with a smile, "David will tell you all about the ghost," turned back.

Accordingly as we pursued our way over the bare green moorland hills, I asked David, "What about the ghosts?" He told me that he could not himself speak as to ghosts, only on the authority of his mother-in-law who lived with him. All that he had seen were lights. These, he said, came almost every evening, but only on dark nights. In the summer they saw nothing of them, but about November, when the cold weather and the long nights set in, they came very often, moved about the house, sometimes made it quite light, and then sunk through the floor. His mother-in-law said she saw black figures in the middle of these lights; but for his part, he only saw the lights, and so did his wife. I asked him if they had ever been seen before he came to live there, and he gave the same account that I had received at Thorpe, that old Clamps had always had them; and that numbers of people besides them had seen them often enough.

With this conversation we were close upon the place, and very striking place it was. A deep valley presented itself below us, its sides clothed with woods, and along its bottom ran the winding course of a stream, which now was dry, and shewed only bare, rugged stones. This was the course of that singular little stream, the Hamps, which runs for a considerable distance underground; in winter and after heavy rains having only volume enough to appear as a stream above ground, and after a while disappearing altogether, and then bursting up in a tumultuous fountain at the foot of the cliffs below Ilam Hall, near another subterranean river, the Manifold. Around this deep, wild, solitary valley rose naked hills, and on their side, not far from this cottage, appeared the mouths and debris of lead mines. It was altogether a place apparently much suited for the haunt of solitary spirits. A paved causeway led down to the house, which stood on the edge of this lonely glen amid a few trees. As I approached, it looked ruinous. The end nearest to me had, in fact, tumbled in, and the remains of an old cheese-press shewed that it had once been a farmhouse. The part remaining habitable was only barely sufficient for a labourer's cottage. On entering, I found the old woman who had invoked the aid of the clergyman, seated in her armed chair under the great wide fireplace common to such houses. There were also a stout, healthy daughter, the wife of David, and two or three children.

On telling them that my errand was to enquire into the haunting of which they complained to the clergyman, both mother and daughter gave the same account as David had done. The old woman said that soon after they came to live in the house, where they had now been four years, the lights began to make their appearance; that they would appear most evenings, for months together, and sometimes several times in the course of the evening; that they would appear to come out of the wall, would advance into the middle of the floor, would make a kind of flickering, and sometimes light up the whole place, and then descend into the floor generally at one spot. There was no cellar beneath the floor, but they descended into the solid rock on which the house was built. They described the light as neither like the light of fire, a lamp, or a candle; but they could not express themselves more clearly about it. It did not at all alarm them, and the old woman said that the reason that she went to the clergyman was because the children were now getting so old as to notice the light before they went to bed in the evening, and they were afraid that it might come to frighten them.

What made them think so was that the old woman saw clearly dark figures in the centre of the lights. They were generally three, like short men, as black and as polished, she said, as a boot. Whilst they staid, she said their hands were always in motion, and that occasioned the flickering on the wall. She thought them quite harmless, for they never did any mischief, but seemed to take a pleasure in coming towards the warm fire, and looking at what was going on. She said that at first neither her daughter nor son-in-law saw anything, and laughed at her when she said she saw old Clamps's lights; but she had prayed earnestly that they might be enabled to see them, that they might not think she was saying what was not true, and they soon after began to see them, and now saw them regularly, but only the lights; they could not perceive the dark figures within the lights.

I expressed a great desire to see them myself, but they said it was the wrong time of the year: the nights now had scarce any darkness, and the lights could only be seen during the dark season; that if I should be there towards "the latter end"—that meant, of the year—I might see them almost any evening. I asked if she had ever tried to speak to the dark figures. She said no; she thought it best while they were harmless to let them alone, and let them come and go just as pleased them. I asked if they ever heard them speak, and they said never inside of the house, but that they often heard them speaking outside as they came up to the door. I asked them if they had never been frightened by them, and they replied only once. On a dark night in winter they heard a horse coming down the causeway, dragging a log at its feet. They could hear the distinct striking of its iron shoes on the flagstones, and the jingling of the chain, and lumbering of the log as it was drawn forward. When it came up to the door a fierce dog growled at it, and they were so frightened that one of them jumped up and bolted the door. The sounds then ceased altogether; and on going out to search neither horse nor dog were visible.

I remarked that perhaps a horse had got into their yard; but they said it could not do that, and that they had no dog. On another occasion, the old woman said that the door being open into the next room, which was the sleeping room, she saw a young woman kneeling on the bed with her back towards her, in the attitude of prayer; that she watched her in silence for some time, when all at once she became covered with spots like a leopard, and then disappeared. They had also observed when the flickering of the light on the wall was strong, that drops of blood would seem to trickle down, but no stain was ever left. Such was the substance of the statement of the old woman, her daughter and son-in-law.

On my return to the house where I had taken tea, all were eager to know what I had learned. In fact, the hostess, on my setting out for Clamps, had followed me to the door, and particularly pressed me to give them a call on my return. I understood the motive, though no word of the lights or ghosts had been uttered by them or me. They now showed themselves all familiar with the reports of the lights and the figures, yet had never taken the trouble to go and judge for themselves; but said one of their servants, being there one evening, had seen the lights very plainly.

Speaking of these curious circumstances on my return home, one of our friends, Captain D—, a scientific man, observed that he had an engagement in Yorkshire about Christmas, and that he would go round that way, and, if necessary, stay all night at Clamps-in-the-Wood. He kept his word. Taking up his quarters at the excellent fishing-inn, the Izaak Walton at the mouth of Dovedale; in the course of smoking a cigar with the landlord in the evening, he asked if they had any good ghost stories in that neighbourhood. "Oh!" said Mr. Prince, "if you want a haunted house you must go to Clamps-in-the-Wood." Not appearing to know anything of the matter, the gallant captain asked him the particulars, and received pretty much such an account as I have given. The captain asked if he thought, that there was really anything to be seen there, and the landlord replied that he could not speak from personal knowledge, for he would rather go twice as far in another direction; but that it was so commonly reported, and by so many who had been there, that there seemed very little doubt about the matter. On this Captain D— declared that, of all things, he would like to witness something supernatural, and that he would go and pass the night there.

The astonishment of the host and hostess was unbounded. "What, leave a comfortable inn and comfortable bed on a cold winter's night to go nearly three miles into a wild region of hills and moors, and to sit up in a haunted house!" They thought at first that he must be joking, but seeing him throw on a capacious military cloak, they then endeavoured by earnest entreaties to dissuade him from his purpose. They represented the darkness and the intricacy of the way; the almost impossibility of finding the place; the dreary solitude of the spot when arrived at it. In vain, bidding them good night, our friend rushed forth, and took the way which the landlord had described to him, before aware of his purpose.

The undertaking was, indeed, a courageous one. A long march had to be made along a tolerably well-tracked road; then a bypath must be struck to the right ascending into the hills. The manor-house or mansion at which I had called must be found, and beyond that it was not likely that the direction over the moorland hills could be hit upon without a guide. But those things did not daunt a man who had made his campaign in the wilds of hostile tribes. By inquiring at a cottage near the end of the high road, he was enabled to hit the hill-track, reached the manor-house, and there received fresh instructions. Yet he missed the direction in the moorland hills—a way there could be said to be none—and wandered about for some hours in a thick fog. At length, he managed to re-find the manor-house, and then got a boy to guide him. It was ten o'clock at night when he reached Clamps-in-the-Wood.

The astonishment amounting to consternation of the simple inmates at his knock at the door at that time of night in such a place was excessive. When they opened the door, and in walked a gentleman in a large military cloak, they stood in speechless wonder. Captain D—, however, with his affable and agreeable manner, soon put them at their ease, and told them the purport of his visit. Their amazement was, if anything, augmented; but they offered him all the means they had for insuring the success of his visit. He proposed to sit with them till their bedtime, and then, if the mysterious visitors had not appeared, to sit up alone by the fireside. To this they readily assented, and as the hour was already late for them the daughter and son-in-law retired, and the old woman and the captain sate and conversed on the subject of the lights.

During two hours no lights appeared, and the old woman told the captain that the lights were often shy with strangers, but that if he could come in for a few successive evenings, he would see enough of them. As they sate with the light only of a low fire burnt to cinders, and therefore without flame, there came knockings in various parts of the room, now on the walls, then on the table, and then on the floor. Captain D—, who was perfectly familiar with the spiritual phenomenon, vulgarly called spirit-rapping, gave, however, no intimation of this, but asked what these knockings were. The old woman said she didn't know, but they were always heard when the lights were coming. No lights, however, appeared, but presently the Captain saw his cloak, which he had laid on the table, begin to move, and anon it was pulled down and thrown on the floor. The old woman said they were often doing that sort of thing, but they never did any mischief.

When twelve o'clock came, Captain D— insisted on the old woman going to bed, and she went, leaving him a candle to light if he wished, and coal to mend his fire. As the night was cold, he now wrapped himself in his military cloak, and sate in profound silence. There was only just light enough from the fire to make the objects in the room visible, and he could hear that the people in the next room were sound asleep by a full concert of nasal music. He sate till one o'clock; he sate till two, and there was neither sight nor sound, but just as he began to despair, his ear was caught by a sound almost soundless, and turning towards the place, he saw a globular light about the size of an ordinary opaque lamp-globe issue from the wall, about five or six feet from the floor, and advance about half a yard into the room. He was all attention, and so evidently was the intelligence within the light, for there it paused as if become aware of the presence of a stranger. Captain D— remained almost breathless, hoping that it would advance into the middle of the room, but it did not. It remained for about a couple of minutes and then receded again into the wall at the spot whence it had issued. As soon as it was clearly gone, Captain D— lit his candle and examined that part of the wall to see if he could discern any hole or fissure through which the light could have come. There was nothing of the kind: it was perfectly plain and sound. He then examined whether a light could have glanced through the window: that was closely curtained. Next he observed whether a light could have flashed through a chink of the door from the bedroom: there was no light there, and the nasal concert was proceeding as steadily as ever. Convinced, both by these examinations, and by the globular and peculiar light, that it was one of the old luminous visitants of the place, he again wrapped himself in his cloak and resumed his watch; but nothing further occurred.

At five o'clock the old woman made her appearance, and enquired what success. Captain D—told her of the appearance of the light, on which she said that was the real light, but no doubt it was "scarred" at the sight of a stranger; but if he could come again for a few evenings the lights would get over their shyness, and he would see them over and over; but this was not in the Captain's power. He made the old woman a recompense for the trouble he had given, and having a cup of warm coffee prepared by her, he returned to the inn to breakfast.

The captain's success was perhaps as much as could be expected for a single visit. He was quite satisfied that the haunting was founded on fact, and he determined to make another visit in the winter season. Whether he ever will now becomes doubtful, for I learn from the clergyman above mentioned that the people have deserted the house, and Clamps-in-the-Wood is now left to the lights and to ruin. Whether these Berg-Geister may continue their visits to the deserted hearth is equally doubtful; for it must be as cold and cheerless as their own mines, which extend horizontally far into the sides of the neighbouring hills.

But we must not quit Clamps-in-the-Wood without remarking on two or three particulars in this singular narrative which are important. As to the apparition of the lights, that has been a matter of assertion for more than half a century. They were so frequent that the old man, Clamps, had grown attached to them, and many other persons had seen them. They were a settled fact all over the neighbourhood, except among the classes who have been systematically educated to ignore such phenomena, and to deny their existence on the authority of their own ignorance, instead of their own rational enquiries. The old woman had never probably heard of such a country as Germany, much less of its Berg-Geister in her life, yet her accounts most curiously agree with the statements of thousands of German miners. She had never heard of such a thing as Modern Spiritualism, or spirit-rapping, yet she had had spirit-rapping going on for years in her cottage, and knew by experience that it announced the presence of the spirits of the mine.

In her own person, she exhibited the regular operation of well-established spiritual laws. She was undoubtedly a medium, or, as

Reichenbach would term it, a sensitive.[6] She saw the lights before her daughter and son-in-law, and, according to universal human practice, was ridiculed for asserting what she saw. She prayed that her son-in-law and daughter might have their eyes opened to see, and her prayer was heard. But the old woman, who was a hale, hearty, clear-headed old soul of perhaps sixty-five, became further developed, and saw not only the lights but the spirits in them, which her son-in-law and daughter never did see, not being equally open to spiritual impressions. Nor did they ever pretend to see more than the lights, though they boldly and invariably asserted their frequent sight of them. In all their statements to the clergyman, to myself, to the captain, their account was uniform and the same. As to magic-lanterns, I believe there was no such thing within many miles, except it might be in possession of Mr. Watts Russell, of Ilam, or of the clergyman in question. And as to anyone wanting the house over the head of the occupants, the very idea was ridiculous, as it was occupied by one of the labourers of the gentleman farming the property, and lies so drearily, so lonely, and so out-of-the-way, that, independent of its reputation as a haunted spot, it was so little desirable as an abode, that its late tenants have deserted it. Whether it will become the subject of further investigation, or whether the former conditions necessary to such investigation remain, are all doubtful; it is therefore to be regretted that a proper enquiry was not instituted by the educated people of the neighbourhood years ago, when enquiry was so easy, and might have been pursued to any length. What we know of this case, however, is curious, as affording confirmation to like cases on the Continent, which have been asserted as positive facts for many generations.

In the "Facts"—Thatsacken—given at the end of the "Seeress of Prevorst,"[7] in the original German edition, in "Fourth Fact," is

---

[6] Carl Reichenbach (1788-1869) was a scientist interested in magnetism and energy. He theorized that all living things share what he termed Odic force, and certain people, whom he called sensitives, could perceive this force. (His sensitives were also prone to neuroses and delusion.) This is akin to the widespread idea of "ghost-seerers" or individuals with a particularly keen ability to perceive specters.

[7] *Die Seherin von Prevorst* (1829), by Justinus Kerner, is a case study of Friederike Hauffe (1801–1829), a clairvoyant reputed to have healing powers and other miraculous talents. Kerner also presents an in-depth defense of the authenticity of such abilities. An English translation titled *The Seeress of Prevorst* was published in 1845, the translator being none other than Catherine Crowe, whose ghost hunt is featured in Case 3 of this book.

mentioned a spirit often appearing at the house of a watchman at Weinsberg, quite black, and the watchman's wife said to Dr. Kerner, "There often shines out of the wall by night a lustre, round as a plate, and then disappears behind the wall again." This is strikingly like the light, and the manner in which it appeared to Captain D—. In the "Fifth Fact," another spirit appeared to Madame Hauffe, with its head surrounded by a glory of light. In a case occurring at Ammersweiler, five hours' journey from Weinsberg, a spirit used to appear, the face of which emitted a light that illuminated everything in the room; but the rest of the figure appeared only as a grey vapoury column. In another part the same series of "Facts," in the prison at Weinsberg, a spirit for some time went about a particular room, with a star on his breast as large as a man's hand. The figure itself was like a shadow. In various places of the same work spirits came attended by a crackling noise, and with flashes of light, very much like those whose appearance is related by Mr. Coleman in his "American Experiences," in the case of the wealthy banker, L—, and his deceased wife, Estelle, and Dr. Franklin.

Captain D— was informed by the inmates at Clamps, that the light was often seen in dark nights by people going past from the mines, shining out of the top of the chimney.

✤

A NIGHT AT CLAMPS-IN-THE-WOOD[8]

Anonymous

In the present age, when we hear so much about the supernatural, and are informed by a host of witnesses that certain wonderful phenomena can be induced by fulfilling the requisite conditions, it is interesting to examine, when possible, those statements or assertions which seem to indicate that spontaneous mysteries, if we may so term them, occur in various places, or, in other words, that unaccountable facts take place, or are *believed* by certain persons to take place.

There is, we believe, no subject which requires a more dispassionate or searching inquiry than this so-called Supernatural;

---

[8] This appeared in *Chambers's Journal* 1.80 (July 8, 1865) pp. 419-22.

and the person making it should be as much like a machine, bodily and mentally, as it is possible to make himself.

We all know how often our senses may be deceived, or at least one or two of them, and thus we should hesitate before we express an opinion, when the facts seem to tend to the unusual. We have but to look through a stereoscope,[9] and to there see the really flat surface resolved into foreground and distance, to be aware that, had we not the sense of touch, by means of which we can test that our sight is temporarily deceived, we might conscientiously assert that the photograph at which we were looking was a statuesque production, standing out from the paper, and not a mere representation of light and shade.

The ghostly effect of the plate-glass image, again, proves to us that one sense alone is not always to be trusted, but must be kept in check by others. When, however, we bring our five senses to bear upon a subject, it is difficult for us to say whether or not these have been all deceived, for if we grant the possibility of such an event, we must also allow that some doubt must exist as to our own tangibility or identity, for we have no other means of judging as to the substances and events around us than by the five senses with which we are provided.

In addition, however, to the care necessary to guard against a too complete dependence upon any one sense, we must, to be competent investigators, be free from that prejudice which too often induces us to form an opinion very hastily from a slight examination of facts; whilst another equally prejudiced person would come to a directly opposite conclusion, though a witness only to those facts which we also had seen. Again, we should avoid examining any evidence when our object is mainly to prove, or to disprove, according as we wish the result to be. Upon the whole, therefore, it may with truth be asserted, that an impartial investigator, especially on subtle phenomena, is very rarely to be found.

Having, then, a due diffidence as regards the infallibility of the senses with which nature had endowed us, but having tested the capacity of these in various parts of the world, and found that they might usually be trusted, we somewhat eagerly listened to the

---

[9] A stereoscope is a device invented in the early 1800s. It has dual lenses mounted on an arm. On one end of the arm is placed a slide with two pictures of a single scene, taken at slightly different angles. When viewed through the eyepiece, the two pictures appear to merge into *one* seemingly three-dimensional scene.

account of a friend who informed us of strange sights and sounds, mysterious nightly visitations, and other wonders, which were said to take place at a ruined farmhouse, part of which was inhabited, situated in one of the wildest glens in Derbyshire, and entitled 'Clamps-in-the-wood.'

It was a dull January day that we were deposited at the village of Ashbourne, in Derbyshire, and the cold fog seemed to penetrate ruthlessly through the thick overcoat with which we were provided.[10] The nearest hotel to the scene of our investigation was distant from Ashbourne about five miles, and a vehicle having been hired, we were in the space of about one hour deposited at the door.

A visitor during the dreary season of January was rare in this locality; the summer, with its bright warm days and trout-fishing, being considered more attractive. One always finds a welcome in an inn, however, and so we were soon at home, sipping a quiet glass of wine by the fire. We had, however, a work to perform, and we were busily engaged in planning how the first sod was to be turned. Strolling down the passage that led to the landlord's parlour, we asked and obtained permission to enter, and then found ourselves in the presence of the landlord and his wife, the village school-master, a butler or responsible servant of the squire's, and another man, whose occupation seemed to be 'promiscuous.' A little awkwardness at first prevailed, until we frankly stated that we did not like smoking in the parlour, so would take our pipe where we were, if there was no objection. In ten minutes we were all at home, and our train was ready to be fired, and our information illuminated. The friend from whom we had heard of 'Clamps' had stayed at the hotel, and seemed deservedly popular. Having heard his praises sounded, we were at length asked how he was. 'Quite well,' we replied, 'but rather curiously engaged, as we believe he is collecting ghost-stories.' Now this, although not strictly correct, had a foundation, and a good one, on truth, and served to answer the purpose we had in view. Two of the company rose to our cast more quickly than would the least cautious trout at a fly in the stream below.

'Ghost-stories! Then he ought to come to Clamps-in-the-wood; he'd have enough of them there.

---

[10] If comparing this chronicle to the account of Captain D— narrated by Howitt in the previous piece, bear in mind that this writer uses the editorial "we" (something like the royal "we") when referring to himself.

'Clamps-in-the-wood!' we replied; 'what is that?'

'You tell the gent,' said the landlord, referring to the butler.

'I'd rather hear the schoolmaster,' was the reply.

'Oh, I don't believe a word about it,' was the response of the pedagogue.

'And I don't know what to say,' said the landlord; 'for I've heard from so many people who have seen it, that I don't know what to think.'

'But what is there to be seen?' was our inquiry.

'You tell, Joe,' was the address to the unknown man; 'you've been there lately.'

'I'd as lieve be excused, and should like to hear Muster [the landlord] tell us, for he knows all about it.'

Thus called upon, the landlord commenced his tale.

'Well, sir, there's an old, half-ruined house about two miles from here, called 'Clamps,' and living there is an old woman, her daughter, and son-in-law; there's besides two or three young children. The place is very lonely and out of the way—a regular desolate place. For some years, the old woman used to see of a night strange-looking figures come in through the wall, and sink down through the floor; there used to be loud, heavy knocks heard at the same time, and the figures always seemed to be carrying lights. For a time, both the daughter and son-in-law laughed at this statement, though they, too, heard the noises, though they didn't see the figures; but after a bit, both of them saw just what the old woman did, and precious frightened they were, till they found no harm came to them. Then the figures seemed to be making signs, but this none of the three could stand, so they'd shut their eyes. Now, this has been going on a long time, and puzzles people amazingly.'

'But is it only the three residents who see these figures?' we inquired.

'O dear, no, sir; lots of people hereabouts have been there, and some see them—some don't.'

'Do some see them at the same time that others who are present do not?' we asked.

'That I can't say for certain, sir,' was the unsatisfactory response.

'What object can these people have for telling these stories?' we asked.

'None at all, sir; and they'd give anything to be free of these figures and lights.'

'Well, I've heard a good deal about it, but I don't believe a word,' was the assertion of the schoolmaster.

'You've never been there of night,' said Joe ironically.

'No; nor I ain't going to be made a fool of.'

'Then you speak by guess like, and don't know whether it be true or not.'

On the following morning, we started in search of Clamps; and after a somewhat damp journey, discovered the half-ruined house, situated in a wild out-of-the-way place. Having examined the building from the exterior, we took advantage of a slight shower to knock at the door, and to obtain permission to enter, and rest for a while. The interior of the domicile was anything but inviting. Two rooms on the ground-floor, and a sort of loft above, were the inhabited portions of Clamps. The lower floors being of stone, gave a cold appearance to the rooms, which was not in any way relieved by the furniture, all being of the most primitive description. The livestock in the house consisted of an old woman, whose appearance was scarcely prepossessing; her daughter; and two or three children.

Having taken a seat on a rough chair, placed beside the wood-embers that did duty for fire, we remarked to the ancient beldam that the situation was lonely, but pretty, probably, in summer. This remark had the effect of the most apt leading question, and brought forth a regular budget of information.

'Lonely, sir! yes, it be lonely; but I wish sometimes it was lonelier, that I do. You don't know, sir, what we've suffered here for years now. We're marked people, and has to do something, but we don't know what. I've tried to get the clergy to help me, but they don't seem to know what to do, and often times don't believe me. I'd a thought it was my fancy, like, that heard and saw these things, if my daughter and her man hadn't seen them too, and many people besides.'

'But what do you see and hear?' was our inquiry.

'Well, that I don't know. I don't know what to call them; but they are dark figures, carrying lights in their hands, and other things too. They come when it's night, and make signs to me as if they wanted something, and then they goes down in the ground.'

'And do you see them too?' we asked of the robust daughter.

'I do, sir,' was the reply; 'and till I got accustomed to them, I was very frightened; but they don't do us no harm, and so ain't afraid now.'

'Have you never spoken to them, or tried to make signs to them, to find out what they wanted.'

'That I wouldn't dare do, sir: I've heard it's dangerous, and I might get a hurt if I did so.'

After hearing various details from both women, we inquired whether people who came to see ever had their curiosity rewarded; and upon receiving an answer in the affirmative, we immediately asked permission to come that evening, for the purpose of seeing the dark figures. Upon ascending the narrow pathway through the wood, we met a countryman, who, touching his cap, gave us at once an opportunity for inquiries. We then ascertained that he was the son-in-law of the ancient dame, and having for a long time ignored the idea of the dark figures and lights, was at length almost frightened to death by finding them enter the room one evening where he was sitting alone. Since that time, he had very often seen them, and had now, like his wife, become used to them.

The surprise of the worthy landlord was great when we informed him that we purposed passing a night at Clamps-in-the-wood. But having taken a good dinner, provided ourselves with a flask, and a small dagger in case of accidents, we started off about dusk on our expedition in search of a ghost.

The fog on the hills was so dense, that we failed to keep the indistinct path that led in to the wood, and narrowly escaped climbing over a wall, and dropping on the opposite side, some forty feet; but the house was at length reached, and we there found the two females and the man sitting round the fire. Upon joining the party, we commenced a course of cross-questioning, endeavouring to shake the evidence which had been independently given us in the morning; but without effect. We also found that the visits of the 'lights,' &c, was a great source of annoyance to these people, and they believed their health suffered in consequence. No object was apparent for these statements being made, supposing them to be untrue; and the consistency of these illiterate and evidently obtuse people in their evidence was particularly marked.

Upon entering the room, we had placed an extra overcoat on a table at some distance from the fire; and whilst conversing with the man, a slight noise attracted our attention to this coat, when instantly, as though snatched, it slipped off the table onto the floor.

'Horse-hair or wire,' immediately occurred to us; so we took up the coat, examined it carefully, and replaced it in its original position, taking care that the whole coat should lie on the table, to avoid slipping. Scarcely had we retaken our seat, before the coat again fell to the ground. The old woman now volunteered the remark that this had something to do with the figures. Again was the coat replaced, when it remained obedient to the usual laws of matter.

As the hour of midnight approached, we desired to be left alone, and after some persuasion, got rid of the old woman and her daughter; of the son, however, we failed to obtain the absence; but as in half an hour he was sound asleep, we were not much disturbed by his presence.

We had drawn a heavy kind of bench onto the stone, into which, we were informed, the figures disappeared, so that if the dark gentlemen with the lights sank therein, they would have actually to touch us. A slight flickering light was given out by the wood-embers from the fire—just enough to reveal the various objects in the room. Two distinct nasal performances were going on in the loft above, whilst our companion also gave evidence that the god of sleep must be obeyed.

Fully an hour passed without sign of aught; still we were watchful, and ready either to see fact or detect a fraud. Suddenly, the leaf of the table on which our coat was lying moved up at about an angle of thirty degrees, and again descended; we waited for a repetition of this movement, but finding, after a lapse of several minutes, that all was quiet, we lighted a small piece of taper, and examined the said table-leaf, but could detect no means by which the movement had been made.

Again an interval of repose, followed by several dull, muffled sounds, like a drum gently beaten. To state where these noises came from, was impossible: now they seemed in the wall close to us, then outside the house, and at a distance; then, again, they seemed on the floor; then underground. For fully ten minutes these noises were audible, and certainly were puzzling, for though apparently unmeaning, yet they seemed to move here and there, and to alter their characteristics, as though guided by an intelligence.

During the continuation of these noises, our attention was attracted to the solid-looking door, upon which a curious effect was visible. At about five feet from the ground, and close to the door, a dim light appeared, like that exhibited by a moderator lamp turned down to its lowest power;[11] the light, however, was shaded off into darkness *without a cut shade,* the centre of the light being the more intense. For about ten seconds this was visible, when it seemed to die away as though absorbed by the darkness.

Immediately this object disappeared, we walked to the door, scratched a mark with our dagger at the spot on which we had seen the light. The door we found locked on the inside, the key being in the lock: this key we placed in our pocket, and reseated ourselves on the bench. Slowly passed the remainder of the night, until the first faint streaks of daylight roused the females, and brought them downstairs, after which we prepared to take our departure. Before leaving, however, we inquired particularly from the old woman as to the nature of the lights she usually saw; and although her description did not tally with that which we have given, yet there was a similarity between the two. She was evidently disappointed that we had not seen more during our nocturnal vigil, but assured us that if we stopped on watch another night, we should surely see the figures as well as the lights, as those who were 'patient' always did see.

Daylight having now arrived, we examined the door on which we had scratched. It was of solid wood; no artfully-cut trap or opening was there, good old English oak being the material. Our next investigation was directed to the table, the leaf of which had swung up and remained stationary for some seconds. There, also, we failed to detect any artificial means by which the movement had been made; and so, registering the observed facts in our memory, we thanked the trio for their night's lodging, and departed. Alas! We were the slaves of time; we were compelled to leave the neighbourhood on the day after our night-watch, and we could not therefore pursue our inquiries further. Since that period, we have not had an opportunity of visiting the neighbourhood, and therefore Clamps-in-the-wood remains to us a mystery. Our own conclusions or opinion on the observed facts would be valueless to the reader;

---

[11] Invented in the 1830s, moderator lamps used a spring to raise a reservoir of oil to the wick.

we can merely state that we have recorded events as they occurred; and the steps we took to prevent either delusion or being tricked without detection, were such as we have found to amply detect some of the performances of our most apt conjurors. We have merely given a genuine detail of our experiences at Clamps-in-the-wood, leaving the reader to form his own conclusions therefrom.

✤

From "What Spirits Are Amongst Us"

Emma Hardinge Britten[12]

. . . It is well known in certain mining districts, especially in Bohemia and Hungary, that many of the miners cherish faith in the existence of an order of beings who take especial interest in their labours, and help them to find rich leads of minerals, knock, or as they call it, "hammer" away lustily when they are at a fault, and sometimes by these sounds, sometimes by lights, and occasionally by the apparition of *little figures,* point the way to the richest leads of the metals. I have visited the mines in Germany and the Bohemar Wold, where I have heard those knockings, seen the lights, and should have unhesitatingly attributed such phenomena to the spirits of deceased friends of the miners had I not also, not once or twice, but many times, seen little stocky-looking things in the shape of men, very small, and either black, red, or metallic in colour—little chunks of creatures, whom the miners were accustomed to see and call by a name which, translated, signifies "earth spirits." They said they were kind and good; never meddled with them, though they sometimes in sport threw their tools about. These miners told me they often saw lights, and all could hear the knockings, *but few could see the figures,* and in some of the mines I visited, the poor workmen thought more highly of me than ordinary, because I could see their "well beloved little earth spirits." With the light of modern

---

[12] This is extracted from "What Spirits Are Amongst Us?" *Banner of Light* 38.2 (Oct. 9, 1875) pp. 1-2. Britten relates her experience near Clamps-in-the-Wood to support Henry S. Olcott, author of *People from the Other World* (American, 1875), in the claim that "some at least of the spirits most actively engaged in astonishing earth's natives through the processes of materialization, were not of 'human origin' and 'never had a mortal existence'" (p. 1). Apparently, Olcott had raised a ruckus by asserting this in a series of letters to the *New York Tribune.*

Spiritualism to guide me, I easily understood that I, as a medium, could see spiritual apparitions invisible to the eyes of those who were not mediums. I also comprehended why certain of the workmen, their wives or children, being spiritually unfolded, could perceive the forms of those whom their less gifted companions only knew by their knockings or flashing lights.

In William Howitt's charming sketch, called *Berg-Geister,* he alludes to these popular beliefs amongst miners, but he does more, he gives a very graphic account of a certain *Clamps in the wood,* where veritable gnomes figured as the principal personages. Mr. Howitt's narrative is supported by names, witnesses, and sundry details which confirm his own undoubted testimony. As I happened to be one of the privileged few who visited the haunted region which Mr. Howitt writes of, I shall cite my own experiences in the matter, with what I trust my readers will allow to be the honest purpose of making myself responsible for the story.

It is now some few years since, being in the neighbourhood of a lovely valley called Dovedale, in the County of Derbyshire, England, I heard my kind host and hostess, Mr. and Mrs. Hart, expatiating upon the singular phenomena they had witnessed in the cottage of an old labourer (then passed away to the better world), called Clamps; I think, if I recollect right, he had worked for Mr. Hart, who was interested in the mines adjacent to Dovedale. My friends informed me that Clamps had resided for over fifty years in a ruinous old farm-house, only a small part of which was habitable. The place was on the edge of the mines, where the old man in his youth and prime had worked, and where, as I believe, he died. During his long residence of half a century in this place, old Clamps and his associates were accustomed to see strange globular lights, which year in and year out would come and go with all the familiarity of household ghosts.

Mr. Hart, who was somewhat of a sceptic on the subject of my "spirits," as he termed it, declared that if Clamps's lights were spirits of "humans," they must have been those of deceased lamplighters or gas men—for they never appeared by day, and generally chose the long winter nights, or particularly dark evenings, for the periods of their visitations. Old Clamps called them his "glorious lights," and was very particular about returning to his shanty early every night, so that he should not miss seeing them. They came out, or seemed to come, as my friends alleged, from a firm wall, fashioned of rock, and the blocks so solidly cemented together that not a crack or cranny could be discovered. They generally came from two or three to seven or eight in number. Mrs. Hart said that one very cold winter's night she saw as many as ten of these lights. They seemed to fill the little room, and hovered about the fire as if gratified with its pleasant warmth. "They came," said my informant, "out of the wall, some about two feet from the ground, others as high as three feet, but none more than four, and all remained the same height during the time of their stay." They shook, trembled, or *flickered* the whole time, as if they were quivering with fear or cold. They had been seen for years and years, longer, indeed, than the memory of the "oldest inhabitants" of that region could trace them, except the venerable octogenarian Clamps, who affirmed they had always been there as long as he could remember. Their coming was generally preceded by crackling sounds, or direct knockings, and many of the neighbours declared they saw the figures of *little men* just as Mr. Howitt's narrative describes them—namely, "black as a coal, and polished as a boot." One of the neighbours, a woman who had often visited the cottage of Clamps with her children, described the appearance of the little men as being short, chunky, destitute of hair, polished all over, and bearing about the region where the heart lies in human beings a large globular light about the size of an ostrich's egg. It was this light, she said, "which the folks saw," and it was by this light that she and her children saw them. She added, they did not walk, but jumped about, and their incessant restless motions caused the flickerings which the lights always exhibited. My friend Mrs. Hart always beheld the dim outline of little figures accompanying the lights, but the distinctness with which these creatures were seen seemed to depend upon what in our philosophy we term mediumistic endowments. Other forms had been seen at Clamps's, such as dogs, horses, and even wild beasts, but as the cottage was inaccessible to horses, and no other animals of any kind were kept or known to frequent that neighbourhood, these accounts were set down to superstitious exaggerations.

I might fill a volume with the stories related to me of this region, and the matter-of-fact narratives which many of the most intelligent of the miners and their families furnished me with seemed beyond gainsay or denial. Shortly before my visit to that section of country terminated, my friends the Harts proposed to give me an opportunity of witnessing for myself some of the marvels they had discoursed about. They told me old Clamps had passed away; that the cottage he had inhabited had been tenanted for some years by a very decent family of poor peasants, but as the children grew up the elder members of the family, fearing the continual manifestation of preternatural sights and sounds would make them "skeary" and superstitious, had at length moved away, and the place had been abandoned. It was the opinion of the few labourers who had been accustomed to see and had grown familiar with Clamps's "glorious lights," that they would never come out except a fire was lighted there; and as the place was deserted and very far remote from other inhabitants, my friends proposed to take me to a still more distant neighbourhood, and one where, as they knew by experience, my curiosity might have a good chance to be gratified. Starting early one fine October morning we drove about ten miles from home, intending to visit the mines, which commenced about the end of Dovedale Valley, but terminated in the direction my friends pursued. Arrived at a wild and most romantic glen, we left our horses and carriage at a poor tavern called "The Miner's Rest," perched on the very top of the mass of rocks which reared up their craggy heights like sentinels guarding the entrance to the charmed region. Our path was continued for more than two miles aping a rough road broken out of fallen trees and crumbling rocks by the wheels of the heavy wagons used for conveying the mineral from the mines. A more wild, weird, and toilsome journey I never in my life undertook, and in truth I became so fatigued during its progress that we had some doubts whether I should be able to muster strength enough to accomplish our pilgrimage. It was twilight before we gained our point of destination, and glad enough I was to see the glowing fires of what looked more like a little encampment of gipsies than a village, although it was really dignified with that title. My friends guided me at once to a hut more pretentious than the rest, and introduced me to a family who had formerly been servants in their household. It consisted of a man, his wife, mother, and two fine lads, all of whom were employed in different ways in the adjacent mines. As we stated that we had only come to inspect these mines, and that the lateness of our visit was occasioned by the difficulties which attended our journey, the good, hospitable people were at once apprised of the necessity of providing us with some accommodation for passing the night. The women, after busying themselves to provide us with some boiling water for our tea—for we had carried provisions with us—agreed to retire to a neighbour's hut with their boys, whilst the father, who was on duty in the mines, left us soon after we arrived. The shanty was to be at our disposal, then, during the night.

Hart was to be "stowed away" in a cave at the back of the house, hewn out of the rock, and filled with sweet, fresh hay, for the use of the horses employed by the miners, whilst a rude but clean bed was assigned to Mrs. Hart and myself. When all was done the women piled up the logs on the hearth, where a cheerful fire was burning, and prepared to quit us. Just as they were bidding us good night, the logs, which they had arranged with some care, suddenly tumbled down and rolled over and over on the floor. Deeming this a mere accident I took no notice of it until I observed, whilst Maria the miner's wife, was in the act of replacing them, several small, glimmering lights flickering over the wall against which the logs were piled. This might have been the phosphorescent light occasioned by the decay of the wood, I thought; but lo! the logs were no sooner piled up again than down they toppled, and that apparently without any cause. I then observed significant looks passing between the mother and daughter, and an evident disposition to linger and make some explanation as yet unspoken. At this moment a succession of loud knockings was heard on the wall at the back of the room, which I should say, by-the-by, was of stone, and little more than a cave, having been partly formed out of the solid rock.

"Is not that some one knocking?" I inquired; "perhaps it is Mr. Hart. We had better see what is the matter."

"No, ladies," said our hostess, with some hesitation, "it isn't anybody—that is, no one in particular; it's the way of this place."

"But what, then, is the way of the place?" asked Mrs. Hart, merrily, and with an evident wish to encourage the poor woman. But before they could answer, down came the brushes on the wall, the frying-pan, and sundry other things that had been hung up on shelves and hooks. The rude door shook violently, and knockings now resounded from every side of us in quick and irregular showers.

"The wind is rising," said my friend; "I fear we shall have a stormy night."

"Don't be skeary, ladies," said our good hostess, encouragingly, "but I s'poose as how I'd just better say them's not the wind, but just the little hammerers; *you knows who,* marm," she added, nodding mysteriously to Mrs. Hart.

"Oh, yes! I know all about them, Betty," said my friend, addressing the mother; "they won't hurt us, but they seem rather rough to-night. Don't they like our being here?"

"Lord love ye, marm," replied the old woman; "it's all along of they's joy to see ye that they're making this to-do. I think they be mortal glad to see the young lady. Only look'ee there, marm!"

I did look, and there, to my astonishment, and I must confess with a thrill of deeper awe than I could account for or control, I saw a row of four lights as large as the veritable ostrich's egg which adorned the mantle shelf of the humble shanty. These lights were directly behind me, and I did not see them till, attracted by the woman's explanation, I turned round and faced them. They were bright, globular in form, vapoury in substance, and nebulous, thickening towards the centre, and deepening in colour almost to a dull red. The faint outline of a miniature human form appeared in connection with each light. They were of different sizes; none of them, however, were higher than four feet. They jumped up and down, and threw out something which resembled hands toward me, and as they moved the lights danced and shimmered. These wonderful *things* at length retreated into the solid wall behind them, and the place where they had been was illuminated only by the light of the wood fire. For two hours the women (who stayed with us at our earnest request), Mrs. Hart and myself, watched for the reappearance of these spectral lights in vain. In the interim the knockings continued, and a few stray gleams like stars shone out from the other side of the apartment, but immediately vanished. A kitten which was attempting to sleep in the warmth of the cheerful fire, would raise its head at the sounds of the knockings, and occasionally make a dart at the shimmering lights, which, as if perceiving the animal, would retreat quickly back into the wall. I repeatedly passed my hand over these walls to ascertain if they were damp, or whether any chinks were there from which phosphorrescent emanations could proceed. The walls were dry, solid, and smooth, and whilst I was pursuing my examination the knockings would thrill the solid stone beneath my very hand. At the expiration of two hours an exclamation of the elder woman called my attention to the hearth, where two large globular lights were hovering midway between the floor and the table, and just above the little kitten, who, with back and tail erect and eyes gleaming fiery red, manifested the most pitiable signs of terror and amazement.

Once again, and this time far more distinctly, I saw the little men I had before but imperfectly beheld. They were grotesque in shape, with round, shining heads, destitute of hair, perfectly black, and more human about the head than the body. I saw their faces, and recognised a sort of good-humoured expression in them, and saw them throw somersaults several times as if for my amusement. A strange duck with each little head ended the performance, and then they sank into the ground made of planks laid down upon the rock of which the house was built.

"There," cried the younger woman, "they won't mislest ye again, ladies. When they goes down, they never comes again the night. It's the end of their game to sink down like that."

The woman was right. Though at our entreaty both mother and daughter remained with us all night, sleeping soundly, curled up on shawls and garments, and though we, lying awake, and—must I confess it?—shivering and trembling from head to foot, kept our eyes open, straining them in every direction, and with bated breath and ears sharpened by fearful anticipation, listened until we could hear the deep silence of that long, long night—we neither heard nor saw any more of the "little hammerers."

The morning came at length. Oh! what an age it was coming! Mr. Hart joined us as we were waiting for the morning meal. He had heard knockings, he said, but concluded it might be the re-echo of the labourers' hammers from the mines so close to us. The miners were not at work, and no hammering came from them, our host told us, with a significant smile at the rest of his family. The adventures of the night were now recounted and talked over. They were not strange, nor even alarming to the miners. The two lads declared they had "fine fun with the hammerers' lanterns," though they acknowledged they had never seen the little men, but plenty of others had, they said, and "they wouldn't part company with them for nothing," for they were famous guides to the spots where the richest lodes of metal lay. The women, too, spoke of their appearance with indifference. "They came often," they said; "and though they cut up now and then, throwing things around like, they were only in fun, and never did any harm, except to the animals they had." They thought somehow they did not like dogs or cats, for they couldn't keep any; they either ran away or died suddenly. They didn't expect, they added, to keep this kitten long. I agreed in this opinion, for, judging of the terror the poor little thing displayed on the previous night, I was not surprised to find it moping in the morning, and averse to touch the food the boys prepared for it. I found, although these lights and knockings were common enough in the mines *at times,* they only seemed to come at special periods, and did not frequent or haunt any other house than the one we visited, and that of old Clamps, many miles distant. There seemed to be many evidences that these apparitions, be they what they might, either attached themselves to or made themselves manifest only in the presence of mediumistic persons. The family we visited were far too ignorant to understand anything of mediumship, although they were not unacquainted with the idea and theory of "ghost-seeing." They were not afraid of their well-beloved "little hammerers," but they were all "terribly scared" by the occasional manifestations of a spiritual character, which they narrated to me with a simplicity which impressed me with a conviction of their veracity. I have never seen this family and never visited that region since. . . .

Case 5: Mr. Dickens' Disappointing Adventure

Investigation: conducted by Charles Dickens, John Hollingshead, Wilkie Collins and William Henry Wills at Cheshunt, England, in late 1859.

Manifestations: none reported; none experienced.

Pertinent Facts: Charles Dickens, the author of *David Copperfield, Great Expectations, Bleak House,* and some of the best ghost stories in the English language, began a new magazine titled *All the Year Round* in 1859. In August of that year, he ran a series titled "A Physician's Ghosts." The anonymous physician's argument is that ghosts are really psychic impressions transmitted to a loved one at the moment of death. William Howitt, who was involved in Cases 2 and 4, wrote to Dickens to express his disagreement, and he reprinted that letter in *The British Spiritual Telegraph.* In a private reply, Dickens explains, "I don't adopt my contributor's theory. . . . I have always had a strong interest in the subject, and never I knowingly lose an opportunity of pursuing it." The letter goes on to say that, along with his *interest* in ghosts, he has reservations about *believing* in them. In a follow-up letter—interestingly dated Oct. 31st—Dickens asks Howitt for a list of sites reputed to be haunted. He was arranging a ghost hunt![1] Howitt complied, and Dickens chose a house in Cheshunt, not too far from London. Unfortunately, Dickens and his team found neither a ghost nor even the house itself. This was then reported in a journal called *The Critic,* where it was used as evidence against the reality of ghosts. The article is included below, along with another of Howitt's letters, this one saying

---

[1] The series of articles that sparked Howitt's ire is in *All the Year Round* 1.15 (Aug. 6, 1859) pp.346-50; 1.16 (Aug.13, 1859) pp. 382-84; and 1.18 (Aug. 27) pp. 427-32. His letter of protest appears in *The British Spiritual Telegraph* 4.10 (Oct. 15, 1859) pp. 143-48. Dickens' replies can be found in *The Letters of Charles Dickens,* Vol. 9, ed. Graham Storey (Clarendon, 1997) pp. 116, 146.

the ghost hunt was poorly conducted. Though the investigation was a bust, the exchange it sparked exemplifies the debate over ghosts at this period.

∞

From My Lifetime

John Hollingshead[2]

About this time the Master[3] had got somehow into a public discussion with William Howitt on the question of "Haunted Houses." Mr. Howitt was an avowed spiritualist, and had the habit, too common at that period, of calling everyone an Atheist who did not quite agree with him. I came to the rescue of my distinguished employer with a *bond fide* offer. I was ready to occupy any house, in any part of the town, no matter how "haunted," on one condition—I was to have a moderate lease of the house, rent-free, giving an undertaking to live in it, and test it as a tenant.

This offer was duly made to Mr. Howitt, and it is surprising how his supply of "haunted houses" decreased immediately. Before that, they were supposed to exist in every street; now, they were as difficult to find as the site of the Holy Sepulchre. The house in Berkeley Square, which was a mystery for many years, until it was recently converted into flats and residential chambers, was spoken of, but possession was not, at that time, to be obtained at any price. A tumble-down pot-house in Holborn was one of the rookeries on order; but when inquiry came to be made, it was only haunted by the claims of brewers and distillers, and it was not to be given away, either with or without a demoniac license.

At last, after much correspondence, a house was found, or supposed to be found, at Cheshunt, Herts— if "Dickens's young man" would not object to that healthy but haunted township? "Dickens's young man" did not object to Cheshunt, and an excursion was arranged, to visit the property. Wilkie Collins and W.H. Wills were sent down in a brougham, wisely provided with fish, as Dickens did not care to trust altogether to the local hotel or

---

[2] This is extracted from *My Lifetime* (Vol. 1, Sampson Low, Marston & Co., 1895) pp. 110-12. Though this autobiography was published *after* the documents that follow, Hollingshead recounts the events that occurred *prior* to their publication.

[3] As noted, the year was 1859. "The Master" was a nickname for Dickens.

inn. Dickens and I walked down—a fair toe-and-heel walk of sixteen miles, through Stoke Newington, Stamford Hill, Tottenham, etc. I had only recently recovered from a rheumatic attack, and was a little stiff on my "pins," but when I got warm I was quite equal to the task, although the mechanical pace, marked by milestones and a watch, rather bored me. Many people passed us at intervals, who recognised the Master; one or two saluted him, and he replied with an extra twinkle of the eye.

We arrived at Cheshunt, and began to make inquiry. No one had heard of any "haunted house," or anything so disreputable in the town. Cheshunt rather prided itself on its trim respectability. At last, we had to fall back upon the oldest inhabitant. He was not very old, but quite old enough for our purpose. Diving into the recesses of his memory, he remembered a house, about thirty years previous to our visit, that once had a reputation for ghosts—either masculine, feminine, or neuter, he could hardly say which. I suggested that it might have been the ghost of the unfortunate Greenacre, the "bogie" of my childhood, with whom and one of his "parcels" I believe I once travelled in a Paddington omnibus.[4] He rather thought it might have been; but, anyway, the house had long since been pulled down, and a semi-detached villa, worthy of Bayswater, had been erected in its place. Dickens stood him a friendly quart, and we went to dinner, the Master changing his walking-boots for a pair of shoes, which had been brought down in the brougham. The dinner was a substantial meal, after Dickens's own heart, and the ale was nectar. This began and ended the first and only chapter of "Ghosts" according to the gospel of William Howitt.

✤

---

[4] Greenacre, a small grocer in the Old Kent Road, having had a row with his housekeeper, Mrs. Browne, gave her an unlucky blow, which killed her. In his trepidation he cut her up in sections, and dropped these in various places in the form of brown paper parcels. He was hanged for murder, owing to the parcels; and his name for years was a "bogie" to frighten unruly children. [Hollinghead's footnote.]

From SAYINGS AND DOINGS

Anonymous[5]

We have no doubt that most of our readers have by this time made themselves acquainted with the contents of the extra Christmas number of *All the Year Round* called *The Haunted House,* and it must have struck most of them that there is an air of *vraisemblance* about the way in which the stories of which it is composed are introduced, which betokens that Mr. Dickens had some particular house "in his eye" at the time when he resolved upon that device. This we believe to be really the case. Not that any such party of friends really did occupy the house under such circumstances, and more than Mr. Dickens really spent an evening and stood punch at the house of the Seven Poor Travellers. Still we believe that, when these tales were in preparation, Mr. Dickens had, or fancied he had, his eye upon a real substantial house of brick and timber.

A short time ago there was a story afloat about a house at Cheshunt, which was haunted to an extent surpassing any since the never-to-be-forgotten mansion in Cock-lane. There were noises, and "eyes," and ringing bells, and peripatetic furniture, and tenant after tenant had been spiritually ejected; even the name of a definite person, the sister of a well-known actress, was mentioned as having been the last victim to the Cheshunt ghost. It was upon this foundation, we believe, that *The Haunted House* was constructed,[6] and the result has been one of the pleasantest contributions to our Christmas reading that we have enjoyed for some time past. The sequel, however, is perhaps the best part of the whole story. Having made such excellent literary capital out of the house, Mr. Dickens took it into his head the other day that it would be a desirable thing to know something more about it, and accordingly proceeded with some friends to Cheshunt. What did they find? We are told, nothing. There was no house, no ghosts, no noises, no eyes, neither was there ringing bells nor saltatory bed-steads; at least, nobody at Cheshunt, not even "the oldest inhabitant," has heard of any such matters. So

---

[5] This is extracted from the "Sayings and Doings" column of *The Critic* 18 (Dec. 17, 1859) p. 599.

[6] In another of their letters, Dickens assures Howitt that *The Haunted House,* which appeared in the Christmas issue of *All the Year Round,* and his visit to Cheshunt "are two perfectly distinct things. I went to Cheshunt to make enquiries, the very day before the Christmas No. was published, and when it had been at press ten days" (*The Letters of Charles Dickens,* p. 181).

that unless we are to believe that the ghosts have removed the house bodily, and have bewitched the inhabitants of Cheshunt, so as to destroy all their recollection of it, we must presume that such a house has never had existence.

It is curious, though not surprising, to find how these monstrous phantoms vanish whenever they are approached and touched. In the introduction to *The Haunted House,* Mr. Dickens himself declares that he once saw the apparition of his own father: "He was alive and well, and nothing ever came of it, but I saw him in the daylight, sitting with his back towards me, on a seat that stood beside my bed. His head was resting on his hand, and whether he was slumbering or grieving I could not discern. Amazed to see him there, I sat up, moved my position, leaned out of bed and watched him. As he did not move, I spoke to him more than once. As he did not move then, I became alarmed and laid my hand upon his shoulder, as I thought—*and there was no such thing.*" We are told that with the Cambridge Club, instituted for the purpose of investigating ghostly matters, the ghosts have it by a large majority. But have the majority acted in this wise? Let them lay their hands upon the shoulders, *as they think,* and perhaps they, too, will find that there is no such thing.

Latterly a vast amount of curiosity has been excited about these spiritual matters. Mr. Howitt's communications to the public prints, the War-office Ghost,[7] and many other causes, have contributed to this, and in many circles and coteries about England there is now quite a range for investigations to this kind. We ourselves dropped in the evening upon a circle of literary gentlemen who had been entertained by two illiterate females, styling themselves mediums, and the account we heard of the spiritual manifestations (for the mediums had departed and the spirits with them) bordered on the ludicrous. Among other personages, Dr. Samuel Johnson had been there in the spirit, but had behaved himself in a most ungrammatical manner, spelling his words in a

---

[7] The War-Office Ghost involves Captain Wheatcroft, a military man. After his regiment had been sent to India, Wheatcroft's wife, in England, awoke to witness the apparition of her husband. The ghost was mute, but seemed to be in pain. Mrs. Wheatcroft was prepared, then, when she afterward received notice that her husband had been killed. However, the date of death was designated as November 15, 1857, while her dream had occurred on the night of the *14th*. Then a London medium said that she, too, had witnessed his apparition *on the 14th*. An investigation ensued, one which concluded with confirmation from the War Office that, yes, the captain had died on the 14th, not the day after. See Robert Dale Owen's *Footfalls on the Boundary of Another World* (J.B. Lippincott, 1860) pp. 411-16.

style much more suited to the acquirements of the mediums than to those of the great lexicographer. Again, a very few nights back, another party of literary gentlemen assembled to hear a lecture from a gentleman who has often interwoven the laurels of dramatic triumphs with the fog-wreaths of meta-physics, on the subject of the junior Fichte's theory of Psychological Manifestations—with what enlightenment to their understanding we know not. Another alarming symptom is that on the 1st Jan. 1860 is to appear a new magazine, to be called *The Spiritualist,* in which articles will appear by Mr. W. Howitt, Mr. E. Rich, Judge Edmonds, Dr. Ashburner, Dr. Dixon, Hon. Robert Dale Owen, Mrs. Crowe, Mr. D.D. Home, Rev. T.L. Harris, and other able contributors. Finally, the peace of the world is threatened with a book, which is to appear in America, also on the 1st Jan., from the pen of Robert Dale Owen, called "Footfalls on the Boundary of Another World."

❖

MR. HOWITT AND MR. DICKENS

Anonymous[8]

In reproducing the following masterly letter of Mr. Howitt to *"The Critic"* on the subject of a certain house at Cheshunt, which was haunted for many years, and from which successive occupants were driven after short tenancies, we desire to say a few words on the general question of Mr. Dickens's supposed scepticism of such cases. We can hardly believe that Mr. Dickens does really disbelieve in haunted houses, nor in other phases of spiritual phenomena and operation. At all events if he do, he is certainly neither very comfortable nor very confident in his disbelief. It rather would appear that he is a believer, from the frequent reference he makes to the subject in his publications; in fact he can neither accept fully the facts, nor let them alone. They form the favourite framework of his stories; he inserts well-attested ghost stories from literary contributors in his periodical; and when appealed to by Mr. Howitt, as to whether they are not dished up for his readers as well-written jokes or hoaxes, he solemnly assures him that they are neither the one nor the other, but on the contrary, are well attested and well-believed accounts by his able contributors.

---

[8] This appeared in *The Spiritual Magazine* 1.2 (Feb., 1860) pp. 58-62. The letter it reproduces had appeared in *The Critic* 18 (Dec. 31, 1859) 647-48.

His own earlier works, in which his genius was more fresh, and smacked less of the mercantile element than it does now, contain beautiful touches of the higher forms of spiritual life. He is now a middle-aged genius, and the fire does not flash through him as of yore. Perhaps when he penned the most beautiful passages, even his outer man was but dimly cognizant of the truths with which in his best moments his spirit was inspired. What did he mean when he said, "It would almost seem as if our better thoughts and sympathies were charms, in virtue of which the soul is enabled to hold some mysterious intercourse with the spirits of those whom we dearly loved in this life. Alas! how often and how long may those patient angels hover over us watching for the spell which is so seldom uttered and so soon forgotten!"[9]

Will Mr. Dickens kindly tell us in plain words, if he believes this passage in his writings, or is it a deliberate piece of what in America is called "bunkum"? No—in his best moments he not only writes so, but believes so; and it is a pity that he does not more cultivate those higher portions of his soul, and give us the benefit of his deeper intuitions of the holy truths.

It is nothing uncommon for men of genius to cover up their inspirations till they themselves deny their existence. But all genius, as it is called, is nothing but inspiration, or the deep intuitive perceptions of the soul, when under favorable conditions it sees beyond this realm of sensuous limitation.

We think that in conceding to Mr. Dickens's modest request to be furnished with ghosts to order, it would be better first to have put the question to Mr. Dickens, whether or not he denied altogether the fact of haunted houses, spirit appearances, and the whole range of spiritual phenomena. Whether in the face of all that has been written and said, giving detailed accounts of such things, in this and other countries, he believes or disbelieves the alleged facts, all and each of them. One of such facts is as good as a thousand. Let him say aye or no to this—If aye, then we are satisfied; if no, he will at all events be pinned to his answer, and be made, by his own act, a scarecrow and a warning to others of that meagre race which kicks against the pricks.

One of our first points against him would be to ask him to reconcile his denial with the closing words of his last Christmas haunted-house story, in which he invokes his Christian readers "to believe in one another, and in that great Christmas book, the New Testament." Does he overlook the fact, that besides being a great

---

[9] From Dickens' novel *Nicholas Nickleby* (Chapman and Hall, 1839) p. 425.

Christmas book, it, as well as the Old Testament, is a great spiritual book, dealing with the spiritual things of the soul, and filled with spiritual facts, such as we are now pressing upon our readers? We shall want him to point out the cognate differences between the man of to-day and the man of the Bible, and the precise time when the spiritual possibilities of the soul, which we see exhibited in the Bible, were cut off from mankind. Above all, what is meant by the promises of spiritual gifts there made by the Redeemer of mankind? There were "haunted houses" then; and men saw the spirits and angels then as now who "haunted them," as the phrase is. Are they all untrue? Does Mr. Dickens dare to disbelieve them?

Then again, as to his advice to "believe in one another." His own conduct is a practical refutation of his advice. Does he believe in another's evidence? Oh, no! He has a high respect, he says, for his informants, but he doesn't believe a word they say on the subject. In other words, he sets up his ignorance against their knowledge. And suppose that, after all, the great Mr. Dickens did condescend to announce his belief in a fact now well known to actual millions in Europe and America. What then? Is he so much more clever and so superior to other persons who have eyes and ears, that they will all with one accord believe him in preference to Mr. Howitt or to A., B., or C.? We have seen nothing in either Mr. Dickens or his writings to mark him out as "the coming man," who is to settle all these things by the mere word of his breath. No, Mr. Dickens is only one person after all, and by no means so entirely above his fellow-men that they will recognise him to the extent he fondly thinks. We know scores of instances in which the most determined sceptics have been convinced; and the only consequence is, that when they tell their friends of their convictions, the friends won't believe them, and insist on being converted themselves. In fact, men do not believe in one another, any more than Mr. Dickens does.

If scepticism had only one head, however much timber there might be in it, we should enter upon the business of convicting it with great alacrity and confidence of success; and even now we will throw down a serious challenge to the literary and philosophic world, that if they will appoint Mr. Dickens to investigate for them, and will be bound by his statements, we will take some personal trouble with him for the sake of the whole.

We are however keeping too long from Mr. Howitt's letter to the *"Critic,"* the Editor of which, is content to be one of Mr. Dickens's lacqueys, and to applaud the shortcomings of his master. We hope in an early number to enlighten the public, as to these gentlemen of the press and "their manners and customs," for we are well acquainted with their natural history.

To the Editor of the "Critic."

Sir,—I am quite sure that you would not go on, week after week, propagating the grossest untruths, if you knew them to be so; yet in your journal of December 17, you say that Mr. Dickens and some friends of his took it into their heads to go down to a reputed haunted house at Cheshunt, "and they found *no house,* no ghost, &c. ... So that, unless we are to believe that the ghosts have *removed the house bodily,* and have bewitched the inhabitants at Cheshunt, so as to destroy all their recollections of it, we must presume that such a house *never had existence.*"

Again, in your number for December 24 you repeat the same thing. "Here is a tale about a house, locality named, witnesses named, ghosts described, and lo! when the matter comes to be closely examined, not only do the ghosts disappear, but the house with them, and no one can be found near the indicated spot who knows anything about it."

Your statement resolves itself into two assertions—that there was no house to be found, and that nobody had ever heard of a haunted house at Cheshunt.

What are the facts? Mr. Dickens wrote to me some time ago to request that I would point out to him some house said to be haunted. I named to him two—that at Cheshunt, formerly inhabited by the Chapmans, and one at Willington, near Newcastle. The former, I told him, I had never seen; the latter I had, and that Mr. Procter, the proprietor, was still living, a member of the Society of Friends, highly esteemed in his neighbourhood for his clear, sober sense and high moral character. That Mr. Procter had always shown every disposition to gratify inquirers into the extraordinary phenomena which had taken place for years in the house whilst he inhabited it. That I had seen and conversed with various people, all of superior intelligence, who had visited him and been witnesses of the most undoubted marvels. Mr. Dickens, however, chose to visit Cheshunt as the nearest. Neither he nor I knew the condition in which it now was, nor, (as the proprietor was said, years ago, to threaten to pull it down) whether it positively still remained. Mr. Dickens, therefore, had no right to be disappointed if he found the conditions formerly predicated now changed, and had only to turn his steps elsewhere, if disposed to still go ghost-hunting.

Now hear what he says as to the house in a note to me, dated December 17: "The house in which the Chapmans lived has been greatly enlarged, and commands a high rent, and is no more disturbed than this house of mine."

So then, there was the house, the same house to which I directed him, and so far from having been whisked away by the ghosts, "greatly enlarged."

Very well, that point is clear: contrary to your repeated statement, the house was there. The next point is, that they could find no persons near the indicated spot who had heard of this house being haunted. If that had been strictly true, this *not hearing* could not set aside the positive evidence of the Chapmans themselves and their celebrated relatives. Their negative evidence could not annihilate this positive evidence. You say, "witnesses were named," and even the name of a definite person, the sister of a well-known actress. So far, quite correct. The witnesses are the Chapmans themselves and their celebrated relatives—Mr. and Mrs. Kean. The account given at p. 332 of Mrs. Crowe's "Night Side of Nature " was written down from their own mouths by a gentleman equally eminent as a publisher and author. I have his copy of Mrs. Crowe's book now before me, with the whole of the names of place and parties written by him in the margin.[10]

That same account, only fuller and with all the names, was detailed to me by the same near relatives of the Chapmans long after, and has by them been told to many others.

Here, then, to the positive evidence that this house is still standing, you have the equally positive evidence of the Chapmans who lived and suffered in the house. Its not being haunted now is a mere accident, which, if Mr. Dickens and his friends had ever acquainted themselves with the laws of pneumatology, would have been perfectly intelligible to them. Surely a ghost is not bound to remain in any particular spot for ever; surely he may be allowed to leave his accustomed haunt, just as much as Mr. Dickens and his friends were it liberty to leave their own homes to go ghost-hunting. I have given Mr. Dickens a perfectly parallel case, where a house known by me and numbers of other persons from actual observation for years, being partly pulled down and rebuilt, was wholly freed from the visitation; and neither "the contagious fear of servant," nor any machinery of rats, cats, old hats, rusty weathercocks, or Ikeys,[11] could to this day ever again raise a ghost there—the ghost having in fact departed.

But you say they could find no person who ever heard of this house being haunted. It would be wonderful, when a set of jovial and quizzical authors and artists go down into the country, ready with a ludicrous array of rats, cats, old hats, rusty weathercocks, and Ikeys, to laugh at the ghosts they professed to seek, that they might figure in a funny Christmas number, if they *did* find any sober old gentleman willing to incur their ridicule by confessing to the weakness of ghost faith. We know, some of us, those in London tolerably high in art and literature, who, whilst they affect to laugh at the superstition of belief in ghosts, really, like some other

---

[10] Only a few days ago, Mrs. Chapman asseverated to a friend the truth of all there stated, *and much more.* [Editor's footnote.]

[11] According to John Farmer and W.E. Henley's *A Dictionary of Slang and Colloquial English* (George Routledge & Sons, 1905), when capitalized, this is a derogatory term for a Jew (p. 235) or a purchaser/receiver of stolen goods (see "Fence," p. 156). Uncapitalized, it can mean a clever rogue (see "Downey-cove," p. 142). I like to think Howitt had this last meaning in mind.

gentlemen to whom I should be sorry to compare them, "believe and tremble." What wonder, then, if the ghost-hunters in question found nothing? But did they learn nothing? Mr. Dickens says in his note to me, that "the well-informed" accounted for the reports about Mr. Chapman's house "by rats, and a certain man, Frank by name, who was addicted to poaching for rabbits at untimely hours!" Our ghost-hunters prove too much.

It certainly did not need a journey to Cheshunt by a knot of jolly fellows, though I hear it was a merry day, to learn the rumour of this haunting, from people who know that neighbourhood. Without crossing my threshold I hear it. Soon after receiving Mr. Dickens's note, announcing that the ghost was out when he called, a military officer born in that vicinity, and who had lived in and about Cheshunt for years, a gentleman of first-rate education and endowments, came in. I asked him, "Did you ever hear of a haunted house at Cheshunt?"

He replied, "Yes, often, and for many years!" I showed him the statements in the Critic, where it says they could not even find the house. He said, "Where did these gentlemen go to? I think I know every person of consequence there, and I tell you the report is common enough."

Thus every one of your statements receives positive contradiction. Mr. Dickens and his friends did find the house—did hear that the reports were accounted for by rats and a man Frank. The parties who lived at the time specified, have put their solemn and substantive statement on record, and a person well acquainted with the locality testifies to the report of this case of house-haunting. I have already still further proofs offered.

Allow me on my own account to say that, my name having been lately much connected with ghosts without my own seeking, but merely to oblige ghost-hunters, I have no particular taste for these particular forms of spirit-life, but am just as willing to hear evidence on their behalf, as I should on behalf of Brown, Jones, and Robinson if their entity and identity were denied.

And now, Sir, allow me a word or two of more seriousness. The theory of apparitions maintained in all ages, and by greater minds than any we can boast among us at present, is but the lowest fringe in the sublime mantle of mystery which wraps the universe; but it is still a real fringe. As for Spiritualism, I would recommend those who desire to know what it really is, not to form their judgment by the idiotic animal which Mr. Dickens introduces into his Christmas Number, and which sort of creature he professes the highest respect for, but to go and listen to Mr. Harris, the celebrated American medium, at the Marylebone Institution, in Edward Street, Portman Square, where he will preach for the next ten or dozen Sundays, at 11 a.m. and 6½ p.m.; and if they do not return with very different ideas of Spiritualism, I shall be much surprised.

Mr. Dickens, in his Christmas Number, concludes with the pious desire that we may all "have faith in that great Christmas Book, the New Testament, and in *one another*." Amen! a very fine sentiment; but how does he carry it out? By devoting the whole of that number to destroy our faith in one another, and to ridicule Christianity. I say to ridicule Christianity; for, whether Mr. Dickens and our literary caterers for mere amusement know it or not, Spiritualism is but a reassertion of primal powers and privileges of the Christian faith. It is but the assertion of our charter as immortal beings to enter into daily communion with God and his Christ, and with those spirits which every Church, however formal, professes to believe are "ministering spirits to all those who shall be heirs of salvation."

That was the faith of George Fox; that has always been my faith: it is nothing new with me, but has, I thank God, been most consolingly confirmed by the striking phenomena and beautiful revelations of spiritualism. Sir, I value more one simple and affecting communication of a departed brother, yearning to atone for past injustice and unkindness, than I do all the sermons that were ever preached and all the literature that was ever penned. And if we have minds amongst us yet muscular enough to grasp the faith of Luther, of Milton, of Pascal, and of Fenélon—minds which are not completely emasculated by the frivolities of a literature of mere amusement, or rendered deaf by the mere squibs and crackers of the poor pantomime of our superficial life—they may yet feel a sense of that tender spot left often in the most callous and secularised heart, when they think of all the souls who have gone into eternity, who would give years— aye, cycles of their existence—to carry back to those on earth, words of reconciliation, confessions of forgiveness, or assurances of pardon; to wipe from the sacred ground of life, the pollution they have left there to fester and become pestilence; to rekindle faith in the souls of beloved ones which they have darkened with words of materialistic death. Such minds may then conceive, perhaps, why the poor despised table has become in thousands of domestic circles a genuine family altar, through which still flow the oracles of God and "the communion of saints," so continually prayed for in our churches. Why, thousands and tens of thousands, by means of this reassured and confirmed faith, care nothing for the sneers and mockeries around, because they have heavenly light in their dwellings, and the peace of eternity in their souls. Take my word for it, that this despised power will yet dash to atoms the mere figure of traditionary faith, all its forms of brass and its feet of clay, and will roll over the mere shell of a defunct formalism, crushing it into the dust. Let us see whether we have yet masculine minds among us capable of receiving its great truths, or the mere weeds of the literary stubble-field, which will be burnt up in it as the weeds of a tropical plain by the sun—whether we are yet capable of the heroic daring of a Paul and the childlike but deep-souled faith of a Newton, or merely of grimacing on a rubbish-heap of rats, cats, old hats, rusty weathercocks, and vulgar Ikeys.—I am, Sir, yours, &c.

William Howitt.

West Hill Lodge, Highgate, Dec. 26, 1859.

Case 6: A Residue which Science Cannot Explain

Investigation: conducted by Sir William Fletcher Barrett at Derrygonnelly, Ireland, in 1877.

Manifestations: knocks; communication with raps; a rain of stones; pranks with boots; candles, lamps, and other household items stolen.

Pertinent Facts: William F. Barrett (1844-1925) taught at the Royal College of Science for Ireland and was elected a Fellow of the Royal Society, the UK's science academy whose members include Isaac Newton, Charles Darwin, and Albert Einstein. Primarily a physicist, Barrett also explored "fringe" sciences, and he wasn't alone, as the editor of the *Dublin University Journal* notes in the following article. A pioneer in evolutionary biology, Alfred Russel Wallace (1823-1913) claimed that he had observed evidence of a spirit writing on a physically inaccessible slate. Chemist and physicist William Crookes (1832-1919) stated that he had photographed a spirit named Katie King. Of course, there was opposition from other scientists, and the editor nods to physiologist and marine biologist William Benjamin Carpenter (1813-1885), who attributed such phenomena to purely natural causes.[1] Despite such resistance, Barrett and other scientists dared to publish their unusual pursuits in the 1870s and laid a foundation for the Society for Psychical Research, established in 1882.

---

[1] Alfred Russel Wallace, "Slate-Writing Extraordinary," *The Spectator* (50.2571 [Oct. 6, 1877] pp. 1239-40. William Crookes, *Researches in the Phenomena of Spiritualism* (J. Burns, 1874) pp. 108-12. William Benjamin Carpenter, *Mesmerism, Spiritualism, &c. Historically and Scientifically Considered* (Longmans, Green and Co., 1877).

Case 6: A Residue which Science Cannot Explain

THE DEMONS OF DERRYGONELLY

W.F. Barrett[2]

Philosophers are prone to reject all philosophy but their own and few men are free from unconscious bias. Before my story is read I would ask consideration for the following paragraph from Abercrombie ("Intellectual Powers," 7th edit, pp. 74 and 76):

"While an unbounded credulity is the part of a weak mind, which never thinks nor reasons at all, an unlimited skepticism is the part of a contracted mind, which reasons upon imperfect data, or makes its own knowledge and extent of observation the standard and test of probability. In judging of the credibility of a statement, we are not to be influenced simply by our actual experience of similar events; for this would limit our reception of new facts to their accordance with those which we already know."

Amid the multitude of extraordinary letters which it has been my lot to receive during the past two years, the post brought me some few months ago a strange communication from a gentleman residing in Enniskillen. The writer, who was only known to me by the geological and archaeological contributions he had made to some of the learned societies, informed me that the cottage of a small farmer in one of the most secluded spots in the County Fermanagh had, for some months, been the seat of various strange and inexplicable disturbances; in a word, that the cottage was reputed to be haunted! Furthermore, that not only had some of the most veracious and shrewd people in the neighbourhood testified to the reality of the disturbances, but my correspondent, in utter skepticism and ridicule, having gone to expose the credulity of his neighbours, had returned convinced that no trickery was at work. Confounded with the results of his inquiry, and utterly unable to throw any light on the matter, he wrote to beg me to visit the place; pointing out that even if the haunted house should go the way of its predecessors, still the beauty of Lough Erne, and the extraordinary

---

[2] This appeared in the *Dublin University Magazine* 540.90 (Dec., 1877) pp. 692-705.

limestone caves of the district might repay me for the journey.[3] Not withstanding that the romance of haunted houses does provokingly vanish when they are investigated, rats being found at work, or boys at play, I agreed to go; for even if my private misgivings were confirmed, still, as my correspondent remarked, the scenery and the caves would assuredly remain.

So a wet Friday afternoon found me in Enniskillen, and the evening was spent in discussing plans for the morrow. Both the "caves" and the "haunted house" were far away from the town, in a desolate region to be reached only by foot or car. However, the next day we were on our way. The morning was spent blasting the stalagmite floor of the caves; a beautifully made and very ancient, though still perfect bone pin, numerous fragments of coarse pottery and bones of wolf and deer, rewarded our labours. Before the sun set we left our digging for the still stranger quest the results of which I am about to narrate. A lovely drive of some nine miles had previously brought us to the village of Derrygonelly; turning sharp to the left after passing through the village, the road faced the magnificent limestone cliffs of Knockmore; a couple of miles farther and we were at a gate opening into field that led to the haunted house. A more lonely spot could hardly be found in this country. Across the bog that lay before us rose the huge pile of Knockmore, its steep side crowned by an escarpment of over-hanging rock, fully 300 feet in height, hollowed here and there into those vast caves, the abodes of pre-historic man, to which allusion has already been made. No house could be seen anywhere, for the cottage we were in search of lies hidden in a hollow, and was further screened from

---

[3] I may mention that my correspondent was Mr. Thomas Plunkett of Enniskillen. If Mr. Smiles is on the look-out for a new hero to add to his self-made men, let me take the liberty of commending him to my correspondent. Mr. Plunkett has, from his boyhood, been an earnest student of books and of nature. He has collected a large and excellent library; has actively encouraged education among the peasantry; has mastered and thrown light on the geology and ancient glaciation of the entire district; has discovered and explored with persistent energy and success the extraordinary limestone caves of Fermanagh; and out of his little leisure and narrow means has himself unearthed some eleven or twelve cwt. of cave bones, many of ancient animals and of pre-historic man, with the usual accompaniment of rude pottery, flint flakes, and bronze implements. I am glad to say that at the last meeting of the British Association a grant of £30 was awarded to aid Mr. Plunkett in the continuation of his cave explorations. [Barrett's footnote. Mr. Smiles is Samuel Smiles, author of *Self-Help: with Illustrations of Character, Conduct, and Perseverance* (John Murray, 1859). "Cwt." is an abbreviation of hundredweight, a unit equaling 100 pounds—and that's a lot of bones!]

observation by the foliage of the trees that surround it. The only neighbours to be found are in the scattered farms that dot the wide-sweeping and poor valleys. It was now evening, and, added to the loneliness of the place, gloomy shades were cast by the clumps of trees and the tall hedgerow beside our path.

At last we reached the door of the farmer's cottage and found him within. He gave us a friendly greeting, and whilst he was making up the turf fire, and his daughters preparing, with Irish hospitality, to get us a cup of tea, we looked around. The cottage did not differ in its size or arrangements from that belonging to any other of the small farmers in the country districts of Ireland. The front door opened into a roomy kitchen, with a low ceiling, in great part open to the blackened rafters of the roof. The floor was of hardened earth, and on a large hearth-stone there burnt against the wall a turf fire, the smoke ascending through the primitive and ample chimney. A small window let enough light in to discern, by the fire-side, a door, opening into a bed-room, and in a corresponding position on the opposite side of the kitchen was the little parlour. The farmer himself was a grey-headed man, with a careworn look; he spoke with a quiet and simple dignity totally different from the voluble utterance that betrays insincerity. He had lost his wife a few weeks before Easter last, and the loss had greatly affected both himself and his children. The family now consisted of four girls and one boy, the youngest about ten, and the eldest, a girl, Maggie, about twenty years old. It was chiefly in the neighbourhood of Maggie that noises were heard, and hence it was of interest to regard her a little more closely. Her appearance was most picturesque: without shoes and stockings to hide her white and well-formed feet and ankles, her gown neatly tucked up, a little red shawl thrown across her shoulders, her hair simply and tidily arranged, and her whole attitude graced by a manner instinctively gentle and modest; to this was added an intelligent and interesting face which wore a somewhat sad expression, though the healthy, open countenance gave no evidence of a character which could pursue a systematic course of deception.

By this time Maggie had the tea ready, and we went into the little parlour; none of the family, however, would partake with us, nor would the elder children sit down in our presence, actuated by that sense of respect and politeness which is inborn amongst the Irish peasantry. Whilst at tea, I questioned the old farmer closely as to any suspicions he may have had to account for these sounds. He was perfectly frank with me, and told me how unable he was to find any clue to their origin, and how gratefully he would thank me if I helped him to discover their source and banish the disturbances. All he knew was that as soon as the girls had lain down noises and rappings began, and often continued all night long, and this, too, when he had sat in their room with a candle, and watched closely both within and without the house.

In order to gain further information, I begged the old man to give me as slowly and carefully as he could the history of these disturbances. In the course of the evening he complied, and as he spoke I wrote down his words, which I will give without alteration or addition in the sequel.

Our primitive tea being over we went back to the peat fire in the kitchen, where I questioned, aside, each of the children, but all gave me substantially the same story of the noises. Maggie now left us to put the children to bed, and afterward she herself bade us good night, saying she would merely lie down on the bed without undressing, so that if the noises came we might, if we chose, carefully examine the bedroom. A few minutes after she had retired a pattering sound was distinctly heard, as if made upon some soft substance. This was followed after an interval by at first gentle, and then gradually louder and louder raps, coming apparently from the walls, the ceiling, and various parts of the inner room; and this again was succeeded by scratchings and other indeterminate sounds. Naturally, the first thought was that we should find Maggie, or one of her little sisters, making these sounds within, or someone making them at a given signal without. Quietly stealing outside the house, every corner was examined. No one was found, but the noises were still clearly heard within the inner room. Upon returning, we obtained permission to go into the bed-room. When we entered with a candle the noises ceased, but they returned on our quitting the room!

This was provoking and uncommonly like, if not demonstrably, trickery. Had some of my medical and physiological friends been with me they would have argued that there was no need for further wasting our time. Maggie, they would have said, was evidently one of that numerous class of hysteroid sufferers who, without moral obliquity, are impelled to trick and cheat and play foolish pranks under the morbid influence of a well known disease. The case, they tell us, is by no means rare; in fact, it is extremely common among girls at her age; sometimes one dominant idea takes possession of the patient, sometimes another. Every physician has had experience of it in some of its phases. Let us, therefore, go home. But I remembered when first the Holtz electric machine came to this country an eminent, but incredulous man of science remarked to me he would not believe its powers unless he saw with his own eyes that sparks of a foot long could be obtained by merely the rapid revolution of a couple of glass discs without any rubber or other apparent source of electricity. I procured and tried the machine, and when the sparks were leaping from the terminals I sent for my friend. He came at once, but on his opening the laboratory door the noisy discharges instantly ceased, the mimic thunderstorm of a moment ago had vanished utterly. Vigorously we turned the machine, but uselessly. My friend was as triumphant as I was crestfallen. He smiled when I told him that the sudden change was unaccountable, and goodnaturedly remarked he was always unlucky in seeing wonders; so with many thanks he wished me good morning. Subsequently, it was found that so trivial a thing as opening a door might precipitate on the plates of the machine particles of moisture or of dust instantly fatal to the generation of the high electric tension evoked by the machine.

The danger of jumping to a conclusion taught by the foregoing experience crossed my mind when the introduction of the candle stopped the playful devilry in Maggie's room.[4] Instead of going home at once, satisfied that the noises were a practical joke, I begged permission to make another trial. Taking the lad (who had all the time been by my side) with me, and putting the candle on the little window sill in the kitchen, I stood, along with the father, just inside the open bed-room door. In a few moments the sounds recommenced, but in a timorous sort of way; gradually they became stronger and stronger. Taking the candle in my hand they ceased again, but after a minute or two once more returned, as if growing accustomed to the presence of the light! When at last, after much

---

[4] It is hardly necessary to point out the unphilosophical attitude of mind of those, who before becoming acquainted with a new group of phenomena, postulate the conditions under which those phenomena ought in their opinion to be produced. It is no more incredible that strong light should be fatal to the particular sounds here investigated than that the glare of daylight is fatal to the appearance of the stars. [Barrett's footnote.]

patience, the sounds were heard in full vigour, we moved towards the bed, and, candle in hand, closely watched the hands and feet of the girls; no motion was apparent, and yet during this time the knocks were going on everywhere around; on the wall, on the chairs, on the quilt, and on the big four-post wooden bedstead whereon they were lying. Returning to the door and placing the candle just outside, enough light was cast into the room for me to see every object distinctly. Whilst in this position the knockings and scratchings came with redoubled energy, and yet the closest scrutiny failed to detect any motion on the part of anyone in the room.

Now came a very staggering and marvellous affair—one of those things which, as Robert Houdin said of a somewhat similar occurrence,[5] are simply stupefying, in as much as they defy any ordinary explanation. I found my request to have a certain number of knocks was obeyed, and this, too, when I made the request more and more inaudibly. At last, I mentally asked for a certain number of knocks: they were slowly and correctly given! To check any tendency to bias or delusion on my part, I thrust my hands in my coat pockets, and said, "Knock the number of fingers I have open." The response was at first merely a loud scratching, but I insisted on my request being answered, and to my amazement three slow, loud knocks were given—this was perfectly correct. The chances, of course, were one in ten of its being right if trickery were at work. Again, I opened a certain number of fingers, and bid it tell me the number open; five was knocked. This, too, was right, and the chances of both times being right were one in one hundred. Again, I opened other fingers, and the number was correctly rapped; the chances were here one in one thousand. Again I tried, and six was knocked, which also was right; and here the chances for all four cases being correct were as but one in ten thousand. Let it be noted that my hands were entirely hidden in the side pockets of a loose overcoat; no one but myself could possibly know the number of fingers I had open; and the enormous chances against being right four times running—if the knocks were due to trickery—gave me, I think, just ground for believing that, after all, there might be here something in operation not dreamt of in medical science, nor

---

[5] Jean-Eugène Robert-Houdin (1805-1871) was a pioneering and celebrated stage magician.

compatible with a purely materialistic philosophy.[6] After the last number had been correctly rapped, and I expressed aloud my great surprise, the knocks increased in vigour and in variety of character. A loud rattling was heard like the beating of a drum, the pattering on the bed-clothes was incessant, and violent scratching and tearing sounds added to the diabolical hullabaloo.

This, said the old man, is how it has been going on nearly every night, and often all the night through, "and it frights and puzzles us greatly, sir." Certainly I was as puzzled as the old man: such uncanny sounds might well scare the lonely little household. By degrees I got the whole of the story from the old farmer, and the following account contains his *ipsissima verba,*[7] verified, as I have already remarked, by cross questioning his children:

"My poor wife," he began, "died in March last, and after her death we were all very lonesome and sad, and fretted a good deal. On Good Friday night, just three weeks after her death, after I had gotten to bed I heard a little wee rapping at the door forenenst where I lay, and it kept on rapping till about two o'clock in the morning. I thought it was our cats, or some rats, and that it would go away soon, but it didn't. The next night it began again, so I fetched a light and got up to see what it was, and it then ceased: but when I lay down again it began again. Then I got a stick, thinking I would scare it away, so when it began again I hit the door a crack with the stick, but instead of scaring it, it struck harder than before at the door, and when I struck again it struck too. Then when I found I couldn't daunt it, just a wee dread came over me, for I knew then it couldn't be rats or mice. So I got up and searched all the house; the cats were surely asleep by the fire and no one was about.

---

[6] What a change in the last twenty years! The weird legends of our childhood are vanishing; their superstitious glamour, which we are both glad and sorry to lose, is being replaced by the conscientiously gathered minutiæ of the scientific investigator. We doubt whether, since they were chronicled in a matter-of-fact way in Egypt five thousand years ago, ghostly occurrences have found tellers free from imaginative terror until now. This scientific age is realistic in its ghost stories. Mr. Wallace catches a small sprite at work in hinged slate, Mr. Crookes photographs one by the electric light. We are waiting anxiously for Dr. Carpenter to meet with the genie of the Arabian Nights, who fills the sky with his giant frown and refuses to be replaced in his bottle. When the haunts of the "Krakens" of the supernatural are found, science will have some fun, and we may expect some good stories. [Editor's footnote. See "Pertinent Facts" at the beginning of this chapter regarding the three scientists mentioned.]

[7] A Latin phrase meaning "the very words."

Then I began to take a thought what it was, but could pass no opinion. Then I woke the children, but when I went to bed again it kept on rapping till day-light, when it went away till next night. After this a great dread came over us all and we kept a candle burning all night, but the knocks would still come when the light was burning, though not so loud. Then we all laid ourselves down in the same room, and now it wrought on the quilt of the bed, making sounds like tapping the quilt, and touching my daughter Maggie, so she says. One morning we found fifteen or sixteen small stones had been dropped on her bed. The noises and the tapping continued nearly every night, and once it wrought all night till the children were getting up in the morning; and so it went on, and with the dread and the loss of sleep we all felt very sick. Then it began to steal. We found this first on May 24th—I know it was that day, because it was Derrygonelly Fair. It first took a pair of boots and an odd one from out of the press in our sitting-room, and we searched the house for them everywhere, but could not find them; and we looked in the fields, but never a one of them could we find. Then one of us said, Let us ask the raps to tell us. So that night I said, If the boots are in the house, give a rap; and instead of rapping it gave a scratch; then I said, If the boots are out of the house, give a rap, and it gave a loud rap. Then I said, Give a rap if they are in Garrick's field, and it gave a scratch; then I asked other places, and at last I said, Are they in the plant field? And it gave a loud rap; and I said, What o'clock will they be there? as I had searched the plant field already. Then it gave six knocks. So a little before six in the morning I went out and searched the plant field again, but could find nothing; then I came in to see the clock, and it do be only just six; so I went out again, and I found them in the very place I had looked before. And sure, sir, I am of this. The three boots were all tied together with a bit of selvage wound round and round them, and with a string of knots we couldn't undo; so we had to cut them apart, and they were quite dry as if from the fire. Then we locked up all the boots, but it did no good, for another night it took a boot from a locked drawer, and after a great search we found it in a chest of feathers in the loft.

"Other things besides boots it stole; somethings it took in daylight, and many of them we have not found yet. It took a pair of scissors, and then it began to steal our candles. First it took a pound of candles; then we had to light the little lamp; it then stole the lamp chimney and after that three more lamp chimneys, so we couldn't get our lamp to burn. Then we borrowed a lamp which burnt without a chimney, and it stole the bottle of lamp oil. None of these things could we find, nor would it tell us where they were, but kept on scratching and seemed to get angry. We got some more oil, and it came that night and stole the lamp we had borrowed, and this vexed us badly. Then Jack Flanigan came and lent us his lamp, saying he would engage the devil himself could not steal it, as 'he had got the priest to dip it into holy water.' But that did no good either, for a few nights after that it stole that lamp too. We were then forced to get more candles, and the children hid them in the byre [the cow-house], in a little hollow between the thatch and the rafters, so that no one could have found the candles, they hid them so close; but *it* seen them, and I think too it heard us speaking of the good way we had managed to trick it this time, for when we went to get a candle from the byre, an hour and a half after they were hid, they were all gone; so we were forced to leave our candles in a neighbour's house till we wanted one, but it was very troublesome, for there is no house very near, and we couldn't keep a candle at all unless it do be burning, for it would take the candle end away if the light were put out. It tried to keep us in darkness, so that it should be able to make most disturbance.

"One day I bethought me of putting a candle in a lantern, and tying the lantern up to the ceiling. So I bought a candle of a woman who comes this way to sell things, and I put the candle in the lantern, shutting the door tight down myself, and then tied up the lantern, and set the two young children after watching it, like a cat would a mouse; but they didn't keep their eyes on it all the time, but every now and again they looked up. We were down working in the bog, and before night came the children came running down to us, saying the candle had gone out of the lantern; and sure it had, for when I got home there was no candle in the lantern: it had been stole out, though the lantern door was close shut all the time, and no neighbor had come nigh the house. After that I said it was no use getting more candles, so we had to use the light of the turf fire. Lately, however, it has left off stealing, and we can now keep a light, though every day we fear it will be taken.

"Many people came now to see us and hear the knockings, for the news of it had gone about, and some said it was only rats, and others thought it were trickery, and some said it was fairies, or maybe the devil. Several neighbours wanted us to get the priest, but we are Methodists, sir, and believed the Bible would do more good. A class leader one day told us to lay the Bible on the bed; so we did in the name of God, but a little after we found the Bible had been placed on the pillow and was laid open at the book of Jeremiah. Then I got a big stone, about 28lb. weight, and laid it on the Bible in the window sill, for I was afeard it might take the Bible away; but before long we found the Bible had been moved and we found the big stone laid on the pillow and the Bible open on top of it. After that it moved the Bible and prayer-book out of the bed-room and tore seventeen pages of the Bible right across, as you see, sir, here."

The old man had now finished his story, though other circumstances would occasionally recur to him as the evening went on. It was time, however, for me to ask, "Is it not possible some of your children were playing tricks all the time?"

"Ah, sir," he replied, "they were in too great trouble, and no trickery could be in their heads, as they were sorrowing over their mother. Then, sir, I know them too well for that; they would not keep their old father awake and trouble him so, for it's many a night we have had no sleep, but have been kept worrying over this till morning. And, sir, how could they be at trickery, for since it began I have laid down on chairs in the same room, right forenenst them, and the candle was burning, when I heard it rapping and scratching or rattling like a drum at the head and the top and the foot of their bed, and the children were lying still all the time."

"Might it not be some troublesome lads outside?" I asked.

"Well, sir," he answered, "if the lads could lie inside a wall they might, for there are no windows beside the bed; and why would lads keep up the noises, for I say truth, sir, when I tell you that for two months it never missed a night from the time we all laid down; sometimes only a quarter of an hour it would go on and then stop entirely. After two months it kept away some nights, and now it comes chiefly on Saturdays and Sundays, but oftentimes other nights also."

"Well, what do you think it is?" said I.

"I would have thought, sir, it do be fairies, but them late readers and all knowledgeable men will not allow such a thing, so I cannot tell what it is. I only wish you could take it away."

"Why do you not ask it the question who or what it is?" I replied. "You might spell over the alphabet, and ask it to knock at the right word."

"Yes, sir, so someone told us to do; but it tells lies as often as truth, and oftener, I think. We tried it, and it only knocked at L.M.N. Some of our neighbours say it do be my wife's spirit haunting the house; but this I am sure, sir, that if the Lord would send her spirit wandering on earth, it's not for to trouble us in this way, but to make us happy and protect us she would come."

Tears stood in the old farmer's eyes, and I felt that before me was certainly one who had no hand in the noises, and it seemed inconceivable that his children could have the physical endurance, even if they *could* have had the cruelty, to inflict such continued suffering and disturbance on the little household, and that, too, in the midst of the great calamity that had so recently over taken them. If I had not personally tested every plausible hypothesis I should have said that the family, unstrung by this very calamity, had readily given way to superstitious fears, their imagination building upon the weird sounds that occur in that bleak and desolate region. But *my* nerves were not unstrung, and my hearing certainly did not deceive me. *Could* it be anyone "larking"? The experience I have narrated seems to render such an idea impossible. Nevertheless, I determined to go again, and meanwhile wrote to ask a friend to join me.

The next occasion I visited the house nothing occurred, though I waited till past midnight. The friend to whom I had written—the president of one of our learned societies—promptly responded, and upon his sobriety of judgment and accuracy of observation the reader may confidently rely. We visited the house together, and heard the noises as before, though not so loudly manifested as previously, yet our united and strict vigilance failed to detect imposture, and equally certain were we that we were not the victims of hallucination for my friend's experience and my own coincided in every detail. We searched round the house; no one was, or could have been concealed; none of the family were absent; and if the readers concludes they *must* have been the agents at work, the question *cui bono*,[8] and the absence of any morbid ailment among

---

[8] A Latin phrase meaning "for whose benefit?"

them seemed unanswerable replied to that point—even if my own careful observations be omitted.[9]

Thus I left the neighbourhood fairly puzzled, and on my way home could not help reflecting upon the extremely curious simi-

---

[9] As might be expected, the family have been greatly pestered with idlers, and with some visitors calling themselves gentlemen, who, uninvited, have come to partake of the free hospitality of these poor folk, and then have behaved in an unseemly way, and when rebuked, have left the place proclaiming they had found out the "whole trick," and denouncing the family as gross impostors. Although such are not likely to be found among the readers of this magazine, yet I have suppressed the farmer's name, as it may prevent intrusive letters. I may add that extensive inquiry among his neighbours confirmed my impression that he was a thoroughly upright, God-fearing man. As this paper was passing through the press, I wrote to the farmer, asking him if any further light had been thrown on the noises. Unable to write, and with difficulty to read a letter, Maggie wrote for him as follows (the spelling and punctuation only are altered): "The disturbances is still going on, we hear it some nights, about once in three weeks we hear it: we have no talk about it now and our nearest friends does not know but it is gone, we are not afraid of it now but I hope it is going away." Furthermore, my Enniskillen friend, at my request, has within the last few days again visited the once troubled household: and I also learn from him that the knockings are still heard, but they are feebler and less frequent than they were. The family are, he says, very reticent about the matter, not only being anxious to avoid further intrusion, but also because their experience has led them to the correct conclusion that the more persistently the noises are disregarded the less troublesome they are, so that in time the sounds will doubtless entirely fade away. This conclusion is singularly verified by the two cases referred to in the last foot-note but one in this paper. In one of these cases, that of a little girl whose parents were annoyed by the sounds, and who eventually let them go on unheeded, the knocking slowly disappeared, and have not returned. In the other case great interest was excited, and sittings were regularly held for nearly two hours every night during the last three years; here the sounds have steadily grown in vigour and variety, and at the present time are tolerably certain in their bold recurrence, *in full light,* directly a passive or expectant state is assumed by the so-called "medium"—not necessarily by the inquirer, who is, or ought to be, in an attitude of the utmost vigilance. But there are cases in private families of high respectability, who not only would be insulted by the idea of taking, directly or indirectly, any payment, but who hush the matter up as far as possible, being naturally anxious to avoid the ridicule of society and the aspersion of their characters by physiologists imbued with a "dominant idea." Numerous similar cases exist, to my certain knowledge, in various parts of England. I am no advocate for indiscriminately encouraging these phenomena; far from it, whatever their explanation, their effect upon *the ignorant and credulous* is an unmixed evil. Viewing with concern the inevitable progress and havoc of "spiritualism" among uncultured minds, I view with still greater concern the flimsy explanations, varnished with half-truths, that pass muster at the hands of those psychologists who arrogate to themselves the sole right of instructing the public on this subject. [Barrett's footnote.]

larity between these phenomena cropping up in remote part of Ireland, where, as I ascertained, neither the name of Spiritualism, nor the report of any of its prodigies had ever penetrated, and the rappings that so mysteriously arose thirty years ago across the Atlantic, in the family of a respectable farmer, also members of a Methodist church,[10] and living in a lonely country district of the United States. I allude to the well known case of "Kate and Maggie Fox,"[11] of whom their Irish counterparts had never heard.

What, then, is this lurking mystery that yields neither to holy water nor scientific inquiry? Are we, in the midst of our nineteenth century science and civilisation, to be expected to believe in the fairies and hobgoblins of our childish imagination? Are we seriously to give heed to the village

> . . . Stories told of many a feat,
> How fairy Mab the junket seat—
> She was pinched and pulled, she said;
> And he, by Friar's lantern led,
> Tells how the drudging goblin sweat
> To earn his cream-bowl duly set,

---

[10] The reader will remember the knockings and disturbances at Epworth Parsonage where the Rev. Samuel Wesley (father of the founder of Methodism) was then rector. These sounds, investigated by his son John Wesley, and described in Dr. Priestley's and Dr. Adam Clark's Life of Wesley, defied every attempt at explanation, and they still remain a mystery, as the foregoing occurrences seem to me at present. The naturalistic philosopher might say that the story of the Epworth knockings had found its way into Methodist literature (as is the case, I believe) and had been read by the children of both the American and Irish farmer (in the latter case I found this supposition was correct), and so they tried to get up notoriety by imitating the wonders that happened in the family of the famous founder of their sect. My rejoinder is that even this hypothesis did not escape me when conducting my inquiry on the spot, and yet the enigma remained still unsolved in my mind. I cannot, of course, expect my readers to be equally convinced that no trickery was at the root of the matter. [Barrett's footnote.]

[11] The attempts made to asperse the character of these ladies (the former is now the wife of an English barrister, Mr. Jencken, the latter the widow of Captain Kane, the Arctic explorer) have signally failed; and concerning the so-called "exposure" of their powers in America, the recent correspondence in the columns of the *Athenæum* has proved it to have been a baseless fabrication. For a full and excellent description of these "Rochester rappings" see Dale Owen's "Footfalls on the Boundary of another World," page 204, *et seq.* [Barrett's footnote. The exchange about the Fox sisters being exposed starts with a positive book review of Carpenter's *Mesmerism, Spiritualism, &c.*; proceeds to Fox Jenkens' denunciation of it; and ends with Carpenter's reply. See *Athenæum* 2587 (May 26, 1877) pp. 666-67; 2589 (June 9, 1877) p. 737; and (2590 (June 16, 1877) p. 767.]

When in one night, ere glimpse of morn,
His shadowy flail hath threshed the corn
That ten day-labourers could not end;
Then lies him down the lubber fiend,
And stretched out all the chimney's length,
Basks at the fire his hairy strength,
And crop-full out of doors he flings,
Ere the first cock his matin rings.
Thus done the tales, to bed they creep,
By whispering winds soon lulled asleep.[12]

But if anyone believes these rappings to be beyond the power of visible mortals to produce, may we not have our household demons around us still, up to any pranks and fun? The conclusion is too absurd for the modern mind. Society has grown out of ghosts and goblins. It has made up its mind they cannot exist. Haunted houses have been relegated to the pages of the novelist or to the limbo of obsolete superstitions. And it matters not whether it be a ghostly apparition, or ghostly knockings, or ghostly noises and freaks of furniture—all are equally foreign to the enlightened opinion, the scientific wisdom, and the strong commonsense of the present day. Does not the voice of philology as well as philosophy assure us that the country ghosts of our forefathers have disappeared under the influence of surface drainage?[13] We must go to the chemist, not to the dark and lonely marsh, to see the objective ghost of to-day. But the chemist is not the only exorcist. The physician has laid the more numerous tribe of supernatural visitants which, in all past ages, mankind *thought they saw.* Apparitions, wraiths, and spectral lights are readily explained by "sensorial deception"; haunted houses and the like are the product of a "dominant idea"; possession, obsession, and exalted powers of mind or body are the results of "hysteria" and its congeners; in fine, ancient necromancy and modern Spiritualism are sad illustrations of "epidemic delusions"!

---

[12] From John Milton's "L'Allegro" (1633).

[13] It is almost needless to say that our modern word *gas* is the equivalent of the Anglo-Saxon *gast,* and the German *geist*—literally, ghost or spirit. The Will-o'-the-Wisp, Milton's "Friar's lantern," is no longer a tricksy sprite, but well known to be due to the spontaneous ignition and wafting to and fro of inflammable gas produced by decaying animal and vegetable matter; the gas itself every school-boy knows under the name of marsh-gas. [Barrett's footnote.]

Thus it comes to pass that no one who values the good opinion of his friends, or cares to lose the reputation of being a sensible man will venture to express the smallest belief in a ghost. It is not a subject in which reasonable men can be expected to take any serious interest; and yet ghost stories of one sort or another still persist, and new cases incessantly recur. No superstitious fear now prevents belief or checks inquiry. Fear of the unknown is out of place at the present day. The reason for modern incredulity is that we know, or think we know, everything. Under the guise of profound humility as to our ignorance of the particular discoveries of the future, there lurks the most arrogant assumption as to the definite boundaries of our knowledge. The world that our senses reveal is all that is, or was, or ever will be. A belief in the supernatural is a relic of the past. Let us eat, drink, and study evolution, for tomorrow we die. In future ages our descendants may be angels, and may have learnt the secret of immortality, but to-day we are as the animals that perish. An unseen universe is a philosophic delusion, and a faith that looks forward to life in the invisible is a priestly snare!

Such is the practical materialism that now runs, more or less hidden, throughout society. Hence any evidence that may be given for the existence of phenomena that elude rigid scientific inquiry, or for which no materialistic hypothesis can be framed, whether that evidence relate to past times or the present, is invariably received with a feeling of settled distrust, or else pushed aside with a motion of impatient contempt.

Notwithstanding this, almost every family has within its knowledge some perplexing occurrence, bordering on the confines of the supernatural, some private mystery rarely spoken of to the outside world. Still, even such people sit in the seat of the scornful when any similar inexplicable phenomenon outside their experience is related to them by their friends. Doubtless in the case of dreams or presentiments, mere coincidence covers much of the ground; but not in all, for cases have come under the writer's notice where the chain of coincidences would have to be stretched to such an unbelievable extent that any alternative is preferable, and some supersensuous influence acting upon the mind of the sleeper becomes a far easier hypothesis. And in the case of apparitions and the like, a disordered state of the nervous or digestive system unquestionably affords, in general, a simple and rational subjective explanation. But here, too, medical scrutiny sometimes hopelessly breaks down, and with it every "naturalistic" suggestion, so that we must either abandon our common sense and disbelieve evidence that in a criminal case would hang the most virtuous man in Christendom, or accept the simpler explanation that amid the multitude of phenomena which time and space present, there exists a residue which science cannot explain. Facts are slowly but surely accumulating which seem to indicate that the whole civilized world up to a couple of centuries ago might, after all, have had some good ground for the once universal belief that activity, intelligence, and personality can have and do have an existence in an unseen state; a state between which and us there is a great gulf fixed. And yet it would almost seem that certain mental organisations, or the conjunction of special circumstances, in which we can trace the operation of no recognized law, form at times a frail and fleeting bridge which enables that gulf to be momentarily spanned. When in support of this the overwhelming testimony of the past and of the present day is borne in mind—testimony which every honest critic feels it most difficult to gain say—such a conclusion can hardly be felt to be extravagant by any rational and unbiased mind.

But here we are arrested by two opposite phases of thought. On the one hand we find those who, whether from their environment or conviction, find no intellectual difficulty in a belief in the supernatural,[14] accepting the general creed of Christendom, and attributing any contact of the unseen with the seen to the operation of diabolic agency. Accordingly they steadily shun all post-Johannine evidence of the supernatural that may be adduced, not from disbelief but from dislike. On the other hand we find the hardened sceptic, who refuses to believe in any unseen world of intelligent beings, but who professes a readiness to believe in such a world if it could be proved, albeit he closes the question by asserting the existence of an unseen world can *never* be proved; for, he argues, any proof we have must come through the evidence of the senses, and thereby the object of proof has ceased to belong to the unseen. Among some exact thinkers such skepticism is fortified by the conviction that if an unseen world does exist in the background of the world with which science deals, any nexus between the two, however slight or transitory, would be attended by

---

14 This is a bad word, of course, but it conveys what is meant, and its use does not imply agreement with its etymological signification. [Barrett's footnote.]

intellectual confusion: in as much as those great natural laws which scientific inquiry has established would at any moment be open to invasion, and therefore periodic destruction, by an unseen enemy. To such, therefore, an unseen universe is practically non-existent.

It is not probable that any remarks of mine are likely to affect the attitude of mind of either of these opposite schools of thought. Nor, if I had the power, would this be the place or time adequately to notice them. But perhaps I may be permitted to say this much. Among Christians the dread they feel is, *in general,* nothing more than a survival of the superstitious fear of the unknown which in former times characterized both savage and saint. To me, it seems that a bold and manly Christian courage should welcome any evidence which throws light on the pneumatology of the Scriptures, and so far from playing the ostrich with these phenomena, Christian thinkers should surely seek to co-ordinate them with the facts of revelation.[15] And turning to the sceptic, whose philosophy is based on the absence of this old superstitious fear, where terror usurps the place of reason, ought not such an one to make himself *quite sure* that the evidence of every supernatural occurrence is valueless before he denies the possibility of an unseen world, and stakes such weighty issues upon his denial. I do not pretend that the case I have narrated in these pages is sufficiently sifted to allow of no alternative but that of the operation of superhuman agency. Such a conclusion could only be admitted after the most laborious and protracted inquiry by experts more competent than the present writer. But these facts—taken in conjunction with similar manifestations that have been submitted to investigation, so long and patient, that we are assured every other alternative has one by one had to be abandoned—do seem to point to a high degree of probability in the direction of such a conclusion.[16]

---

[15] Upon this point the reader will find a masterly and interesting excursus on the "Scripture Doctrine of an Evil Superhuman Agency concerned in the Destruction of Mankind," in the second book of that valuable work, "Life in Christ," by the Rev. E. White (Elliot Stock.) [Bartlett's footnote.]

[16] It is irrational to contend that because the *physical* phenomena are so utterly contemptible, therefore they are not worthy of inquiry. A knock at the street-door is an absurd thing in itself, but it may be the precursor of an exalted guest. To establish the fact that physical or mental action is possible across space would in itself be a great advance in our knowledge of the universe. Two cases have come under my notice which have carried conviction to my mind that intelligent physical action can and does occur at a distance, *i.e.,* from any perceptible agent.

That an unseen universe does exist the leaders of physical inquiry are agreed upon purely scientific grounds; from it they trace the genesis of life and of everything that our senses reveal.[17] Moreover, do we not find in our own microcosm the mingled mystery of matter and spirit, so unlike and yet so closely knit? What, then, may we not expect to find in the macrocosm of the world around? Already we know definitely that it presents us with gross matter free from, as well as united to, consciousness; may it not also present us with the converse—consciousness free from gross (*i.e.,* perceptible) matter? The vagueness of idea which engenders skepticism as to how consciousness, personality—in a word, spirit— can exist free from tangible matter, is surely lessened when we admit, as every man of science does admit, that interatomic as well as interstellar space is filled with matter, of a substance not gross enough to affect our senses, or the finest instrumental appliances. And the incredulity which arises from the difficulty of conceiving how spirit freed from its association with tangible matter can act upon such matter so as to appeal to our consciousness through it, is truly no greater than the difficulty which meets us in the action of our own will over the gross cellular tissue of our brain, and thus over our entire bodily frame. Is not the greater difficulty rather that of conceiving of the life-long conjunction and mutual influence of gross matter and individual consciousness, and not that of their separate existence?

After all, the problem the sceptic has to solve is not whether the immanence of the supernatural is credible or incredible, or comprehensible or incomprehensible, but simply whether the evidence in support of such a statement is conclusive; in fine, whether the facts are *true*. Let us put aside clamour, misrepresentation, and vituperation; let us also put aside the *idola tribûs*, whose worshippers believe all the laws of existence in this wide

---

These cases I have investigated with extreme jealousy and care, and can affirm that none of the numerous hypotheses, suggested by Dr. Carpenter and others are competent to explain away the facts. The strongest evidence in the case narrated in these columns is that of *mental action at a distance;* concerning this question of *supersensuous* perception I hope very shortly to publish ampler and more decisive evidence. [Bartlett's footnote.]

[17] *Cf.* the utterances of the late Sir John Herschel and Professor Faraday, and of Prof. Clerk Maxwell, Prof. P.G. Tait, Prof. G.G. Stokes, Prof. Balfour Stewart, Prof. S. Haughton, and others, in various discourses and writings. [Bartlett's footnote.]

universe are to be found within the covers of certain physiological manuals; and the *idola specûs,* at whose shrine truth is so often sacrificed; and seek for *instantiæ crusis* of super- or infra-natural phenomena, if such exist, in the dry and pure light of truth. Be the conclusion as it may, the story I have here narrated, even if it goes no deeper, may perhaps furnish some of my readers with a Christmas tale, or a subject for fireside speculation.

Case 7: In the Manner of the SPR

Investigation: Supervised by Frank Podmore with assistance from Charles Downing, Eleanor Sidgwick, Alexander Macalister, and others.

Manifestations: disembodied sighs, whispers, groans and footsteps; rustling of a silk dress; phantoms of various description.

Pertinent Facts: Frank Podmore (1856-1910) was one of the most innovative and controversial members of the Society for Psychical Research. His argument that phenomena experienced at haunted sites can be explained as telepathic—if not as perfectly natural occurrences misinterpreted as supernatural—irked those who saw ghosts as empirical evidence of survival in the Afterlife. His report on an investigation of an alleged haunted house gives a sense of how the SPR handled such cases: with thorough documentation, cautious analysis, and *mostly* amiable teamwork (with exceptions to the latter discussed in Cases 8 and 9).

⁜

HAUNTED HOUSE.[1]

Members and Associates desirous of occupying for a time a small house reputed to be haunted, with a view of investigating the phenomena, are invited to communicate with F. Podmore, Esq., 14, Dean's Yard, S.W. It is not, of course, guaranteed that arrangements can be made with all applicants. The house is partly furnished, and is in a pretty part of the country, not very far from London.

✤

---

[1] This appeared in the *Proceedings of the Society for Psychical Research* 1.15 (April, 1885) p. 324.

An Account of Some Abnormal Phenomena
Alleged to Have Occurred at B— Lodge, W—

Frank Podmore[2]

In the autumn of 1884 the Society received accounts of some abnormal phenomena which were said to have occurred at a house in W—, a small village about 40 miles from London. The house—a modern one, having been built, I believe, within the last half century—stands flush with the high road, having a garden on one side and at the back, and a barn, which separates it from a row of cottages, on the other. On the ground floor, to the right and left of the entry respectively, are a drawing-room and dining-room; behind each of these is a kitchen: the kitchen behind the dining-room communicates with a small scullery, which leads into the barn above referred to. The barn, which has no window, possesses another door, opening to the high road. Beneath the house are dry and spacious cellars.

The first floor contains four rooms; situated as shown in the plan subjoined. On the second floor there are three bedrooms, corresponding to the front rooms on the floor below; the rest of this floor is occupied by two windowless garrets, one of which contains the cistern.

ROUGH PLAN OF FIRST FLOOR OF B— LODGE, W—

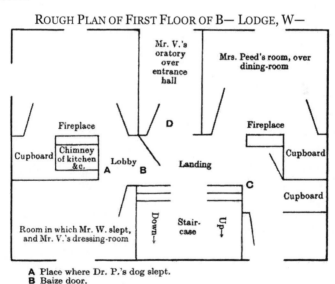

A Place where Dr. P.'s dog slept.
B Baize door.
C Place where Mrs. H. (then Mrs. Peed) states she saw the figure.

---

[2] This appeared in the *Proceedings of the Society for Psychical Research* 2.25 (Feb., 1886) pp. 196-207.

From 1870 to 1876 the house was occupied by a Mr. and Mrs. Peed. Mr. Peed died in 1876, and Mrs. Peed—who subsequently became Mrs. H.—left the house in 1877. During her occupancy she received as lodgers, successively, the Rev. H.A.S., and the Rev. E.G.P., who acted as curates to the rector of the parish.

The following letters from the Rev. H.A.S. were written in answer to our inquiry whether he had had any unusual experience in the house during his stay there:

July 28th, 1885.

I regret that I am unable to offer much information in reply to your inquiries concerning B— House, W—.

I do, however, distinctly remember hearing on many occasions sounds of footsteps upon the stairs, and especially upon the little landing, at various hours during the night. The inhabitants of the house then were Mr. and Mrs. Peed (the former paralysed and unable to leave his room without assistance), myself and a maid named Emma Matthews. At first I thought the maid must have been secretly entering or leaving the house for objects best known to herself, but as she was always thoroughly respectable and discreet, and 25 years of age, I could not easily understand these proceedings. Moreover, I could never discern the object of the footsteps themselves. If they descended, I waited vainly for sounds of ascending; if ascending, I might vainly listen for any sounds of descent. For obvious reasons I was unwilling to emerge upon the stairs *en deshabille*.[3]

Finally, I asked my landlady, Mrs. Peed, if Emma walked in her sleep; but no satisfactory solution of the matter appeared, and I ceased to notice the ordinary sounds.

On one occasion I remarked to my landlady that I heard people "scuffling in the garden at the back door, and could hear their feet on the gravel." She went to the door and perceived nothing. She became a widow shortly after I left W—; then married a farmer, who has also died, and she is now living at W—. From her some further information might perhaps be derived.

Of course I had often heard rumours about the house—a more modern and practical house could not exist—but know nothing further of my own knowledge.

H.A.S.

P.S.—I ought to mention that the footsteps on the stairs nearly always proceeded to or emerged from the top story of the house, where no one lived but the maid. I never heard either back or front door opened at night, though I often waited for that object.

---

3 A French phrase meaning "in a state of undress."

July 31st, 1885.

I began to reside in B House, W. (probably) about July, 1871, and left the house finally on August 27th, 1872.

H.A.S.

The next account is from the Rev. E.G.P., D.D., who appears to have succeeded Mr. H.A.S. in the curacy. This account was written by Mr. C. Downing from notes taken at a personal interview, and has been corrected by Dr. P. himself.

I began residence as curate of W— at B— Lodge, December 29th, 1872, and left May 10th, 1875. I was then fresh from Oxford, and a boating man. The house was of moderate size, built plainly of red brick, and had nothing in any way suggestive of "ghosts" in its appearance. It was neither lonely nor gloomy looking.

I was not aware, upon taking possession of my apartments there, that any history was attached to the house; but have since learnt that an old gentleman of no great reputation once lived there, who was supposed to have had an illegitimate child, and to have made away with it. There were some peculiar stains on the floor of an upper room in the house, and on the occasion of the kitchen chimney catching fire, what looked much like charred fragments of a child's bones came down. It is also said that the house is built upon the site of an old inn (17th and 18th century) which was frequented by the outlaws of the Chiltern Hills, and in which several murders were committed.

A Mrs. Peed (now Mrs. H.) was the landlady. Her husband was paralytic, incapable of moving by himself. He died July 20th, 1876. *The phenomena have continued since his death.*

The only other person in the house was Emma Matthews, the servant, a taciturn and trustworthy woman, of Puritan family and religious disposition. *One night, when she was away in the village,* at the sick bed of her mother, the usual occurrences took place, in a more pronounced way, if anything.

There was a second floor. My sitting-room on the ground floor was beneath my bedroom, and Mr. and Mrs. Peed had a dining-room beneath theirs.

On retiring to rest, I always bolted the lobby door, leaving my bedroom door open. I was thus shut off from the rest of the house. My dog—a Yorkshire fox-terrier, pedigree breed—slept in a basket in the lobby.

Almost immediately after I began to live there I noticed strange noises at night, both in my own rooms and all over the house, especially in the room at the top of the house, where the stains were. These noises, however, were not very easy to localise. They were at first slight, but afterwards increased in intensity. They were essentially unearthly, and it is very difficult to describe them. There were loud explosions, sounds like the falling of trays, stampings, rustlings, sounds of heavy furniture being moved. When I sat in the room below, it seemed as if there were a lot of schoolboys "larking" in the bedroom above. There were also sighs and groans; but no knockings. Nor did I ever attempt to communicate with what I considered to be an evil power. Strange to say, and this was noticed by previous and subsequent occupants of the house, the noises seemed to be greatest towards the full of the moon; and there were considerable intervals in which they were not heard at all. The dog apparently heard nothing.

On the night of May 14th, 1874, I had retired to rest, quite ignorant that a dear friend of mine was dying. I was awakened by a noise in the corner of the room, like the clashing of cymbals, followed by other strange sounds. I had become used to my visitants by this time, was in no way frightened, turned away and went to sleep again.

On the night of May 31st, 1874 (the moon then being at the full), an old gentleman, Mr. W., my friend and adopted father, as I was wont to call him, was staying with me. He slept in the dressing-room, and burnt a light. Both our doors were open, but I am as certain as I can be that the lobby door was fastened as usual. Mr. W. knew nothing of these noises. In the middle of the night I was aroused by the most extraordinary clamour in the lobby; sprang out of bed and entered the dressing-room. As I did so I saw the dog was gone, and the lobby door wide open. Mr. W. was much agitated; said that he had been greatly alarmed, but should be better presently. It was not till shortly before his death (December 28th, 1875) that he told me that he had awoke just before I entered and seen the figure of a tall man, in a grey woollen dressing-gown, standing at the foot of his bed. This appearance, I believe, coincides with what has been seen by others. My only feeling at the moment was that of great anger at being thus continually disturbed, and upon this night especially, in a manner which was worse than all that had gone before. Taking the light, I went out on the landing, where the noise still continued, followed it closely *wherever it seemed to go;* drove it, so to say, down stairs, seeming to hear the stamp of feet upon each stair, together with an indescribable sound in the air, just where the head of an invisible being, the height of a man, might have been. From the stairs it proceeded, still stamping, into the dining-room, which I also entered, with nerves braced for the worst that could befall, and thoroughly determined to cope with this now insupportable annoyance. In the middle of the room it ceased, and I adjured it in the Name of God. There was no answer, and in a moment or two, with more terror than I had ever felt before, I returned upstairs. The dog was at D. (on the plan), crouched in a condition of the utmost fear, foaming and bristling, every hackle on end.

After this night the noises *kept at a distance and were never in the same room with me.*

Mrs. Peed and Emma Matthews heard noises, though I cannot say whether they were heard at the same time by everybody. Mrs. Peed has seen the apparition twice, I understand; also that an old lady who came down from London afterwards and took the apartments, having previously inquired whether any one else lived in the house, and been answered in the negative, complained on the morning after the first night passed there, that the landlady had deceived her in this particular, for in the middle of the night she was awakened by a tall man, in a grey woollen dressing-gown, who was moving the ottoman in her bedroom. Near this ottoman I used very often to hear noises.

I may mention that before Mr. V. took the house he had heard from me, at St. Augustine, what experiences I had there. He was rather inclined to laugh at me, and for some five months after he began to live in it this intimation seemed justified. But no longer than five months, as you will doubtless hear from him. I never saw anything there myself though I have constantly had the feeling of someone being in the room with me, behind my shoulder while I was writing, &c. Neither before nor since have I had any hallucination. If any trickery were practised it was far too clever for me to discover. If rats could do this they could do anything; at least, they would never have alarmed my dog. I never listened for or fearfully expected to hear noises.

[Dr. P. was asked whether his friend, Mr. W., heard the noises, and replied in the affirmative.]

Mrs. H. declined to write out any account of her own experiences in the house, but she had no objection to relating them *vivâ voce*,[4] and the following account was written by Mrs. H. Sidgwick immediately after an interview with her:

B— Lodge, W—.,
September 28th, 1885.

I have just come back from a long interview with Mrs. H. She entirely declines to write out an account of what she saw, or to sign any account written by me, so we must be satisfied with a second-hand account.

She lived in this house from 1870 to 1877, with her first husband, Mr. Peed, who was an invalid—paralysed, I think—and who died in 1876. Very soon after she came to the house she used to hear noises of various kinds and especially noises like a person creeping or shuffling about the house. Mr. S., the curate before Dr. P., who lodged with her, said he was sure someone came shuffling into his room at night, and thought her servant walked in her sleep. But she did not think much of the noises till Dr. P. seemed much impressed by them. She saw the ghost only once, in July, 1875, after she had been five years in the house, and about a year or 18 months after Mr. W. (Dr. P.'s adopted father) saw it. It was about 8 o'clock in the evening. She had been giving her husband his supper in the room over the dining-room, the servant had gone out to fetch her some stout for her own supper—when going out of the room she saw a tall figure standing against the door opposite. It was a tall figure dressed in white—like a surplice. She did not see the hands. It was an old gentleman with a bald

---

4 A Latin phrase meaning "vocally."

head, fine forehead and beautiful blue eyes. They looked straight into each other's faces—she caught its eye. She said to herself, "So it's you that goes about the house," looked down to the ground a moment, and when she looked up again it had vanished, or she would have spoken to it. She would know it again anywhere, but never saw the face before. She told no one at the time. Her servant remarked on her paleness when she came in, but she did not explain. A little later—a few weeks, I think—she heard a great rustling, as of silk dresses, just as she was starting downstairs. It seemed as if something was "coming on her back," but she saw nothing. This frightened her a good deal more than the other, I think. It was at the same hour in the evening. After this she prayed to be delivered from it, and was never troubled again. She continued to hear sounds, but did not mind them.

The servant, Emma Matthews, once heard a silk dress brush past her, and go upstairs and shut a door while Mrs. Peed and Dr. P. were at evening church, and Mr. Peed and his daughter were in the dining-room. It was darkish. She thought it was Miss Peed—so much so that she went into the dining-room immediately after *without knocking,* to take in candles or something. Miss Peed was there, and said she had not been up, but that Mrs. Peed had come in and gone upstairs—she had heard her silk dress, &c.

Mrs. Peed once saw an old woman with a cap and hooked nose, who held her down in bed. She had not been in bed long. She thought it was a nightmare, but after it had happened three times in rapid succession on the same night she got up to see whether anything was there and found nothing.

This was also at B— Lodge. She never saw anything, nor had any psychical experiences anywhere else, and disbelieved in ghosts before she went there.

She half thinks that the ghost was concerned in throwing her downstairs on one and perhaps two occasions, but on one of them it is believed by others to have been Mr. S.'s cat.

One sound that she describes as occurring in the house consisted in three heavy sighs in perfectly still weather; and once at night, in the dark, a voice whispered at the foot of her bed, "Three more stages and then death," hissing at the last word. This frightened her, and she has not liked to sleep in the dark since. I think it was before she saw the ghost.

Others have heard the sighs who had never been told about them, she believes, viz., a visitor of hers now dead, who thought it said "Ann, Ann," and a third word which I have forgotten. The servant, too—another one, not Emma—was found by Mrs. Peed, when she came in, looking out at the back door, to see if a thrashing machine was preparing for work, but it was not. She had heard three sighs quite loud, and apparently close to her, and had tried to account for them as caused by the thrashing machine. These sighs were not heard during Mr. V.'s tenancy.

Eleanor Mildred Sidgwick.

The next account comes from the Rev. J.F.V., who has also kindly related it *vivâ voce* to some of us on the spot. The distressing nature of Mr. and Mrs. V.'s experience is proved by the fact that they moved at some personal inconvenience into a much smaller house rather than complete the term of their tenancy of B— Lodge.

We took up our abode in B— Lodge in September, 1882. The house fronts the London Road. Two steps lead up to the front door, a garden runs along behind and to the right of the house ending in the stables, divided by a high brick wall from the road on one side, and by a stiff hedge from an orchard on the other. The house has had the reputation of being haunted for at least 10 or more years past. When we entered the house we were aware of its ill name, but did not treat the matter very seriously. We resided there till Michaelmas, 1884. During this period various phenomena took place which may be divided into two kinds :—

I. Visible apparitions.

II. Unaccountable and mysterious sounds and noises.

I. 1. The first time an apparition took place was about December, 1883. Mrs. V. was awake in the night after getting out of bed to give the baby his food. She was thoroughly awake and had been so for some time, when she felt a cold blast like an icy wind pass over her hands, which were outside. She felt an impulse to turn and face the door. The door was seen to be about a foot open, and a man's hand grasping it, and his head and his body down to his waist, in a white dress, as if a night-dress, looking in. He looked full at her. She was terrified and tried ineffectually several times to call her husband by name; when she succeeded, the door shut noiselessly. Mr. V., when awakened, saw that the door was shut, as his wife's first words were to ask him if it was open, and after assuring her that it was all fancy, without more ado fell asleep again.

2. Sarah S.,on going upstairs to light our bedroom fire at 9 p.m. saw a man in white coming out of the dressing-room door. She stood by to let him pass, thinking it was her master in his surplice (which he sometimes wore in the oratory, and which hung in the dressing-room). His clothes seemed to brush her; the figure disappeared into the cupboard at the end of the landing. (Mr. V. was out at the time, or, at any rate, nowhere near.) Sarah S. told this experience to Mrs. V. She has repeated her account to Mrs. V. since she left (about one year after the event), and is unshaken in her conviction. [She is believed to be thoroughly trustworthy.]

3. Sarah S. was carrying water across the hall about 9.30 one morning when, on hearing a noise, she turned towards the front door, which was a few yards off. She saw come out of the dining-room door, and pass into the drawing room, shutting the door behind it, the figure of a tall woman in black wearing a dress made like a "sacque," with her hair twisted upon the top of her head, her face turned towards the door, and wearing shoes on her feet. Sarah S. was much astonished, and went into the kitchen and reported what she had seen to Lizzie P., the cook. Mr. V., who was upstairs, heard her recounting some tale or other, and the cook laughing

incredulously, but he did not know what about. He then went out, and the servants came and reported the matter to Mrs. V. They all three went then into the drawing-room and found the door, which had been left open, shut, but nothing else peculiar. Mr. V. soon after came in and examined both rooms without making any discoveries. If anybody came in, the entry must have been (1) noiseless; (2) through the dining-room window; (3) in broad daylight; and the exit must have been out of the drawing-room window. Mr. V. felt quite satisfied that it was morally impossible for anyone to have got in and out under these conditions.

4. Lizzie P. disbelieved, or affected to disbelieve, Sarah S.'s story. Sarah soon after left, and Annie C. took her place. On the night of April 9th, 1884, about 9 p.m., Lizzie was in the first or upper back kitchen—there being a light in the room—on her way to the lower back kitchen to fetch a dish from the rack, when suddenly a figure rose up in the doorway before her. The figure was of a woman in a long black dress, a face very white, eyes shining red, like a ferret's. It seemed to stand and look at her and she at it. She was too terrified to move, but at last managed to cry out "Oh! Clara!" to the girl ironing in the kitchen. At her cry the object vanished with a sort of rushing sound, but no steps. Mrs. V. heard the cry in the drawing-room, the door being shut, and found Lizzie in a state of great agitation and unable for some minutes to speak. After some little time she burst out crying, and her first words were that she could not stay in the house. She then described what she had seen. Just after Annie C. came down stairs ignorant of what had happened, and passed through the back kitchen, unbolting the last door and the door into the barn into which she went to get some coal. She returned without having noticed anything. Lizzie was so terrified by what she saw that she seemed in danger of a fit. The four women were so panic-stricken that they spent the night in the same room. Mr. V. happened to have gone away the same day, and heard nothing of the event till his return on the following Saturday. The only exit from the back kitchen, excepting the one leading into the hall, visible from the kitchen, was by the bolted outer door.

5. Clara M. was ironing in the kitchen by herself about 4 in the afternoon. She heard someone coming down stairs, apparently wearing high-heeled shoes and a silk dress which rustled. She saw through the open kitchen door a shadow of a person on the cupboard door, which faced the bottom of the stairs. She went on with her ironing and listened, thinking Mrs. V. was coming down. She then saw the door into the back kitchen open and close again. She could only see the hinge portion of the door. Hearing the footsteps stop she went out to see who it was, but no one was visible. She then called out, but no one answered. She then went into the back kitchen and looked, finding nothing. She then went upstairs and asked who had been down. Finding that no one had she was much astonished and reported to Mrs. V. what she had heard and seen. This took place May 3rd, 1884.

6. Mrs. V. was in the kitchen one morning ordering dinner; there came a noise like the crashing of tin trays from the back kitchen. She said "What

is that, Lizzie?" thinking a dog had come in to help himself to the pig-bucket. "Oh, we often hear that!" she said. The noise was repeated; the third time both went out to see, and on going out through the kitchen door saw in the back kitchen something black, as if the end of a dress, in the air, vanish away towards the door. They went to the doors, found nothing moved, the doors fast.

7. About August, 1884, Annie C. and Lizzie P. were in the spare room on the top floor, above Mr. and Mrs. V.'s bedroom, about 9.30 p.m. Annie had just been into the cupboard to take out the bath. On going to the bed to turn it down she faced this cupboard and saw a man in white standing against the black clothes which were hanging there, facing her and "looking very cross." Lizzie P. saw her face turning white and her terror-struck appearance, but nothing else. After a few seconds Annie called out "Oh, Lizzie, there's a man in the cupboard." While she spoke he vanished away.

II. Noises strange and manifold have taken place at all times of the day and night, and at all parts of the house. Some have been incidentally mentioned. Noises have been heard, e.g., as of the dashing of fire-irons close by when they were seen to be quite still, as of a person walking about, as of one packing up over head, as of coals falling into the grate, as of some one thumping under the floor while the family were at prayers, as of a box being put down in the room with a crash, as of boards falling down on one another, as of a person groaning or wailing in agony. A few cases may be singled out for special remark.

a. One night Mr. and Mrs. V. were either awake or awakened by a loud crash in the centre of their bedroom, apparently, as if some one had dropped some large coals on the floor. Mr. V., surprised, got out of bed and went to the grate thinking some coals had dropped out of the fire-place. Nothing of the sort had occurred, there was nothing in the grate but small ashes, nor was there any discoverable ground for the noise.

b. Mr. and Mrs. V. have heard noises as of a person packing a box in the bedroom above, where a sister slept at the time—having, as she alleged, been perfectly still all night; of a person moving up and down quietly under the same circumstances.

c. A moan was heard as if on the stairs by Mrs. V. and Lizzie P., half moan, half scream of horror, April 9th aforesaid about 11 p.m. They were on the first floor. Mrs. V. thought it was Annie, called her, and found she had made "no noise."

d. Mr. V. heard a similar agonised, indescribable, horror-stricken moan one evening when he was going down stairs. The noise was impossible to localise and unearthly in its peculiar tone and character.

e. Sunday morning, September 14th, 1884, Mrs. V. was at home sitting in the dining-room alone in the house. Mrs. P., who had succeeded Lizzie P., *pro tem.*,[5] was in the garden with the baby. Mrs. V. heard a noise who scrubbing the floor or grinding a coffee mill on the top floor. Mrs. V.

---

[5] An abbreviation of the Latin phrase *pro tempore,* meaning "temporarily."

listened for some time; the noise grew louder and louder without being continuous. Mrs. V. called in Mrs. P. to listen, and she heard the same, and even the baby heard it, and made his little remarks. No investigation was made as they felt too much alarmed to go up. The door of the spare room opened and shut and banged of its own accord, although all the windows were shut. Mrs. V. watched the door and it stopped moving. She stood nearly a quarter of an hour watching. As soon as she left off it opened again, and banged loudly, shaking the whole house. Doors on the top floor have at various times done the same thing for no apparent reason. Mr. V. has watched them also, but never caught them *in flagrante delicto.*[6]

f. In September, 1884, Mr. V. awoke one night. He was fully awake, and became vividly conscious of some evil presence close to him, apparently striking with a sharp instrument against the bedstead close to his head, making a ringing noise. He silently commanded the being three several times in the name of God to desist, and the noises ceased. Mr. V. said nothing to Mrs. V. about it, but he became aware that she was in a state of great agitation, and asked her what was the matter. He found that she had been awake, and declared that some being had passed round the bed, and touched her foot on the way. She lay still and without speaking, and felt some one holding his hands close to her face. Mrs. V. also heard, she afterwards said, this sharp knocking against the bed. Mr. V. lighted a candle, but, as they expected, nothing was visible. But the strange sensation did not pass away for some little time. Mrs. V. was so disquieted that Mr. V. promised there and then to leave the house. Next day he gave notice; his wife's health and nerves had begun to be seriously affected by what she had seen and heard, and before the month was over they had left the house never to return.

Remarks.—The above is a bare and uncoloured narrative of the phenomena which took place in the house during its occupation by Mr. and Mrs. V. Mr. V., the writer of the account, wishes to record his strong personal conviction that the phenomena admit of no natural explanation. Mr. V. is of opinion that the house is either under a curse or in some way under the influence of diabolical agency, or of departed spirits who have not found rest. Neither Mr. nor Mrs. V. nor any of their fellow sufferers, as far as they know, have enjoyed any experiences of the kind at any other time.

Upon this evidence it was decided in the spring of 1885 to take the house for six months. A member of the Society undertook to defray the necessary expenditure. The Society's time commenced on Lady Day,[7] and the house was occupied continually from the 30th March till the 4th May by Major H.M. Hughes and three or

---

[6] Another Latin phrase, meaning Mr. V. never observed the doors in the act of banging.

[7] Lady Day falls on March 25th and commemorates the archangel Gabriel's telling the Virgin Mary that she would give birth to Jesus Christ.

four friends. From the 7th to the 18th May it was occupied by the Misses Porter, and from that date until the end of September, 1885, when the six months' tenure expired, it was occupied at intervals by various members of the Society, and others, for periods varying from one to five days. The sum of these shorter periods was about 25 days, and about 50 persons in all appear to have slept in the house during the six months. Only two occurrences during that period appear to me to call for any remark. In the middle of September a party of four ladies and two gentlemen were staying in the house, and after they had retired to their rooms hurried steps were heard to descend the stairs. On the gentlemen proceeding to investigate the matter it was discovered that the door leading into the garden—which had been closed and bolted a short time before— was standing open. They inferred that some one from the village had concealed himself in the house with the object of playing the ghost.

The other incident referred to consisted in the occurrence of violent manifestations during dark séances held in the house by a party of gentlemen accompanied by the well-known medium, Mr. Eglinton, but the details of these appear to belong rather to the question of Mr. Eglinton's mediumship than to that of the haunting of B— Lodge.[8]

The following letters from Mrs. Sidgwick and Professor Macalister may be held to suggest a possible means of accounting for the noises heard by Dr. P. and other witnesses; but the apparitions seen by Mr. W., Mrs. V. and others, if they were not simply hallucinations generated by expectancy or anxiety, seem to require some less obvious explanation, and should, I think, be referred to the class of phenomena treated of by Mrs. H. Sidgwick in her paper on the "Evidence for Phantasms of the Dead." (Proceedings, Part VIII.)

Hill Side, Chesterton Road, Cambridge.
July 27th, 1885.
Our visit to W— was quite uneventful. We encouraged the ghost as much as we could by sitting in the dark, &c., but to no purpose. The house seems to me one well adapted for strange sounds, on account of its extreme nearness to the road. I think some one made this remark before, but I was

---

[8] A chronicle of the Eglinton séances titled "Proceedings at a Haunted House in W—" was published in *Light: A Journal of Psychical, Occult, and Mystical Research* 5.253 (Nov. 7, 1885) pp. 541-42. After reading it, one is likely to agree with Podmore's curt dismissal of the séances as revealing more about the medium than about the haunting.

certainly surprised to find how extremely audible outside sounds were, and the idea that outside sounds have been mistaken for inside ones is rather supported by Dr. P.'s statement that the manifestations occurred more about full moon, because then people are out at night so much more.

Eleanor Mildred Sidgwick.

[It was bright moonlight when Mrs. Sidgwick was there.]

Anatomical Schools, Cambridge.
October 27th, 1885.

My notes of the house are rather in the form of a criticism of the evidence submitted to me than of positive results of investigation.

During the period that we stayed there (five days from June 26th) we neither saw nor heard anything noteworthy.

Since that time I had the opportunity of reading Dr. P.'s narrative, which, however, contained nothing but what was known in the neighbourhood, and the substance of which I had learned from Mrs. H. and Mr. V.

The value of the narrative is much lessened by the small amount of personal observation in it, and Mrs. H. stated to me that Dr. P. was not at home when the kitchen chimney took fire nor for some days afterwards. "Had he been at home I should not have let him sleep in his own room, as the smell there was so bad." (I noted her words.) She also said that some dirt came down the *kitchen* chimney, but no bones that she could see. She could not specify the year, but thought it was about 1875.

The stain on the boards in the top room I cut a small bit of, and brought it home; it is paint. Probably some paint pot had been standing on the board and stained it.

Two men in the neighbourhood (Mortimer and the landlord of the Red Lion) told me that the old inn was not on that site but a little further down. The local traditions of "some murders" resolve themselves into a story of one pedlar who was seen to enter the inn and was not seen to leave it. There was a later homicide in a house south of the King and Queen Inn, but that was the result of a quarrel, and the house is at some little distance.

Mrs. H. stated to me that she had only seen the apparition once. Her account of the old lady's vision differed from Dr. P.'s as to the character of the apparition.

We made a number of experiments on noises in the house, which creaks like a basket on very slight shaking. Mr. Hill, of Downing College, who stayed there with us the last night we were there, said that after we had gone upstairs, walking rather heavily on purpose, the stairs creaked at intervals with a series of "recoil creaks" for a while. We also noticed this ourselves.

When I stamped or jumped in one of the top rooms I set the whole house quivering, and the sounds as heard below were quite disproportionately loud; specially was this the case at midnight.

One of the nights was windy, and when one of the top windows was left open we had noises, with window flapping, creaking, and doors slamming, quite enough to frighten a nervous man. When the door of the dark room at the top was left partly open and the window open, it produced a most eerie noise when the wind blew.

It was altogether one of the noisiest houses I ever slept in, but every sound we heard had an evident physical cause.

I do not know whether Mrs. H.'s evidence has been taken down; it should be, for the story of the lady visitor, as well as that of the first servant, rest on her evidence alone, also the story of the kitchen chimney.

Her narratives were graphically told, especially the incident that standing by the foot of her husband's bed one evening she heard the words, "Three stages more and then death," the last word prolonged and hissed as through the speaker's teeth. Mrs. H. came up and showed me the places where these incidents took place. Her account of the appearance was a tall bald-headed man with side locks of long grey hair, clothed in a long, grey dressing gown, and with bright blue eyes. He was solid, although there was a window behind him, and it was yet light (eight o'clock p.m. in July), yet she could not see through him.

Alex. Macalister.

Our readers may be interested in comparing with the foregoing accounts the following specimen of second-hand evidence, which is taken from a local newspaper:—

Letter From The Rev. J.Y.

Previous to the year 1874 rumours of appearances were common, always at one particular house (which your neighbour and my friend, Mr. —, has, with me, examined), and nowhere else in this town. In the year 1874 Mr. and Mrs. H. went to live in the house. Mr. H. ("a tall, thin gentleman") was ill a long time, and died in the house. After his death, Mrs. H., the widow, saw, as she says, "the ghost," and her description of it is nearly enough a true description of her own departed husband. She says the ghost breathed faintly her name. Mrs. H. soon after left the house, and is living now at W., five minutes' walk from my house. Whatever construction may be put on Mrs. H.'s story, there can be no doubt whatever that Mrs. H. is a clearheaded, well-informed Christian lady, in whose veracity perfect reliance may be placed. The house was next occupied by a curate, who frequently heard something but saw nothing. The house was then tenanted by a Mr. T. and family for about 18 months, I believe, and they neither saw nor heard anything. Next a Mrs. G. occupied it. She "frequently heard something but saw no appearance." Then the present curate, the Rev. Mr. V., and family occupied it. Mrs. V. saw the ghost (as an old gentleman in long white robes) so many times that she durst not stop in the house any longer. She was able one night to wake up Mr. V. (who had not up to this time seen the "ghost") before its disappearance, and he saw it. They got out of the house as quickly as possible after this unpleasant experience in 1884. For several months last summer the house was occupied by deputations from the Psychological Society in London successively, each company numbering from four to five persons. It is believed they neither saw nor heard anything particular; but I am not quite sure that they have made public all their experiences. . . . The house is a substantially-built brick building, and looks like a comparatively modern structure, very remote from what we would expect as being a haunted house. There is a large, lofty wooden structure adjoining the house on one side, which has not been made much use of for years, and is in a somewhat dilapidated state This old wooden building, in such close contiguity to the house, is, to my mind, quite sufficient to account for anything that may have been heard.

Then, as to what Mrs. H. saw (or fancied she saw) after the long, weary watching at the sick—ultimately death—bed of her husband, after his decease, was it wonderful that she (in her weakness, sorrow, and loneliness) should in the dark and silent hours of the night meditate on the trial and scenes through which she had so recently passed, and so vividly realise the very presence and form of her departed husband? I have no belief whatever in ghost stories of this sort.

In conclusion I may add that we have been unable to ascertain that there is the slightest ground for attacking the reputation of the old gentleman who "once lived" in the house before the Peeds, and think it not improbable that the stories against him have their foundation in the supposed blood-stain, ascertained by Dr. Macalister to be paint.

Case 8: Some Theories
Regarding the Ghost Question

Investigation: conducted by Ada Goodrich-Freer at Hampton Court
Palace at Richmond upon Thames, England, in 1894. Two
earlier ghost hunts are also mentioned, but dates and locations
are left unstated.

Manifestations: apparitions of Queen Jane Seymour and her nurse;
the screaming ghost of Catharine of Aragon; the grip of a
spectral hand; a luminescent apparition of a woman who
kneels.

Pertinent Facts: Often signing her writing simply X, Ada Goodrich-
Freer (1857-1931) was a member of the Society for Psychical
Research—until 1897. That's the year she served as coordinator
for a three-month probe of Ballechin House, and one of several
visiting investigators made a very public pronouncement that
"the most haunted house in Scotland" was haunted only by
noisy pipes. The SPR distanced itself from the ghost hunt and
severed its relationship with Goodrich-Freer. Not long
afterward, her reputation was tarnished and eventually she
abandoned ghost hunting. First, though, she went ahead and
co-authored a book about the Ballechin investigation, resulting
in one of the few book-length chronicles of a single ghost hunt.[1]
Her investigation of Hampton Court Palace, presented here,
occurred earlier, but even so the surprising results she claims
to have gotten during her single night at the palace might make
one wonder how truthful she is being. Still, her article provides
a useful review of some prominent theories regarding haunted
houses, and at least in that regard, Goodrich-Freer reveals a lot
about how ghosts were understood and debated in the 1890s.

---

[1] A. Goodrich-Freer (Miss X) and John [Crichton-Stuart], Marquess of Bute,
K.T., *The Alleged Haunting of B— House* (George Redway, 1899).

Haunted Houses

Ada Goodrich-Freer[2]

Of all departments of psychical research there is, perhaps, none which commands more general interest and attention than that of haunted houses. It often happens, when dealing with the "occult," that we have to begin by explaining what we mean and why our subject is interesting. But here is a subject which most people think interesting, even when they do not know what it means.

As to knowing "what it means" in the sense of accounting for the phenomenon, few of us would venture to lay claim to that; but it is well, at starting, to make it clear what in the present case our title of "Haunted Houses" is intended to mean.

WHAT WE MEAN BY A HAUNTED HOUSE.

In that monument of industry, Mrs. Sidgwick's "Report on the Census of Hallucinations," the term "haunted" is used in its widest sense, the local visitations, not only of the dead, but of the living.[3] For lack of space, and for that reason only, I resist temptation, and narrow our term "haunting" so as to exclude phantoms of the living, and confine myself to phantoms of the dead, or what (though the term is one which begs the question) are commonly known as "ghosts." For the same reason I exclude the hauntings of places other than habitations, such as crossroads, churches, churchyards, battlefields, the sites of gallows, the scenes of outdoor murders, as well as hauntings by creatures other than human, or post-human; fairies, elves, phantom-animals, boggarts, banshees, kirk-grims, gabble-retchets, and the like.

Further, I would not classify a house as "haunted" merely because a vision had been seen in it, on some few occasions, of some

---

[2] This appeared in *Borderland* 1.6 (Oct., 1894) pp. 523-28. A much expanded version appeared in *Essays in Psychical Research* (George Redway, 1899) pp. 27-74. In the latter version, Goodrich-Freer goes further into theories explaining haunted houses without expanding upon her own ghost-hunter experiences.

[3] "Phantoms of the living" can include apparitions of people at the brink of death or in some other crisis. In a massive survey conducted by the Society for Psychical Research, out of 17,000 informants, 1,684 people claimed to have experienced paranormal apparitions. The lengthy report was published in *Proceedings of the Society for Psychical Research* 10 (1894) pp. 25-422.

person or persons, dead or living; otherwise, for such of us as are habitual "seers," it would be true in another sense than that of Longfellow's, that "all houses wherein men have lived and died are haunted houses."

In many cases, the person seeing, rather than the place, seems to be the motive-cause of what we call "hauntings." What we have to deal with here are those houses which are alleged to be habitually visited by phantoms supposed to be those of former inhabitants.

THE ORIGINS OF HAUNTED HOUSES.

Probably there are few persons who could not point out a house with which some such story is connected. A house gets the reputation of being haunted almost as easily as a dog gets "a bad name"; and in either case, hanging, or its equivalent—desertion is often its ultimate fate. If a house remains for a few years unoccupied, so that its chimneys fall, its roof becomes lichened, and its garden-paths moss-grown, it is sure to get the reputation of being haunted, and the condition, which at first was the cause, soon gets talked of as the effect of its evil reputation. If a travelling tinker takes advantage of its deserted condition, and lights his fire under the shelter of its outhouses, there is the added phenomenon of ghostly lights, and perhaps noises. Some sight or sound, easily explained if occurring elsewhere, is interpreted in favour of the theory; the "oldest inhabitant" recalls some tradition of a forgotten crime, suspected or perpetrated, and the "evidence" is complete.

THE MYTHICAL GHOST.

Where, however, the house has been in continuous occupation, when the common place details of domestic life have been uninterruptedly carried on, the problem of the origin of the story becomes a little more difficult. The thing must have had a beginning; there must have been a day when the occupants first recognized that their home had become "no canny," and, however much the story may subsequently grow and strengthen with perpetual restatement, whatever may be the degree of exaggeration and misunderstanding and unconscious self-deception, it is interesting and instructive to examine, when we can, the beginnings of such traditions, the seed out of which the full-grown blossom is ultimately produced.

Unfortunately, the blossom is the more interesting and romantic of the two; in fact, the seed is seldom very exciting. The sheeted ghost, smelling of sulphur or mildew, who clanks chains and reveals secrets in a hollow voice, is now relegated to "Christmas Numbers"; he exists in his full beauty in the old-fashioned annuals—the Keepsakes, and Forget-me-nots, and Garlands, where we have him in company with the One-Handed Lady and the Smuggler's Revenge.

THE GHOST UP-TO-DATE.

The ghost of the Society for Psychical Research and other collectors of first-hand evidence, is on the whole comparatively thin and pale; but if, on the one hand, recent systematic inquiry lends us some help in *explaining* the ghost, on the other it makes it the more possible to preserve a reputation for sanity, without being obliged to *explain him away.* We have now several possible hypotheses other than lying, indigestion, insanity, a morbid state of health, rats, bats, owls, hot-water pipes, bell-wires, a snail on the window, the wind in the chimney, vibration, ordinary sounds misinterpreted, or the result of fear and expectation. At the same time it is impossible to emphasise too strongly the absolute duty of every ghost-seer to examine every one of these hypotheses, and fifty others which his friends will undoubtedly suggest, with the utmost care and conscientious scrupulosity, before allowing it to pass into history that he has "seen a ghost."

HAUNTED HAMPTON.

Before generalizing further, let us carefully consider a single example. I take for illustration an experience of my own, not because it is in itself of especial interest, but because it has come under my personal notice, and because it is connected with a place no less historical than Hampton Court. I do not offer it as evidential; it is not susceptible of proof, there is no possibility of corroboration, it rests entirely on the word of the narrator; but as the same may be said of a very large proportion of "ghost stories," and as it is at least first-hand, it will serve as well as another as a peg upon which to hang my observations.

I recently found myself the guest of a lady occupying a pleasant suite of rooms in Hampton Court Palace. For obvious reasons I cannot specify the name of my hostess, the exact date of my visit, nor the precise whereabouts of her apartment.

THE LATEST APPARITIONS.

Of course, I was familiar with the Hampton Court ghost-legend, as told by Mr. Law in his valuable history of the Palace, as well as with more recent stories related in *Cassell's Magazine* and quoted in *Borderland* for July.[4] I examined the scene of the occurrences, and was allowed to ask questions at will. The "ghost," I was told, visited habitually in a dozen different rooms—not, however, in the bright, dainty drawing-room in which we were chatting, and where it was difficult to believe that we were discussing recent history.

As a matter of fact, it was very recent indeed. But a few nights earlier, in a certain small but cheerful bedroom, a little girl had been awakened out of her sleep by a visitant so dramatic that I wondered whether the child had possibly gone to sleep again after her original fright, and dreamt the later and more sensational part of the story.

SLEEPING IN A HAUNTED ROOM.

My own room was quaintly pretty, but somewhat peculiar in arrangement, and lighted only from the roof. I have seen "ghosts" before, have slept for months together in haunted rooms; and though I find such visitants somewhat exciting, I cannot say that my prospects for the night filled me with any degree of apprehension.

At dinner and during the evening ghostly topics were avoided; there were other guests, and music and chat occupied us till eleven o'clock, when my hostess accompanied me to my room. I asked

---

4 In the first of his three-volume *The History of Hampton Court* (George Bell and Sons, 1885), Ernest Law discusses the ghosts of Queen Jane Seymour and her son's nurse, Sybil Penn, pp. 195-200; along with the screaming specter of Queen Catherine Howard, pp. 223-25. A writer known only as "The Owl" begins with that screaming ghost and then adds her own and others' experiences with locked doors opening by themselves, pillows being pulled away by bedside figures, and many other ghostly sights, sounds, and touches in "Royal Ghosts in Hampton Court Place," *Cassell's Family Magazine* 20.8 (July, 1894) pp. 631-33. The article that quotes it is in *Borderland* 1.5 (July 1894) pp. 449.

various questions as to my neighbours above and below, and the exact position of other members of the household, with a view to knowing how to interpret any sounds which might occur. About a third of the ceiling of my room was skylight, a servant's bedroom being situated over the remainder. Two sides of the room were bounded by a corridor, into which it opened, a third by the wall of the state apartments, while the fourth opened by folding doors upon a room for the time unoccupied (except by a cat, asleep upon a chair), out of which there opens a door leading by a secret passage to the bank of the river.

I ascertained that the folding doors were locked; moreover, a heavy table stood against them on the outer side, and a wardrobe on the inner. The bedstead was a small one without curtains; indeed, the room contained no hangings whatever. The door into the room opened so near to the head of my bed that there was space only for a very small table, upon which I took care to place two long candles and a plentiful supply of matches, being somewhat addicted to late and early reading.

BIMETALLISM AS AN ANTI-SOPORIFIC!

I was very tired, but a sense of duty I owed *Borderland* demanded that I should not sleep through the witching hours, so I sat up in bed and gave my best attention to Lord Farrer's problem, "Shall we Degrade our Standard of Value?" in the current number of the *National Review*, and on the principle of always trying to see both sides of a question, thought of several reasons why we should not, with the author, come to a negative conclusion. The matter did not, however, excite me to the pitch of wakefulness, and when I finished the article, as the clock struck half-past one, I considered myself absolved from further responsibility, put out my lights, and was asleep before the next quarter sounded.

AWAKED!

Nearly three hours later I was suddenly awakened from dreamless slumber by the sound of the opening of a door against which some piece of furniture was standing, in, as it seemed, the empty room to my right. I remembered the cat, and tried to conceive by what kind of "rampaging" she could contrive to be so noisy. A minute later there followed a thud apparently on this side of the folding doors, and too heavy for even the prize animals of my home-circle, not to speak of a mongrel stray, newly adopted and not yet doing credit to her keep. "A dress fallen in the wardrobe" was my next thought, and I stretched out my hand for the matchbox, as a preliminary to inquiry.

THE TOUCH OF A SPECTRAL HAND.

I did not reach the matches. It seemed to me that a detaining hand was laid on mine. I withdrew it quickly and gazed around into the darkness. Some minutes passed in blackness and silence. I had the sensation of a presence in the room, and finally, mindful of the tradition that a ghost should be spoken to, I said gently, "Is anyone there? Can I do anything for you?" I remembered that the last person who entertained the ghost had said, "Go away, I don't want you!" and I hoped that my visitor would admire my better manners and be responsive. However, there was no answer—no sound of any kind; and returning to my theory of the cat and the fallen dress, though nevertheless influenced by the recollection of those detaining fingers as not to attempt to strike a light, I rose and walked round my bed, keeping the right hand on the edge of the bedstead, while, with my left arm extended, I swept the surrounding space. As the room is small, I thus fairly well satisfied myself that it contained nothing unusual.

THE APPARITION AND ITS LIGHT.

I was, though somewhat perplexed, about to grant myself license to go to sleep again, when in the darkness before me there began to glow a soft light. I watched it increase in brightness and in extent. It seemed to radiate from a central point, which gradually took form and became a tall, slight woman, moving slowly across the room from the folding doors on my right. As she passed the foot of my bed I felt a slight vibration in the spring mattress. At the further corner she stopped, so that I had time to observe her profile and general appearance. Her face was insipidly pretty, that of a woman of from thirty to thirty-five years of age, her figure slight, her dress of a dark, soft material, having a full skirt and broad sash or soft waistband tied high up, almost under the arms, a crossed or draped kerchief over the shoulders, sleeves which I noticed fitted very tight below the elbow, and hair which was dressed so as not to lie flat to the head, either in curls or "bows," I could not tell which. As she appeared to stand between me and the light, I cannot speak with any certainty as to colour, but the dress, though dark, was, I think, not black. In spite of all this definiteness, I was, of course, conscious that the figure was unsubstantial, and I felt guilty of absurdity in asking once more, "Will you let me help you? Can I be of use to you?"

THE GHOST KNEELS AND DISAPPEARS.

My voice sounded preternaturally loud, but I felt no surprise at noticing that it produced no effect upon my visitor. She stood still for perhaps two minutes, though it is very difficult to estimate time on such occasions. She then raised her hands, which were long and white, and held them before her as she sank upon her knees and slowly buried her face in the palms, in the attitude of prayer—when quite suddenly the light went out, and I was alone in the darkness.

I felt that the scene was ended, the curtain down, and had no hesitation in lighting the candle at my side.

I tried to examine the impression the vision conveyed. I felt that it was definitely that of reproach, yet of gentle resignation. There was no force, no passion; I had seen a meek, sad woman, who had succumbed. I began to turn over in my mind the illustrious names of former occupants of the chamber. I fixed on one—a bad man of the worst kind, a bad fool of that time of wickedness and folly, the Regency[5]—I thought of the secret passage in the next room, and began to weave an elaborate romance.

"This will not do, here and now," I reflected, as the clock struck four, and as an act of mental discipline I returned to my *National Review*. I read a page or two of "The Poor Man's Cow," and though I delight in cows—more, perhaps, than in poor men—I could, under the circumstances, feel no enthusiasm about credit co-operation. I turned to Mr. Myers' article on "The Drift of Psychical Research," which I had already read; it seemed at least more to the point.

I read:

---

[5] The Regency era was from 1795 to 1837, immediately preceding the Victorian era.

"...Where telepathy operates, many intelligences may affect our own. Some of these are the minds of living persons; but some appear to be discarnate, to be spirits like ourselves, but released from the body, although still retaining much of the personality of earth. These spirits appear still to have some knowledge of our world, and to be in certain ways able to affect it."[6]

Here was, so to speak, the text of my illustration. I had quite enough to think about—more than I needed for that occasion. I never heard the clock strike five.

VARIOUS VISIONS.

Let us try to examine this, a type of many ghost stories.

In earlier papers I have classified my visions of persons, whether seen in the crystal or otherwise, as—

1. Visions of the living, clairvoyant or telepathic, usually accompanied by their own background, or adapting themselves to mine.

2. Visions of the departed having no obvious relations to time and space.

3. Visions which are more or less of the nature of pictures, such as those which I voluntarily produce in the crystal from memory or imagination, or which appear in the background of real persons as illustrative of their thoughts or history. This is very often the case when an impression reaches me in visual form from the mind of a friend who, it may be, imperfectly remembers or is imperfectly informed as to the form and colour of the picture his mind conveys.

GHOSTS AS VISUALIZED THOUGHTS OF THE DEAD.

Again I emphasise the fact that I am speculating, not dogmatising—that I am speaking from internal evidence with no

---

[6] From Frederick W.H. Myers, "The Drift of Psychical Research," *National Review* 24.140 (Oct., 1894) p. 193. As suggested above, Myers' piece is in the same issue as Thomas Farrer's "Shall We Degrade Our Standard of Value," pp. 165-89, and Henry W. Wolff's "The Poor-Man's Cow," pp. 253-62. However, given that this issue is dated the *same* month and year as the issue of *Borderland* that includes this very article, one *might* raise an eyebrow in regard to Goodrich-Freer staying at Hampton Court, writing of her experience there, and that article being published all in such rapid succession.

possibility of corroboration, and that I am perfectly aware that each reader must take this for what it seems to him worth. Such being the case, I venture to classify the vision under class III. Again, to borrow from Mr. Myers, I believe that what I saw may have been a telepathic impression *of the dreams (or I should prefer to say "thoughts") of the dead.* If what I saw were indeed veridical or truth-telling—if my readers will agree to admit that what I saw was no mere illusion, or morbid hallucination, or imagination (taking the word in its commonly accepted sense)—then believe that my visitor was not a departed spirit, such as it has before now been perhaps my privilege to meet, but rather an image of such, just as the figure which, it may be, sits at my dining-table is not really the friend whose visit a few hours later it announces, but only a representation of him, having no objective existence apart from the truth of the information it conveys, a thought which is personal to the brain which thinks it.

THE ONE INCREDIBLE HYPOTHESIS.

I have already said that, preconceived notions apart, or as far apart as in subjective analysis it is possible to put them, I had no impression of reality. I recognized that what I saw and felt was an externalization of impressions unconsciously received, possibly from some discarnate mind. But further, and this I cannot hope to establish as anything but mere personal sentiment, my whole being, and experience, and hope and aspiration, protests against the notion that for years, sometimes, it has been alleged, for centuries, those who have suffered here should be compelled to revisit the scene, often to re-enact the tragedy of their lives. That, for example, the criminal should be doomed to have before his eyes the earthly surroundings of his crime, that he should perpetually rehearse the foul deed, is in some degree thinkable; but that the victim, often it would seem, the innocent victim, should, for no obvious purpose, be debarred from "the rest that remaineth," should not await, at least in peace, "the consummation of all things," is an idea which, by subtracting from the hope of the future, adds yet another sorrow to the present and the past.

OTHER HAMPTON GHOSTS.

I have not dwelt upon the possibilities of thought-transference from the living. What I saw had been seen by no one else, and the "hauntings" of these particular rooms are quite apart from the historical ghosts of the Palace, Jane Seymour and Mrs. Penn, the mother and nurse of Edward VI., who haunt certain rooms in the clock court, as well as from that of Queen Catherine Howard, whose ghost shrieks up and down a certain gallery, as is written in Mr. Law's valuable volumes.

The author of a very interesting article in *Cassell's Magazine,* quoted at length in *Borderland V.,* deals with the rooms in question. She assumes, from external probability, mainly the near neighborhood of a certain doorway leading to Queen Catherine of Aragon's apartments, that the visitation of her rooms is associated with that unhappy lady. I am not, however, persuaded that there is anything in this beyond conjecture, as the phenomena—mainly consisting of lights and noises—do not point to any particular origin. The little girl "who saw the ghost " a week or two ago, said "it was dressed like the pictures of Catherine of Aragon"; but the statement might conceivably be influenced by expectation.

As the figure which visited me was not dressed in the Tudor fashion at all, and as I heard none of the orthodox sounds of jingling glass and knocks at the door, I do not think I need personally discount much, either for thought-transference from those about me, or for expectation.

THE INFLUENCE OF EXPECTATION.

Speaking for myself, on that very complex question of expectation, the expectation of phenomena in my own case tends rather to discourage than to force experiences. Of the danger of expectation I am entirely aware, and, in fact, am probably only too much alive to its possibilities, so much so that I am conscious that the critic in me often absorbs the energy and stimulus which ought in justice to belong to the seer. We talk and write so much about ghosts and hauntings that at first sight it seems curious we should know so very little about them. But there are certain obvious impediments to the study of these—one might perhaps say, of all psychical phenomena.

The material, however plentiful, is not to be commanded; ghostly visitations are seldom continuous, though now and then one hears of a ghost who keeps an anniversary. Personally, I regret that I know of none such; but in most cases you may watch for a score or a hundred nights without seeing anything. Not that this proves there is no ghost; indeed, in all probability, he will come back on the twenty-first or the hundred-and-first night, and remain till the night preceding your return!

THE PODMORE THEORY.

It has been my privilege lately to accept the hospitality of two owners of haunted houses. The first was one already described in these pages as the resort of "Old Fadanny." This is a case which I should describe as, if not purely Podmorean, at all events mixed. The theory of haunting, invented by Mr. Podmore, is one, I think, of frequent, but by no means of universal application. He thinks that the story of a haunting is begun by some subjective hallucination on the part of a living person, which lingers on in the atmosphere, and is telepathically transmitted to the next occupant of the room or house in question.[7] Thus, for example, future occupants of my room at Hampton Court Palace should, on his theory, be likely to have visions of a kneeling woman in a dark dress, possibly sensations of detaining hands, and sounds of opening doors, and a falling body; and this, whether I really saw, or only imagined that I saw, or only mistook what I saw.

"OLD FADANNY."

In the case of "Old Fadanny," the infection, so to say, was, I believe, more direct. There is first-hand evidence for very

---

[7] Goodrich-Freer discusses the "Old Fadanny" haunting in "Haunted Houses of To-day: 'Old Fadanny,' of Norfolk, and Other Ghosts," *Borderland* 1.5 (July, 1894) pp. 447-50. Frank Podmore introduced his idea that, rather than being spirits of the dead, what we call "ghosts" are telepathic communications between the living in "Phantasms of the Dead from Another Point of View," *Proceedings of the Society for Psychical Research* 6 (Nov. 29, 1889) pp. 229-313. He went on to write a book on his theory: *Telepathic Hallucinations: The New View of Ghosts* (Frederick A. Stokes, 1909). A similar allegation that ghosts aren't evidence of an afterlife sparked William Howitt to write a letter of protest to Charles Dickens, igniting the events chronicled in Case 5 of this book.

mysterious sounds about the house, and careful inquiry in the neighbourhood has elicited the statement that as much as eighty-five years ago the house was "noisy." Whether there is any means of explaining these sounds away I am not prepared to conjecture; it is the sort of problem which demands minute acquaintance with the geography, architecture, and even the manners and customs of the neighbourhood. There is, however, no question, that when my kind host took possession of the house, rumours of hauntings were in the air, and were probably known to that mysteriously omniscient race—the servants.

The first witness for the ghost was a little boy of six, who testified that he had seen "Old Fadanny." The title was of the child's bestowal, and was evolved in the unaccountable way in which a child's mind works. Without resorting to the extreme hypothesis that a nursemaid had been so wicked as deliberately to threaten the child with the ghost, it is quite conceivable that the expectation of some such visitant was telepathically present in his thoughts, and a child's natural powers of visualization will account for the rest. I have a vivid recollection of certain tigers who dwelt, in my youth, under the lace hangings of my mother's dressing-table, and whose paws projected beyond the pink lining, and made brown patches on the carpet. The child minutely described an old man with a cap, whom several witnesses have seen since, all of them being in a state of great alarm. During my visit to the house I saw nothing—not, as I have already said, that this proves anything at all—but I certainly heard the mysterious noises, not, however, in the degree to which other witnesses have testified. For the reasons already stated, as well as for others which I need not particularise, I am inclined to make a present of the "Old Fadanny" evidence to Mr. Podmore.

A GHOSTLY HOUSE.

A third house which I have lately been permitted to investigate is one upon which have not been able as yet to form any opinion. A more "ghostly-looking" place it would be difficult to find. It might well be the original house of Hood's weird poem:

"For over all there hung a cloud of fear,
A sense of mystery the spirit daunted,
And said, as plain as whisper in the ear,
The place is haunted!"

It is buried in trees, reeking with damp, it has mysterious passages
and doors in unexpected places. It knows nothing of sunshine, and
little of fresh air; the rooms are, for domestic purposes, dismally
large; there are superfluous steps which betray you with a sense of
shock; it has been used for a lunatic asylum, and reminiscences of
Charles Reade's ghostly novel inevitably recur to the mind;[8] in
short, not to have a ghost in such a house as that would be waste of
a magnificent opportunity.

I, alas! watched through the witching hours in vain, but others
have been more fortunate. Eleven servants have refused to stay in
the house, the daughters of my host have exiled themselves from
home, the master of the house has been disturbed at his studies, the
mistress in her sleep; visitors have hinted at "another room"; dogs
and cats refuse to sit alone; finally, after but three years' occupation,
my friends have decided to remove elsewhere. As to what is actually
seen, we hope to present our readers with further particulars in a
future number, when the evidence is more complete.

HOUSES NOT OBVIOUSLY "GHOSTLY."

The Norfolk farmhouse, the abode of Old Fadanny, is, on the
contrary, as bright and pleasant a spot as anyone could desire to
dwell in. So, too, is another "haunted house" with which I have been
all my life familiar. It is one as to which I, and many others, could
tell countless stories; not, however, at this time, for I feel doubtful
as to whether it falls properly under our classification, though one
speaks of it, in general terms, as a "haunted house." There is no
association of the things seen and heard with any former occupants,
though it may be instructive to note that the nearest house
(standing in grounds which "march," as the Scots would say, with
those of the house in question) has an exceedingly definite and local
"ghost." Here, however, there has been great variety as to the ghosts
seen and heard; so much so that it might be more correct to say that

---

[8] Presumably, Charles Reade's *Hard Cash* (Bradbury, Evan, & Co., 1868),
which presents a ghastly and gloomy portrait of insane asylums.

it is a house, the occupants of which become haunted, rather than that it is a haunted house. Visitors see the doubles of distant friends; servants describe the persons of former visitors whom they have never seen. Even as a child of eight and upwards, I have frequently had, in the "haunted" room, visions which we should now classify as telepathic—intimations of the death of persons in whom at that age I felt no interest; vivid, I might almost say *intense,* intuitions as to persons and events, otherwise beyond my power of criticism, and which I now know to have been justified. The house has repeatedly changed hands, my friends, like other previous and subsequent occupants, found it a very undesirable habitation, and were glad to get rid of it on almost any terms. No tenants could be induced to remain, and the property has finally been sacrificed at considerable pecuniary loss.

A HAUNTED ATMOSPHERE.

Such a house might perhaps be described as being in a haunted atmosphere. This question of atmosphere is so exceedingly subjective that the sensation is difficult to analyse. It is one of which all sensitives are conscious—both as to places and persons, and I am inclined to think that in both cases the emotion is telepathic. Most of us know, in some degree, the overwhelming sensation of the presence of Westminster Abbey, or, whether we chance to be very loyal or no, of hearing "God Save the Queen" sung by a thousand voices; of the sight of a life-boat; of a relic of Prince Charlie; of a war-horse that has been in action; of the colours used at Waterloo or Balaclava; or of the mast of the *Victory.* We may dismiss the emotion as merely "cosmic," but, I venture to think, that we are overwhelmed because we are, for the moment, the subject of the emotions of others as well as of our own.

I remember as a child hiding with a companion in a dark closet, in the course of a game of " I spy." "Do stop laughing; they'll hear you," said my playfellow. "How can we? you're laughing yourself," I rejoined. "Let us think of dear grandmamma," he proposed. The old lady had, indeed, died shortly before; but the suggestion did not operate. In despair of putting my gaiety under eclipse, I turned my thoughts to the Pyramids, and was sobered immediately. Croly's "Salathiel," or York Minster, or my music-master, of whom, in spite of his wife and family, I always thought as "a lonely man—a child's tribute to genius—were all subjects for reflection equally over-whelming. Psychologically the child-mind is a clue to much we lose sight of in the increased complexities of later life, and I cannot but think that there are persons and things and places surcharged with accumulated emotion of which the sensitive is, so to speak, the heir. And this, I fancy, may be a clue to certain of the sensations of haunting.

THE SENSATIONS OE A SENSITIVE.

It may account for the frequent monition when walking in the streets of London that one is approaching a public house or other unpleasant resort, though of course one might also account for this by unconscious observation, or the alertness alleged of our sub-conscious selves. For myself the loneliness of the wildest moorland has in it more of welcome companionship than Bond Street or Hyde Park. I can conceive of no desert so dreary as the Strand; the sense of impending catastrophe, of suspended apprehension, is ever present in the streets of London; the sense of surrounding humanity with all its unknown sin and sorrow, and unsatisfied longings, is paralysing to mind and body. All around there is a cry for help one is powerless to answer, a demand for sympathy one knows not how to direct. Whereas, in the haunts of Nature, among her wild creatures, where she stretches out hands to those who love her, one finds voice and utterance, and support and stimulus; here in the heavy atmosphere of humanity one is helpless, and blind, and dumb. It may possibly be, unconsciously, for this reason, that in the Hebrides, when passing at night any spot reputed to be haunted, it is considered wisdom to get as near as possible to the sea, which has in it the element of change rather than the lingering atmosphere which surrounds what is more permanent.

Possibly too—for the islander—the sea is a friend, a familiar companion, a source of livelihood, a great living power in his life.

THE HAUNTINGS OE ROME.

I find something of what I have sought to express in the following passage from a recent work of Miss Frances Cobbe:

I believe the Psychical Society has started a theory that when places where crimes have been committed are ever after "haunted," the apparitions are not exactly good, old-fashioned, *real* ghosts, if I may use such an expression, but some sort of atmospheric photographs (the term is my own), left by the parties concerned, or sent telepathically from their present habitat (whatever that may be) to the scene of their earthly suffering or wickedness. The hypothesis, of course, relieves us from the very unpleasant surmise that the actual soul of the victims of assassination and robbery may have nothing better to do in a future life than to stand guard perpetually at the dark and dank corners, cellars, and bottoms of stone staircases, where they were cruelly done to death fifty or a hundred years before; or to loaf like detectives about the spots where their jewelry and cash-boxes (so useful and important to a disembodied spirit) lie concealed. But the atmospheric photograph or magic-lantern theory, whatever truth it may hold, exactly answers to a sense which I should think all my readers must have experienced, as I have done, in certain houses and cities, a sense as if the crimes which had been committed therein have left an indescribable miasma, a lurid, impalpable shadow, like that of the ashes of the Polynesian volcano, which darkened the sun for a year; or, shall we say, like the unrecognized effluvium which probably caused Mrs. Sleeman in her tent to dream she was surrounded by naked murdered men, while fourteen corpses were actually lying beneath her bed, and were next day disinterred? Walking once through Holyrood with Dr. John Brown (who had not visited the place for many years) I was quite overcome by this sense of ancient crime, perpetuated, as it seemed, almost like a physical phenomenon in those gloomy chambers; and on describing my sensations, Dr. Brown avowed that he experienced a very similar impression. It would almost seem as if moral facts of a certain intensity, begin to throw a cloudy shadow of evil, as Romish saints were said to exhale an odour of sanctity.

If there be a city in the world where this sense is most vivid I think it is Rome. I have felt it also in Paris, but Rome is worst. The air (not of the Campagna, with all its fevers, but of the city itself) seems foul with the blood and corruption of a thousand years. On the finest spring day, in the grand open spaces of the Piazza del Popolo, San Pietro, and the Forum, it is the same as in the darkest and narrowest streets. No person sensitive to this impression can be genuinely light-hearted and gay in Rome, as we often are even in our own gloomy London. Perhaps this is sheer fancifulness on my part, but I have been many times in Rome, twice for an entire winter, and the same impression never failed to overcome me. On my last visit I nearly died there, and it was not to be described how earnestly I longed to emerge, as if out of one of Dante's Giri, "anywhere, anywhere out of Rome!"[9]

TRADITIONAL HAUNTED HOUSES.

A very large proportion, of the places which have good evidences of haunting are, as we might expect, places with a history—places of historic interest, or of dramatic associations. It would be easy to compile a list of some hundreds, without going further than the British Isles. The following list is typical only, and makes no pretence of being exhaustive. It does not even include Ireland, Scotland, or Wales:

Yorkshire—Denton Hill; Waddow Hall; Bridge End House.
Northumberland—Cullaby Castle; Dilston; Hermitage Castle; Willington Mill.
Westmoreland—Lowther Hall.
Durham—Crook Hall; Netherby Hall; South Biddick Hall.
Lancashire—Wyecoller Hall, near Colne, "Spectre Horseman"; Clegg Hall; Salmeshury Hall, Blackburn.
Cumberland—Corby Castle, "Radiant Boy."
Hampshire—Hackwood House, Basingstoke; Ewshott House; Hinton Ampnoz Manor House.
Bucks—Creslon Manor House.
Notts—Newstead Abbey, " Goblin Friar."
Derby—Bolsover Castle.
Devon—Berry Pomeroy Castle; Sampford Peverel.
Oxford—Cumnor Hall.
Northampton—Althorpe.
London—Holland House; The Tower,
Berkshire—Windsor Castle.
Cheshire— Combermere Abbey; Ashley Hall.
Norfolk—Rainham; Holt Castle.
Suffolk—Dulton House.
Somerset—Beckington Castle, near Frome.

---

[9] This is extracted from the first volume of Cobbe's *Life of Frances Power Cobbe* (Richard Bentley & Son, 1894) pp. 223-25. In an earlier article, the same author discusses Mrs. Sleeman dreaming of dead men as she slept over fourteen bodies, concluding, "It is easily conceivable that the foul odour of death suggested to the lady, in the unconscious cerebration of her dream, her horrible vision. Had she been in a state of mesmeric trance, the same occurrence would have formed a splendid instance of supernatural revelation" ("Unconscious Cerebration: A Psychological Study" *Macmillan's* 23.1 [Nov., 1870] pp. 31).

Dorset—Bayley House, near Bridport.
Wilts—Market Lavington, near Devizes.

Ghosts and haunted houses appear to be abundant enough. Mr. Andrew Lang, in his essay on the subject, (see *Cock Lane and Common Sense,* p. 127) shows that this supply has never failed.

THE GHOST IS ALWAYS WITH US.

Among classics and savages, Christians and heathens, before the blessed Reformation and after—in spite of science and common sense, of medicine and the church, of his *reductio ad absurdum* at the hands of the Christmas number,[10] of Mr. Podmore, and even of Presbyterianism. He has been relegated to animism and the astral; he has been called a "telepathic impact" and a "morbid hallucination"; he has been explained as the creation of smugglers and coiners, and of people who "have a spite"; he has been "laid" by hypnotism, and with bell, book, and candle; he has been materialised, and de-materialised and rationalised; he has been tabooed and referred to the Horse Marines, and alleged to be an associate of Mrs. Harris ("which I don't believe there never was no such person"); but houses are still "haunted," and the provincial newspaper still chronicles the ghost.

GHOSTS AND THE S.P.R.

In 1884 the Psychical Research Committee, appointed for the Investigation of Haunted Houses, chronicled some four hundred as to which they had information more or less exact. Nineteen stories they regarded as first-class, and many of these are given us in the *Proceedings of the Society for Psychological Research,* Vol. II. They have also reserved for us many other isolated examples with all the detail one could desire. Scarcely a volume of *Proceedings* has been published which does not carry the evidence of its discussion a little farther. In Vol. VI, we have Mr. Podmore's "Phantasms of the Dead from Another Point of View," and in Vol. VIII, we have much debate on the Podinorean theory (for which theory within limits we should

---

10 *Reductio ad absurdum* is a Latin phrase used for an argument that shows the ultimate absurdity of a particular claim. Christmas issues of many Victorian magazines featured fictional ghost stories.

feel grateful). There, too, we have Miss Norton's "Record of a Haunted House," interesting chiefly from the abundance of its detail. In other respects it differs little as to the kind or variety of the phenomena reported from fifty others.

The last manifesto of the Society for Psychical Research, "The Report on the Census," is more exclusive in the matter of ghosts than were the earlier and less experienced investigations.

The number of cases reported is reduced by a careful process of selection to thirty, the number "which" writes Mrs. Sidgwick, "in our opinion afford any *primá facie* evidence of a supernormal origin. . . . In fifteen out of the thirty cases, the apparition was supposed to represent some dead person, whom the percipient had not known."

THE KIND OF GHOST THAT IS WANTED.

Ghosts as we have said, like other things human (I suppose we may regard them as post-human, at all events) never do the things which they should. I should like to draw up a programme for a really well-behaved ghost to follow.

1. He should be a ghost of the good old-fashioned kind. When a passenger who sits opposite to you in the railway train and reads *The Daily Telegraph* suddenly vanishes and turns out to be some one who was killed "on that day year," you feel a little as if you had been "done." I don't want him covered with blue mould, or wearing a shroud (I can never see why an ordinary night garment should be called, under certain circumstances, "a shroud"), but a dress of the last century, or indeed anything distinctive and picturesque, would be suitable.

2. He must be quite dead. I don't call an hallucination of a living person a fair kind of ghost, nor, for my present purpose, do I want to disturb a recent ghost who would excite painful emotions in myself or others. He should have been dead twenty years or so. I should prefer two hundred or two thousand.

3. I don't want to be too avaricious, but if he would talk and explain himself it would save a good deal of trouble. The few who do speak generally say very stupid things, like, "Are those boots paid for?" or, "What have you done with my photograph?" One who

appeared quite lately said, "Where is my pen-wiper with the dog's head on?" If he talks he must talk sense.

By the way the personal pronoun masculine is used only for convenience. I should be quite as glad to see *"her."*

4. This is really important. He (or she) must make an effort to be evidential. Any (or still better, all) of the following methods would serve the purpose:

(A.) If he would communicate some fact not within the knowledge of any one living of a nature which could be verified.

(B.) If he would reveal his identity in some definite manner; such, for example, as directing the seer to some portrait of him elsewhere, which the said seer had never heard of.

(C.) If he would appear independently to two or more good witnesses, neither of whom had heard of the other's experience.

This surely is not a great deal to ask, and I firmly believe that all these things have been done over and over again hundreds of times.

THE HAUNTINGS OF TEN REAL.

It is very encouraging to the ghost-hunter that so serious and impressive a volume as "The Report on the Census of Hallucinations," so often referred to, should conclude its discussion of "Local Apparitions" with such a paragraph as the following:

The cases we have given, in addition to others of the same kind to be found in previous numbers of the Proceedings, constitute, we think, a strong body of evidence showing, that apparitions are seen in certain places independently by several percipients, under circumstances which make it difficult to suppose that the phenomena are merely subjective, or that they can be explained by telepathy, without considerable straining of our general conception of it.

It appears, however, that there is in most cases very little ground for attributing the phenomena to the agency of dead persons, but, as we have said, in the great majority of cases they are unrecognised; and in these cases, if they really represent any actual person, there is often no more reason to suppose the person dead than living. The caution is not superfluous. The more absolutely that we believe in the reality of occult phenomena, the more jealous we are of that which is spurious counterfeit, or even doubtful—the more we feel the significance of that saying of

Tacitus, "Truth is established by investigation and delay." We hesitate over nine-tenths of the stories which reach us, in proportion as we believe unhesitatingly in the significance of the tenth.

X.

Those readers who wish to study the question further are referred, among the multitude of books dealing with the question, to the following among recent literature:

Lang, *Cock Lane and Common Sense.*
Thistleton Dyer, *The Ghost World.*
Baring Gould, *Strange Survivals.*
Proceedings S.P.R., Vols. I. II., V., VI;, VIII.
Ingram, *Haunted Houses.*
Stead, *Real Ghost Stories and More Ghost Stories.*

Case 9: When You Have Eliminated the Impossible

Investigation: conducted by Arthur Conan Doyle and Frank Podmore at a house in Charmouth, England, in 1894.

Manifestations: tossed stones; pranks involving a bouquet of flowers; a loud bang heard during the investigation.

Pertinent Facts: "When you have eliminated the impossible," says Sherlock Holmes, "whatever remains, no matter how improbable, must be the truth." Unfortunately, one person's impossibility is another's improbability—or even probability. Holmes's creator, Arthur Conan Doyle (1859-1930) joined a ghost hunt led by the Society for Psychical Research and then described it in a letter shortly afterward. That letter is now in private hands, but Andrew Lycett reports that, in it, Conan Doyle attributes curious noises heard during the investigation to a young man who lived in the house. About 24 years later, Conan Doyle retold the anecdote in a book titled *The New Revelation* (1918), and here he uses new evidence of bones unearthed at the site to suggest that the ghost was very real—and likely that of a murdered child. He repeated this in later books, adding that the investigation took place in Charmouth, that Frank Podmore (see Cases 7 and 8) was with him, and that he strongly disagrees with Podmore's report to the SPR that the boy was responsible.[1] In other words, Conan Doyle went from agreeing with Podmore that the haunting was a *hoax* to suggesting it was *authentic*. And one ghost hunter's impossibility had become another's probability.

---

[1] Lycett's comments are in *The Man Who Created Sherlock Holmes* (Free Press, 2008) p. 218. Conan Doyle's first "re-telling" of the case is reprinted below, and his subsequent reiterations are in *Memories and Adventures* (Little, Brown, and Company, 1924) pp. 142-44 and *The Edge of the Unknown* (G.P. Putnam's Sons, 1930) pp. 115-16.

From "Poltergeists"

Frank Podmore[2]

Visitations of raps and loud noises, accompanied by the throwing of stones, the ringing of bells, and other disturbances of an inexplicable kind have been known for many centuries. Mr. Lang (*Cock Lane and Common Sense*, p.170) cites a case as early as 856 a.d. In the last century there were many outbreaks of the kind, nor were the manifestations confined to any one country. There was the celebrated Cock Lane case, occurring in London in 1762; there was a tumult of bell-ringing in the Russian monastery of Tzarekonstantinoff in 1753[3]; and we hear of a case, in 1750, in Saxony, of mysterious stone-throwing which lasted for some weeks, much to the annoyance of a clergyman and his two sisters who were the victims of the outbreak.[4] In a small and now rare book, called *Bealings Bells,* published in 1841 by Major Moor, F.R.S., for sale at a Church bazaar, accounts are given, mostly at first-hand, of some 20 cases of this kind. The disturbances described in *Bealings Bells* consisted generally of bell-ringing, but they included occasional noises of other kinds, movements of furniture, throwing of crockery and small objects. The S.P.R. has received many reports of similar disturbances. Two of the most striking have already been published by Mr. Myers in the *Proceedings*. (See *Proceedings* S.P.R., Vol. VII., pp. 160-173, and pp. 383-394—Mr. Bristow's case.) In these two cases no opportunity was afforded of personal investigation; but in several instances Members of the Society have been able, either to be present during the actual occurrence of the disturbances, or to visit the locality and interrogate the witnesses immediately after the events. In the present paper it is proposed to deal with the results of these investigations. . . .

---

[2] This is extracted from *Proceedings of the Society for Psychical Research* 12 (1896-97) pp. 45-115. Podmore reviews eleven cases of poltergeists, each investigated by the SPR. In regard to the year, the family members involved, and the manifestations, the investigation Podmore designates "Case IX" is the only one that comes close to matching Conan Doyle's published accounts of a ghost hunt he shared with Podmore in Charmouth. Another scrap of evidence that Case IX is Podmore's report of the Charmouth case is in *The Edge of the Unknown*, where Conan Doyle states, "I was never asked by the Society for a report of this case, but Podmore sent one in, ascribing the noises to the young man. . . ." (p. 143).

[3] *The Russian Archives,* 1878, pp. 278-9, translated and forwarded to us by T. Bruhns. [Podmore's footnote.]

[4] *Annali dello Spiritismo,* quoted in *Light,* February 22nd, 1896. [Podmore's footnote.]

Case IX

In the autumn of 1894, Mrs. B., a lady living in a provincial town, gave me an account of certain curious incidents which had recently taken place in her house. The occupants of the house—an old one—consisted, besides Mrs. B. and her family, of a widow lady, Mrs. D., and her two children—a girl of about 20, C.D., and a boy of 15, E.D.

Mrs. B., C.D., and E.D. had been in the habit of trying experiments with planchette in the evening.[5] Planchette had given them to understand that the house was haunted by four spirits, a wicked marquis, a wicked monk, a lay desperado, and a virtuous and beautiful young lady. These had, all four, met with violent deaths (minutely described by planchette) at one another's hands in the house. These spirits wrote, through planchette, of treasure concealed in the house; of a hidden chamber; and many other matters. They also promised through planchette, and ultimately gave, objective proofs of their presence. Amongst other proofs were the following: (1) One evening after dark Mrs. B., in accordance with directions received through planchette, went with C.D. and E.D. to the old oak tree in the garden, and standing with the girl and boy on either side, holding a hand of each, she distinctly heard a stone strike the garden-roller a few feet off. The phenomenon was repeated twice; and her companions solemnly assured her that they had no part in the performance.

(2) On another occasion, sitting up in a bedroom (her son's) at the top of the house in the dark, with only E.D. in the room, Mrs. B. was struck by a stone on the temple, heard objects thrown about the room, felt an arm put through hers, and so on. Some of these phenomena also occurred when she was alone in the room—but with the door, I gathered, not shut.

(3) Mrs. B. one morning placed a white chrysanthemum bouquet on the boughs of the oak tree. It disappeared shortly afterwards; and on the next morning two other small bouquets were found there. Mrs. B. asked for whom these were intended, and went away, leaving pencil and paper. On her return she found the paper

---

[5] Planchette is a flat board—often heart-shaped and about the size of a hand—that rests on casters or rounded pegs with an aperture for a pencil. Users gently place their fingertips on it for use in automatic writing/spirit communication. It is the precursor to the device used with a Ouija board.

torn in half, and the initials of her own Christian name, and that of C.D., written on the two halves respectively, with a bouquet on each half.

(4) About this time a new secret chamber was discovered, with the skeleton of a cat crouching in act to spring, and the skeleton of a woman. Asked more particularly about the latter, Mrs. B. said: "Well, at least, a skull and some bones—but it was a woman's skull."

A few days after receiving this account, I went down by invitation to the house. I saw Mrs. D. and her two children, and received from them ungrudging corroboration of Mrs. B.'s marvellous story. In E.D.'s company I penetrated the secret chamber, and found there the mummified skeleton of what might have been a cat—but nothing else. In removing the stains left by this exploit from my person, I contrived a *tête-à-tête* interview with E.D. I at once asked him, "How much did you do of all these things?" He replied, "Oh, not much; I only did a few little things." Pressed on particular points, he admitted having thrown one stone at the garden-roller, and having also thrown a trouser-button against the wall when sitting alone in the bedroom with Mrs. B. He denied having produced the other phenomena on those occasions. Asked as to the bouquets, he said he had not placed them on the tree. Pressed a little more, he said, "If I did it, it must have been without knowing it." (This without any suggestion from me as to possible somnambulism, or unconscious action.) He assured me that his sister had had no hand in this matter. I could not get any more out of him, as he was shortly after called away.

I subsequently learnt from his mother that E.D. was so nervous and delicate that he slept in her room at night; that he was not allowed to do much mental work; that he was subject to attacks of somnambulism; and had, indeed, fallen into a semi-conscious state only a few days before, during a lesson in carpentry.

Subsequently Miss C.D., whilst denying any complicity with her brother in the "physical phenomena," admitted having deliberately co-operated with him in working planchette, and writing answers of their own invention to Mrs. B.'s questions.

These things may seem too foolish to be worth recording. I have recorded them because—incredible as it must seem Mrs. B., an educated woman, did unquestionably believe that she was in communication, through planchette, with four spirits, who looked to her for help and guidance; and saw in a schoolboy's silly tricks special manifestations of spirit power vouchsafed for her enlightenment. On the whole, Mrs. B. was, perhaps, only a little more credulous than some of the other witnesses to the doings of Poltergeists. . . .

✤

From *The New Revelation*

Arthur Conan Doyle[6]

. . . About 1891, I had joined the Psychical Research Society and had the advantage of reading all their reports. The world owes a great deal to the unwearied diligence of the Society, and to its sobriety of statement, though I will admit that the latter makes one impatient at times, and one feels that in their desire to avoid sensationalism they discourage the world from knowing and using the splendid work which they are doing. Their semi-scientific terminology also chokes off the ordinary reader, and one might say sometimes after reading their articles what an American trapper in the Rocky Mountains said to me about some University man whom he had been escorting for the season. "He was that clever," he said, "that you could not understand what he said." But in spite of these little peculiarities all of us who have wanted light in the darkness have found it by the methodical, never-tiring work of the Society. Its influence was one of the powers which now helped me to shape my thoughts. There was another, however, which made a deep impression upon me. Up to now I had read all the wonderful experiences of great experimenters, but I had never come across any effort upon their part to build up some system which would cover and contain them all. Now I read that monumental book, Myers' Human Personality, a great root book from which a whole tree of knowledge will grow. In this book Myers was unable to get any formula which covered all the phenomena called "spiritual," but in discussing that action of mind upon mind which he has himself called telepathy he completely proved his point, and he worked it out so thoroughly with so many examples, that, save for those who were wilfully blind to the evidence, it took its place henceforth as a scientific fact.[7] But this was an enormous advance. If mind could act

---

[6] This is extracted from *The New Revelation* (George H. Doran, 1918) pp. 31-35.

[7] Frederic W.H. Myers, *Human Personality and Its Survival of Bodily Death* (Longmans, Green, and Co., 1903).

upon mind at a distance, then there were some human powers which were quite different to matter as we had always understood it. The ground was cut from under the feet of the materialist, and my old position had been destroyed. I had said that the flame could not exist when the candle was gone. But here was the flame a long way off the candle, acting upon its own. The analogy was clearly a false analogy. If the mind, the spirit, the intelligence of man could operate at a distance from the body, then it was a thing to that extent separate from the body. Why then should it not exist on its own when the body was destroyed? Not only did impressions come from a distance in the case of those who were just dead, but the same evidence proved that actual appearances of the dead person came with them, showing that the impressions were carried by something which was exactly like the body, and yet acted independently and survived the death of the body. The chain of evidence between the simplest cases of thought-reading at one end, and the actual manifestation of the spirit independently of the body at the other, was one unbroken chain, each phase leading to the other, and this fact seemed to me to bring the first signs of systematic science and order into what had been a mere collection of bewildering and more or less unrelated facts.

About this time I had an interesting experience, for I was one of three delegates sent by the Psychical Society to sit up in a haunted house. It was one of these poltergeist cases, where noises and foolish tricks had gone on for some years, very much like the classical case of John Wesley's family at Epworth in 1726, or the case of the Fox family at Hydesville near Rochester in 1848, which was the starting-point of modern spiritualism. Nothing sensational came of our journey, and yet it was not entirely barren. On the first night nothing occurred. On the second, there were tremendous noises, sounds like someone beating a table with a stick. We had, of course, taken every precaution, and we could not explain the noises; but at the same time we could not swear that some ingenious practical joke had not been played upon us. There the matter ended for the time. Some years afterwards, however, I met a member of the family who occupied the house, and he told me that after our visit the bones of a child, evidently long buried, had been dug up in the garden. You must admit that this was very remarkable. Haunted houses are rare, and houses with buried human beings in their gardens are also, we will hope, rare. That they should have both united in one house is surely some argument for the truth of the phenomena.[8] It is interesting to remember that in the case of the Fox family there was also some word of human bones and evidence of murder being found in the cellar, though an actual crime was never established. I have little doubt that if the Wesley family could have got upon speaking terms with their persecutor, they would also have come upon some motive for the persecution. It almost seems as if a life cut suddenly and violently short had some store of unspent vitality which could still manifest itself in a strange, mischievous fashion. . . .[9]

---

[8] As noted above, Conan Doyle adds details to this story in *Memories and Adventures*. There, he writes: "Some years later the house was burned down, which may or may not have a bearing upon the sprite which seemed to haunt it, but a more suggestive thing is that the skeleton of a child about ten years old was dug up in the garden. . . . The suggestion was that the child had been done to death there long ago, and that the subsequent phenomena of which we had one small sample were in some way a sequence to this tragedy." Regarding Podmore's report implicating the son, Conan Doyle insists the son was with them in the parlour when they heard the noise in the kitchen. "A confederate was possible," he explains, "though we had taken every step to bar it, but the explanation given [in Podmore's report] was absolutely impossible. I learned from this, what I have often confirmed since, that while we should be most critical of all psychic assertions, if we are to get at the truth, we should be equally critical of all negatives and especially of so-called 'exposures' in this subject" (pp. 142-44). Almost the same story is told in *The Edge of the Unknown*, but Conan Doyle adds: "I am sorry to say that in some cases the exposure means downright fraud upon the part of the critic" (p. 116).

[9] In 1930, Conan Doyle quit the SPR. In his letter of resignation, he cites a "tradition of obtuse negation" practiced by Podmore and others. He circulated a copy of his letter with additional commentary, presumably to prompt other members to follow his lead. Apparently, this had minimal results. Conan Doyle's letter and commentary, along with a response from the Society's leaders are available in the *Journal of the Society for Psychical Research* 26.463 (March, 1930) pp. 45-50.

Case 10: Tracking the Phantom

Investigation: conducted by "some members of the *Welshman* staff" at Castell Moer (Greencastle), Carmarthen, Wales, in 1895.

Manifestations: an apparition of a man in a three-corner hat and other apparel of an earlier era; an apparition of an elegantly dressed woman.

Pertinent Facts: Most of the chronicles in this book come from magazines or books, presumably written by those with the leisure time to pursue the paranormal. Another kind of Victorian ghost hunter was the newspaper reporter whose professional duties occasionally included tracking down a rumored ghost or—in this case—to investigate what had become of phantoms long since vanished.

GREENCASTLE, OR CASTELL MOEL, NEAR CARMARTHEN
The Ghosts no Longer Seen

Anonymous[1]

In old times nearly every venerable mansion had its ghost, but ghosts are now getting very scarce. It is a pity we should not have a history of some of the most remarkable of them before they become lost to memory as well as sight. An essay on Carmarthen ghosts would be particularly interesting, for here haunted houses were very numerous a generation or two ago. Fifty years ago, if not at a later period, a male ghost used to be seen about the grounds at

---

[1] This appeared in *The Welshman* (Sept. 27, 1895) p. 8. I came upon this article discussed in Mark Rees's excellent *Ghosts of Wales: Accounts from the Victorian Archives* (History Press, 2017) pp. 65-68. My thanks to him.

Ystrad. Among those who saw it was the late Mr. John Davies, of Alltycnap, who had twice that doubtful pleasure. We have all heard of the dark gentleman who, after the death of "Betti 'Sia," the witch, used to visit the cottage in which she formerly lived on the roadside beyond Cillefwr. The old people of Carmarthen all remember Ty'r Bwci (a house which stood on or near the site of the present Longacre Villa) and the female ghost who loved to frequent that place and the lane leading up to Cwmernant. But all these ghosts have apparently retired from public life, and even Greencastle, on the Llanstephan road, once so famous for its unearthly visitants, appears to know them no more. We are an incredulous generation, and the work of frightening even a ten-year-old attendant at the Board School now requires more exertion than an easy-going family ghost of the good old, times cares to put forth.

Our attention has lately been turned to Greencastle by an engraving of the Brothers Buck, which we had the privilege of borrowing from our good friend Mr. Williams, of the Royal Exchange, whose stock of curiosities in the way of old books and pictures seems well-nigh inexhaustible. The engraving, which is dedicated to the then owner of Greencastle ("Thomas Bludworth, Esq., Master of Ye Horse and Privy Purse to his Royal Highness Ye Prince of Wales"), has the following descriptive lines underneath: "This Castle is about two miles to south-west of Caermarthen on a lofty situation commanding an extensive Prospect of the River Towey. It is also call'd Castell Moel, and is suppos'd to be that which is call'd by Dr. Powell in his Continuation of H Lhoyd's History of Cambria, Humffreys' Castle; It is said to be one of those built by Uchtred, Prince of Merionethshire, A.D. 1138. It is at present in the Possession of Thomas Bludworth, Esq., Published according to Act of Parliament, April 5th, 1740." The engraving shows the castle in a state of ruin, not very different from its present condition, although some parts of the walls have since fallen in. On one side is a row of trees running westward, and on the opposite side, running in a contrary direction, is a wall with the top battlemented. A glimpse of Carmarthen and the many windings of the Towy (which appear, by the way, to be rather exaggerated), bearing several full-rigged yachts on its waters are seen in the background. In the distance the tower of St. Peter's Church and Carmarthen Bridge, with seven arches, are plainly delineated. Armed with this engraving, some members of the *Welshman* staff paid a visit to Greencastle the other evening. The twilight hour was chosen in order to give the outing as much of a ghostly character as possible. Mr Jones, whose family has occupied the place for several generations, received the party very kindly, and with his permission Miss Harte showed them over the old Castle, which is really much larger than it looks from the road, without speaking of the outstanding fragments of wall, proving that it was originally a good deal more extensive than would appear at present. The visitors were rather surprised to learn that the present farmhouse (which has walls three feet thick or more) occupies part of the ground covered by the original building, and portions of the walls are probably remains of the more ancient structure.

Encouraged by Mr Jones's kindness, one of the visitors before leaving ventured to ask him if the ghosts had quite forsaken the old place. Evidently Mr Jones, for all the weight of his eighty-nine years, retains not only a good deal of manly vigour but a considerable sense of humour as well. His eye twinkled as he smilingly confessed to having heard "old stories," but he did not plead guilty to having met any ghosts in his own time. The others present were a little more explicit, and Miss Harte said she had heard, not indeed of the fine lady, but of the old gentleman in a three-cornered hat, who appeared there in the early days of the present century to a female domestic. She believed it was in the time of Mr Jones's uncle, whose name, we believe, was David Thomas. This was probably as far back as the battle of Waterloo. One of the *Welshman* party mentioned a certain aged man living in Carmarthen (often referred to in our Town Notes as "Old Inhabitant"), and asked if his mother was not the servant who had seen the ghost. Miss Harte believed it was. She then led the way into an ancient kitchen, where there was an immense open fire-place with a sort of settle on each side. She pointed out where the servant was sitting up late one night with a lover who had come to see her, and told how, on looking out into the middle of the room, both saw the gentleman in his out-of-date attire, including the three-cornered hat.

On returning to Carmarthen, the ghost hunters thought it incumbent on them to glean all the particulars which Old Inhabitant could supply. His story was to this effect. He had often heard of the servant and her lover who saw the ghost at Greencastle. He was not sure that his mother was the girl, but thought it might have been so, though his mother had never told him that she was the person. He knew that his mother was a servant at Greencastle as far back as 1817. The present Mr Jones's mother had told Old

Inhabitant's mother, he added, that she (Mrs Jones) had seen the man on several occasions, always dressed exactly in the same way. The man, or ghost rather, always wore a three-cornered hat, a swallow-tailed coat with a profusion of buttons on it (apparently silver buttons), knee breeches, silk stockings, and shoes with silver buckles. One day Mrs Jones was making bread ("so she told my mother," says "O.I."), when looking up, she saw the man as above described leaning against the pillar in the middle of the kitchen. Recognising her ghostly visitor, Mrs Jones walked out of the kitchen, and when she looked in at the door a moment afterwards he was gone. Miss Thomas, a sister of Mrs Jones, slept in a bed over the staircase, and one night, when the room was so flooded with moonlight that every object was distinctly visible, Miss Thomas was surprised to see a very beautiful lady, handsomely dressed and wearing on her neck, which was quite bare, a lovely necklace. She had a lot of jewellery about her person. At first the thought of an unearthly visitor did not occur to Miss Thomas at all. She thought some fine lady must have called and entered her room by mistake. In a few minutes, however, she was startled to find that the mysterious lady, who never spoke, vanished like morning mist. Nothing more astonished Miss Thomas than the fact that she felt quite unable to speak while the visitor was in the room. About that time Miss Jones began to find it very difficult (so "O.I." says) to find servants who had sufficient courage to remain at Greencastle, and Old Inhabitant's mother received a pound or thirty shillings (a great consideration in those days) over the usual wages paid to servants at the time. She stayed on, having plenty of nerve and being afraid of nothing. "Old Inhabitant" understood that the owner of the property got some one at last to lay the ghosts, and that the operation cost a lot of money, but he was never told how the job was effected. "O.I." remembers his mother often telling how, when she was servant at Greencastle, she could see from the hill there the body of Rees Thomas Rees hanging on the scaffold at Pensarn.[2]

---

[2] On April 19, 1817, Rees Thomas Rees became the last man to be hanged at Pensarn, the site of the Carmarthen gallows. The prisoner, who had served as a preacher, had been convicted of poisoning Elizabeth Jones. According to William Spurrell, "Rees, trusting in his innocence of murder, had surrendered himself, on the 9th of April, at the County Gaol, contrary to the entreaties of his friends." Of additional interest, Spurrell has a chapter on the "Oldest Inhabitant," whom he describes as "a personage whose memory is often found defective. . . . Yet, though his reminiscences are seldom deemed worthy of being committed to print, they are

But earthly work presses rather hard upon us this week, and we must take leave of the ghosts and the interesting old ruin of Greencastle, with thanks to Mr Jones and those in his employ for the kindness with which our meddlesome representatives were received.

---

sufficiently curious, when confined to a circumscribed neighbourhood like Carmarthen, to excuse our recording a few of them." Spurrell then provides a long list of what the "O.I." *does* recall, including such tidbits as "how before the introduction of gas, the inhabitants went to Church and Chapel like glow-worms, each with his lantern" and "the cheese riots, when the exportation of that article of food was prevented by the mob" (*Carmarthen and Its Neighbourhood,* [published by] William Spurrell, 1860, pp. 100, 54-55, 57).

Case 11: A Ghost Hunter's Lament

Investigation: conducted by James John Hissey and his wife at a house in Halton Holgate, England, in 1897.

Manifestations: loud noise as of furniture being moved; the apparition of an old man.

Pertinent Facts: James John Hissey (1847-1921) wrote several books about his trips through England and Wales. He often illustrated these book himself. (The foreboding house on the front cover of this book is one of his excellent drawings.) Sprinkled throughout his books, he notes his attraction to haunted sites, be they houses, inns, castles, streets, or hills. "Hunting after haunted houses is in one sense a dispiriting sport," he laments, "for though haunted houses abound, I never could run down a ghost; at least only once, and then it hastily ran away from me."[1] Perhaps his most detailed account of a ghost hunt involves a farmhouse near a village called Halton Holgate, a case he learned about from newspaper articles like the one in the previous chapter. With a touch of irony, those reporters acting as ghost hunters later stood in the way of Hissey's earnest desire to encounter an actual ghost.

გუ

---

[1] *The Charm of the Road: England and Wales* (Macmillan, 1910) p. 131.

From *Over Fen and Wold*

James John Hissey[2]

. . . We had so far been disappointed in our search after a haunted house this journey, but, nothing daunted, the following morning we set forth on the same errand, having heard that there was "a real haunted house" at Halton Holgate, a village situated about eight miles from Wainfleet. Haunted houses are strangely coming into note and repute again; I really thought their day was over forever, but it seems not so. The good old-fashioned ghost that roams about corridors, and stalks in ancient chambers till cock-crowing time; the ghost of our ancestors and the early numbers of the Christmas illustrated papers; the ghost that groans in a ghastly manner, and makes weird "unearthly" noises in the middle of the night, appears once more much in evidence,—I had nearly said "had come to life again"! He is even written about seriously and complainingly to the papers! In a long letter to the *Standard* that appeared therein on 22nd April 1896 under the heading of "A Haunted House," the writer gravely laments his lot in having unwittingly taken a lease of a house from which he and his family were driven, solely on account of the ghostly manifestations that took place there! The letter, which I afterwards learnt was written in absolutely good faith and was no hoax, commences: "In the nineteenth century ghosts are obsolete, but they are costing me two hundred pounds a year. I have written to my lawyer, but am told by him that the English law does not recognise ghosts!" The reading of this caused me to open my eyes in wonderment, the assertions were simply astonishing. Still the law seemed sensible; if any man were allowed to throw up an inconvenient lease on the plea of ghosts where should we be? The writer of the letter, it appears, was an officer in the English army. "Some time ago," he proceeds, "I left India on furlough, and, being near the end of my service, looked out for a house that should be our home for a few years. . . . I may say that I am not physically nervous. I have been under fire repeatedly, have been badly wounded in action, and have been complimented on my coolness when bullets were flying about. I was not then afraid of ghosts as far as I knew. I had often been in places where my revolver had to be ready to my hand. . . . As winter drew on and the nights began to lengthen, strange noises began to be heard. . . . The governess used to complain of a tall lady, with black heavy

[2] This is extracted from *Over Fen and Wold* (Macmillan, 1898) pp. 274-95.

eyebrows, who used to come as if to strangle her as she lay in bed. She also described some footsteps, which had passed along the corridor by her door, of someone apparently intoxicated. But in fact no one had left their rooms, and no one had been intoxicated. One night the house maid, according to her account, was terrified by a tall lady with heavy dark eyebrows, who entered the room and bent over her bed. Another night we had driven into the town to a concert. It was nearly midnight when we returned. Our old Scotch housekeeper, who admitted us, a woman of iron nerves, was trembling with terror. Shortly before our arrival a horrible shriek had rung through the house. To all our questions she only replied, 'It was nothing earthly.' The nurse, who was awake with a child with whooping-cough, heard the cry, and says it was simply horrible. One night, lying awake, I distinctly saw the handle of my bedroom door turned, and the door pushed open. I seized my revolver, and ran to the door. The lamp in the long corridor was burning brightly, no one was there, and no one could have got away. Now I can honestly say there is nothing against the house but ghosts. It is a roomy, nice, dry house. There are no ghosts. Are there not?" This is truly astonishing reading considering, as I have already stated, that I know the communication was made in perfectly good faith. A brave soldier to be driven out of a very comfortable and suitable home by a ghost—for thus the story ended!

For curiosity I cut out this letter and pasted it in my Commonplace Book. The subject had almost slipped my memory, when, just before starting on our present tour, I read in the *Standard* of 30th August 1897 of another haunted house in Lincolnshire. The account was long and circumstantial; having perused it carefully I took note of all particulars, determining to visit the house, if possible, and to see if by any means one could elucidate the mystery. As it may interest my readers, I venture here to quote the article *in extenso;*[3] the more am I induced to do this as it happened we did manage to inspect the house at our leisure, and had besides a long conversation with Mrs. Wilson, who claims to have actually seen the ghost! But I am getting previous. It will be noted that the account is of some length, and that the story was not dismissed by the editor of the *Standard* in a mere paragraph. This then it is:

---

[3] A Latin phrase meaning "at full length."

From Halton Holgate, a village near Spilsby, Lincolnshire, comes a story which is causing some sensation among the country folk in the neighbourhood. For some time rumours of human bones having been discovered under a brick floor of a farm, near the village, of strange tappings having been heard, and of a ghost having been seen, have been afloat, and it was with the intention of trying to sift the mystery that a Lincoln reporter has just visited the scene. The farmstead where the sounds are said to have been heard, and the ghost seen, stands some distance back from the high road, and is occupied by Mr. and Mrs. Wilson and their servant man. On being interviewed Mrs. Wilson was at first reluctant to make any statement, but eventually she narrated the following story:

"We came here on Lady-day.[4] The first night or so we heard very strange noises about midnight, as though some one was knocking at the doors and walls. Once it seemed as though some one was moving all the things about in a hurry downstairs. Another time the noise was like a heavy picture falling from the wall; but in the morning I found everything as right as it was the night before. The servant man left, saying he dared not stop, and we had to get another. Then about six weeks ago, I saw 'something.' Before getting into bed, my husband having retired before me, I thought I would go downstairs and see if the cow was all right, as it was about to calve. I did so, and when at the foot of the stairs, just as I was about to go up again, I saw an old man standing at the top and looking at me. He was standing as though he was very round-shouldered. How I got past I cannot say, but as soon as I did so I darted into the bedroom and slammed the door. Then I went to get some water from the dressing-table, but 'feeling' that some one was behind me I turned round sharply, and there again stood the same old man. He quickly vanished, but I am quite certain I saw him. I have also seen him several times since, though not quite so distinctly."

Mrs. Wilson conducted her interviewer to the sitting-room where the figure appeared. The floor in one corner was very uneven, and a day or two ago Mrs. Wilson took up the bricks, with the intention of relaying them. When she had taken them up she perceived a disagreeable smell. Her suspicions being aroused, she called her husband, and the two commenced a minute examination. With a stick three or four bones were soon turned over, together with a gold ring and several pieces of old black silk. All these had evidently been buried in quicklime, the bones and silk having obviously been burned therewith. The search after this was not further prosecuted, but a quantity of sand introduced and the floor levelled again. Dr. Gay, to whom the bones were submitted, stated that they were

---

[4] See footnote 7 on page 96. One might wonder if Lady Day is condusive to otherworldly visitations.

undoubtedly human, but he believed them to be nearly one hundred years old.

Now it happened, whilst we were at Boston, that we purchased a copy of the *Standard* of 13th September 1897. On glancing over this our eyes caught sight of the following further and later particulars of this haunted dwelling, now exalted into "The Lincolnshire Ghost Mystery." The account brought up to date ran thus:

A Lincoln Correspondent writes: "Despite all efforts, the Lincolnshire ghost mystery still remains unravelled. That the noises nightly heard cannot be ascribed to rats has been amply demonstrated, and other suggestions when acted upon likewise fail to elucidate the matter. All over the country the affair has excited the greatest interest, and two London gentlemen have written asking for permission to stay a night in the house. Other letters have been received from 'clairvoyants' asking for pieces of the silk or one of the bones discovered under the floor, whilst a London clergyman has written advising Mrs. Wilson to bury the bones in consecrated ground, then, he says, 'the ghostly visitor will trouble you no longer.' The owner of the house in question—a farmstead at Halton Holgate, near Spilsby—has tried to throw discredit on the whole affair, but such efforts have failed, and it now transpires that the house was known to be haunted fully thirty years ago."

The mystery had quite a promising look; and, coming across this second account of it just as we were approaching the neighbourhood of the scene of ghostly doings, raised our curiosity still more, and increased our determination not to miss this rare opportunity of inspecting a genuine(?) haunted house. See it somehow we must! Now it occurred to us that, as Halton Holgate was within easy distance of Wainfleet, our landlord would surely know something about the story and the people, and that he might enlighten us about sundry details. So in the morning, before starting, we interviewed him in his snug bar, and having shown him the cuttings from the *Standard* that we had brought with us, awaited his comments. "Oh yes," he began, "I've heard the story, but do not put much account on it myself, nor do I believe any one else about here does. I think the London papers put more store on it than we do. They say noises have been heard in the house at night. Well, you see, sir, the house stands on the top of a hill, and is very exposed to the wind. I've been told that there is a small trap-door in the roof at the top of the staircase, which is, or was, quite loose, and at the foot of the staircase is the front door, and they say that when the wind blows at all strong it gets under the door and lifts the trap up and down, and this accounts for the noises, perhaps there may be rats as well. I fancy the noises frightened the woman when she first went into the house, and she imagined the rest. At least that's my view of the matter from all I've heard." Manifestly the landlord was unbelieving; truly we too were sceptical, but even so, we thought the landlord's explanation of the nightly noises rather weak, notwithstanding his further remark that he thought the woman was very nervous, and the house being in a lonely situation made her the more so when she was left in it by herself at times, as she frequently was on their first coming there. "But that hardly accounts for her *seeing* the ghost," we exclaimed. "Oh! well, I just put that down to nerves; I expect she got frightened when she went there at first, and, as I've said, imagined the rest. I don't believe in ghosts seen by other people." "And what about the human bones?" we queried. "Well, as to the bones, they say as how when the house was built some soil was taken from the churchyard to fill up the foundations, and that fact would account for the finding of them."

It certainly seemed to us that the landlord's theory and explanations rather added to the mystery than helped to clear it up in any way; his reasonings were hardly convincing. We noted one thing in the landlord's arguments that appeared to us almost as improbable as the ghost story, namely, the way he so readily accounted for the existence of human bones under the floor by the removal of soil from the churchyard, the latter we afterwards discovered being about a mile away from the place; and even allowing such a thing to be permitted at the time of the building of the house perhaps, by rough guess, some fifty years ago such a proceeding was most unlikely, as soil could be had close at hand for the digging.

We felt that now we must wait till we got to Halton Holgate for further details. We had an introduction to the rector of the parish there, and we looked forward to hearing his views on the matter, for surely he of all people, we reasoned, would be in a position to help us to unravel the mystery. Matters were getting interesting; at last it seemed, after long years of search, that we should be able to run a real "haunted" house to earth; and we determined, if by any means we could arrange to do so, that we would spend a night therein. It would be a novel experience; indeed we felt quite mildly excited at the prospect. Failing this, it would be something if we could converse with a person who declared that she had seen an actual ghost, and who would describe to us what it was like, how it behaved itself, and so forth! We had come across plenty of people in the world, from time to time, who declared to us that they once knew somebody who said that they had seen a ghost, but we could never discover the actual party; for some cause or another he or she was never get-at-able, and I prefer my facts—or fiction—first hand. Stories, like wine, have a wonderful way of improving with age; indeed I think that most stories improve far more rapidly than wine. I once traced a curious three-year-old story back home to the place of its birth, and the original teller did not even recognise his offspring in its altered and improved garb! Tradition is like ivy; give it time and it will completely disguise the original structure.

The weather being fine and having finished our interview with our landlord, we started off without further delay, anxious to have as much time as possible before us for our day's explorations. The country still continued level, the road winding in and out thereof, as though determined to cover twice as much ground as needful in getting from place to place. Just beyond Wainfleet we passed, close to our way, the tallest windmill I think I have ever seen; it looked more like a lighthouse with sails attached than a proper windmill; it was presumably so built to obtain all the breezes possible, as in a flat country the foliage of the growing trees around is apt to deprive a mill of much of its motive power. In fact an Essex miller once told me that owing to the growth of the trees around his mill since it was first built, he could hardly ever work it in the summer time on account of the foliage robbing him of so much wind. Then as we drove on we caught a peep of low wooded hills ahead, showing an uneven outline, faintly blue, with touches of orange here and there where the sun's rays rested on the golden autumn leafage, now lighting up one spot, now another. We were delighted to observe that our road led apparently in the direction of these hills, for they gave promise of pleasant wanderings.

Farther on we reached a pretty little village, with its church picturesquely crowning a knoll. Here we pulled up for a moment to ask the name of the place from a man at work by the roadside. "This be I-r-b-y," he responded, spelling not pronouncing the name, somewhat to our surprise; so we asked him why he did so. "Well, sir, you see there be another village not far off called Orby, only it begins with a 'O' and ours begins with a 'I,' and the names do sound so alike when you speaks them, that we generally spells them to strangers to make sure. Often folk comes here who wants to go to Orby, and often folk who wants to come here gets directed to Orby. One of the names ought to be changed, it would save a lot of trouble and loss of temper." Then we asked him how far it was to Halton Holgate, and he said he thought it was about three miles, but he was not quite sure, not being a good judge of distances; "it might be more or it might be less," which was rather vague. Indeed we noticed generally in Lincolnshire how hard it was to obtain a precise reply to any query as to distance. Here is a sample of a few of the delightfully indefinite answers made to us from time to time when seeking information on this point. "Oh! not very far." "Some goodish bit on yet." "Just a little farther on." "A longish way off." "A few miles more." To the last reply a further query as to how many miles only brought the inconclusive response, "Oh! not many."

In due time we bade good-bye to the level country, for our road now led us up quite a respectable hill and through a rock cutting that was spanned at one point by a rustic bridge. It was a treat to see the great gray strong rocks after our long wandering in Fenland. The character of the scenery was entirely changed, we had touched the fringe of the Wold region, the highlands of Lincolnshire "Wide, wild, and open to the air." At the top of the hill we arrived at a scattered little village, and this proved to be Halton Holgate. The church stood on one side of the road, the rectory on the other; to the latter we at once made our way, trusting to learn something authoritative about the haunted house from the rector, and hoping that perhaps we might obtain an introduction to the tenant through him. Unfortunately the rector was out, and not expected back till the evening. This was disappointing. The only thing to do now was to find our way to the house, and trust to our usual good fortune to obtain admission and an interview with the farmer's wife.

We accosted the first native we met. Of him we boldly asked our way to the "haunted house," for we did not even know the name of it. But our query was sufficient, evidently the humble homestead had become famous, and had well established its reputation. We were directed to a footpath which we were told to follow across some fields, "it will take you right there." Then we ventured to ask the native if he had heard much about the ghost. He replied laconically, "Rather." Did he believe in it? "Rather" again. We were not gaining much by our queries, the native did not appear to be of a communicative nature, and our attempts to draw him out were not very successful. To a further question if many people came to see the house, we received the same reply. Manifestly for some reason the native was disinclined to discuss the subject. This rather perplexed us, for on such matters the country folk, as a rule, love to talk and enlarge. As he left us, however, he made the somewhat enigmatical remark, "I wish as how we'd got a ghost at our house." Was he envious of his neighbour's fame? we wondered, or what did he mean? Could he possibly deem that a ghost was a profitable appendage to a house on the show principle, insomuch as it brought many people to see it? Or were his remarks intended to be sarcastic?

Having proceeded some way along the footpath we met a clergyman coming along. We at once jumped to the conclusion that he must be the rector, so we forthwith addressed him as such; but he smilingly replied, "No, I'm the Catholic priest," and a very pleasant-looking priest he was, not to say jovial. We felt we must have our little joke with him, so exclaimed, "Well, never mind, you'll do just as well. We're ghost-hunting. We've heard that there's a genuine haunted house hereabouts, an accredited article, not a fraud. We first read about it in the *Standard,* and have come to inspect it. Now, can you give us any information on the point? Have you by any chance been called in to lay the ghost with candle, bell, and book? But perhaps it is a Protestant ghost beyond Catholic control?" Just when we should have been serious we felt in a bantering mood. Why, I hardly know, but smile on the world and it smiles back at you. Now the priest had smiled on us, and we retaliated. Had he been austere, probably we should have been grave. Just then this ghost-hunting expedition struck us as being intensely comical. The priest smiled again, we smiled our best in reply. We intuitively felt that his smile was a smile of unbelief in the ghost, I mean. "Well, I'm afraid," he replied, "the worthy body is of a romantic temperament. I understand that the bones are not human bones after all, but belonged to a deceased pig. You know in the off-season gigantic goose-berries, sea-serpents, and ghosts flourish in the papers. You cannot possibly miss the house. When you come to the end of the next field, you will see it straight before you," and so we parted. Somehow the priest's remarks damped our ardour; either he did not or would not take the ghost seriously!

Reaching the next field we saw the house before us, a small, plain, box-like structure of brick, roofed with slate, and having a tiny neglected garden in front divided from the farm lands by a low wall. An unpretentious, commonplace house it was, of the early Victorian small villa type, looking woefully out of place in the pleasant green country, like a tiny town villa that had gone astray and felt uncomfortable in its unsuitable surroundings. At least we had expected to find an old-fashioned and perhaps picturesque farmstead, weathered and gray, with casement windows and ivy-clad walls. Nothing could well have been farther from our ideal of a haunted dwelling than what we beheld; no high-spirited or proper-minded ghost, we felt, would have anything to do with such a place, and presuming that he existed, he at once fell in our estimation—we despised him! I frankly own that this was not the proper spirit in which to commence our investigations—we ought to have kept an open mind, free from prejudice. Who were we that we should judge what was a suitable house for a ghost to haunt? But it did look so prosaic, and looks count for so much in this world! The flat front of the house was pierced with five sash windows, three on the top story and two on the ground floor below, with the doorway between—the sort of house that a child first draws.

We did not enter the little garden, nor approach the regulation front door, for both had the appearance of being seldom used, but, wandering around, we came upon a side entrance facing some farm out-buildings. We ventured to knock at the door here, which was opened by the farmer's wife herself, as it proved; the door led directly into the kitchen, where we observed the farmer seated by the fireplace, apparently awaiting his mid-day dinner. We at once apologised for our intrusion, and asked if it were the haunted house that we had read accounts of in the London papers, and, if so, might we be allowed just to take a glance at the haunted room? "This is the haunted house," replied the farmer with emphasis, "and you can see over it with pleasure if you like; the wifie will show you over." So far fortune favoured us. The "wifie" at the time was busily occupied in peeling potatoes "for the men's meal," she explained, "but when I've done I'll be very glad to show you over and tell you anything." Thereupon she politely offered us a chair to rest on whilst she completed her culinary operations. "I must get the potatoes in the pot first," she excused herself, "or they won't be done in time." "Pray don't hurry," we replied; "it's only too kind of you to show us the house at all."

Then we opened a conversation with the farmer; he looked an honest, hard-working man; his face was sunburnt, and his hands showed signs of toil. I should say that there was no romance about him, nor suspicion of any such thing. The day was warm, and he was sitting at ease in his shirt sleeves. "I suppose you get a number of people here to see the place?" we remarked by way of breaking the ice. "Yes, that we do; lots of folk come to see the house and hear about the ghost. We've had people come specially all the way from London since it's got into the papers; two newspaper writers came down not long ago and made a lot of notes; they be coming down again to sleep in the house one night. We gets a quantity of letters too from folk asking to see the house. Have I ever seen the ghost? No, I cannot rightly say as how I have, but I've heard him often. There's strange noises and hangings going on at nights, just like the moving about of heavy furniture on the floors, and knockings on the walls; the noises used to keep me awake at first, but now I've got used to them and they don't trouble me. Sometimes, though, I wakes up when the noises are louder than usual, or my wife wakes me up when she gets nervous listening to them, but I only says, 'The ghost is lively to-night,' and go to sleep again. I've got used to him, you see, but he upsets the missus a lot. You see she's seen the ghost several times, and I only hear him." The wife meanwhile was intent on her work and made no remark. "This is all very strange and interesting," we exclaimed; "and so the house is really haunted?" Now it was the wife's turn. "I should rather think so," she broke in, "and you'd think so too if you only slept a night here, or tried to, for you'd not get much sleep unless you are used to noises, I can tell you: they're awful at times. I daren't be in the house alone after sundown, I'm that afraid." "And you've actually seen the ghost?" I broke in. "Yes, that I have, three or four times quite plainly, and several times not quite so plainly; he quite terrifies me, and one never knows when to expect him." "Ah! that's an unfortunate way ghosts have," we remarked sympathetically, "but good-mannered ones are never troublesome in the daytime: that's one blessing."

Eventually the busy housewife finished her task, and the peeled potatoes were safely put in the pot to boil. At this juncture she turned to us and said she was free for a time and would be very pleased to show us over the house and give us any information we wished, which was very kind of her. We then slipped a certain coin of the realm into the hands of her husband as a slight return for the courtesy shown to us. He declared that there was no necessity for us to do this, as they did not wish to make any profit out of their misfortunes, and as he pocketed the coin with thanks said they were only too pleased to show the house to any respectable person. The farmer certainly had an honest, frank face. His wife, we noticed, had a dreamy, far-away look in her eyes, but she said she did not sleep well, which might account for this. She appeared nervous and did not look straight at us, but this might have been manners. First she led the way to a narrow passage, in the front of the house, that contained the staircase. On either side of this passage was a door, each leading into a separate sitting-room, both of which rooms were bare, being entirely void of furniture. Then she told her own story, which I repeat here from memory, aided by a few hasty notes I made at the time. "Ever since we came to this house we have been disturbed by strange noises at nights. They commenced on the very first night we slept here, just after we had gone to bed. It sounded for all the world as though some one were in the house moving things about, and every now and then there was a bang as though some heavy weight had fallen. We got up and looked about, but there was no one in the place, and everything was just as we left it. At first we thought the wind must have blown the doors to, for it was a stormy night, and my husband said he thought perhaps there were rats in the house. This went on for some weeks, and we could not account for it, but we never thought of the house being haunted. We were puzzled but not alarmed. Then one night, when my husband had gone to bed before me (I had sat up late for some reason), and I was just going up that staircase, I distinctly saw a little, bent old man with a wrinkled face standing on the top and looking steadily down at me. For the moment I wondered who he could be, never dreaming he was a ghost, so I rushed upstairs to him and he vanished. Then I shook and trembled all over, for I felt I had seen an apparition. When I got into the bedroom I shut the door, and on looking round saw the ghost again quite plainly for a moment, and then he vanished as before. Since then I've seen him about the house in several places."

Next she showed us into the empty sitting-room to the left of the staircase; the floor of this was paved with bricks. "It was from this room," she continued, "that the noises seemed to come mostly, just as though some one were knocking a lot of things about in it. This struck us as singular, so one day we carefully examined the room and discovered in that corner that the flooring was very uneven, and then we noticed besides that the bricks there were stained as though some dark substance had been spilled over them. It at once struck me that some one might have been murdered and buried there, and it was the ghost of the murdered man I had seen. So we took up the bricks and dug down in the earth below, and found some bones, a gold ring, and some pieces of silk. You can see where the bricks were taken up and relaid. I'm positive it was a ghost I saw. The noises still continue, though I've not seen the ghost since we dug up the bones." After this, there being nothing more to be seen or told, we returned to the kitchen. Here we again interviewed the farmer, and found out from him that the town of Spilsby, with a good inn, was only a mile away. Thereupon I decided to myself that we would drive on to Spilsby, secure accommodation there for wife and horses for the night, and that I would come back alone and sleep in the haunted room, if I could arrange matters. With the carriage rugs, the carriage lamp and candles, some creature comforts from the inn, and a plentiful supply of tobacco, it appeared to me that I could manage to pass the night pretty comfortably; and if the ghost looked in—well, I would approach him in a friendly spirit and, he being agreeable, we might spend quite a festive evening together! If the ghost did not favour me, at least I might hear the noises—it would be something to hear a ghost! Thereupon I mentioned my views to the farmer; he made no objection to the arrangement, simply suggesting that I should consult the "missus" as to details; but alas! she did not approve. "You know," she said, addressing her husband, "the gentleman might take all the trouble to come and be disappointed; the ghost might be quiet that very night; he was quiet one night, you remember. Besides, we promised the two gentlemen from the London paper that they should come first, and we cannot break our word." Appeals from this decision were in vain; the wife would not hear of our sleeping the night there on any terms, all forms of persuasion were in vain. Manifestly our presence in the haunted chamber for the night was not desired by the wife. As entreaties were useless there was nothing for it but to depart, which we did after again thanking them for the courtesies already shown; it was not for us to resent the refusal. "Every Englishman's house is his castle " according to English law, and if a ghost breaks the rule well, "the law does not recognise ghosts." So, with a sense of disappointment amounting almost to disillusion, we departed. I feel quite hopeless now of ever seeing a ghost, and have become weary of merely reading about his doings in papers and magazines. I must say that ghosts, both old and new, appear to behave in a most inconsiderate manner; they go where they are not wanted and worry people who positively dislike them and strongly object to their presence, whilst those who would really take an interest in them they leave "severely alone!"

Case 12: Into the 20th Century

Investigation: conducted by Violet Tweedale, her husband, and some others in a house in Torquey, England, in 1917 and shortly before.

Manifestations: a sense of being watched; doors that refuse to remain closed, even when locked, or that lock when residents want them to remain open; sounds of screams, footsteps, and brushing; phantom of a woman in a black dress.

Pertinent Facts: As a girl in Scotland, Violet Tweedale (1862-1936) went ghost hunting with her father, who—like her uncle—was a prominent publisher. Tweedale's family was well positioned to launch Violet's life associating with Britain's elite and royalty. In fact, she hobnobbed with Queen Victoria herself! "Being very tall," she recalled, "I had always a certain difficulty in getting down low enough to kiss the tiny Queen's hand."[1] No doubt, this affluence afforded Tweedale the leisure to pursue her interest in the paranormal, her husband adopting the investigative role once held by her father. The married couple figure into the chronicle that follows, and it is here that we see the Victorian ghost-hunting tradition progress into a new century—indeed, up to and beyond World War I.

---

[1] Violet Tweedale, *Ghosts I Have Seen and Other Psychic Experiences* (Frederick A. Stokes, 1919) p. 34.

149

From *Ghosts I Have Seen and Other Psychic Experiences*

Violet Tweedale[2]

I have never yet met any one who was not interested in haunted houses. Even the most blatant skeptic always wants to "hear all about it," though he has predetermined to treat the story with his habitual scoffing incredulity. Of all the departments of psychical research none commands more general interest than a "spooky" house, and there are few people who cannot name a dwelling which has acquired the reputation for being haunted by denizens of the other world.

Of course, any house that falls into serious disrepair, and remains unoccupied for some long period, any dwelling whose owner permits decay to proceed unchecked, and dilapidation to run its course, at once suggests the thought to the beholder, "what a haunted looking old place," and rumor, in such cases, quickly supplies all the old phenomena, even though tradition be totally absent. Tramps are always on the lookout for such shelters, and their damped-down fires catch the eye of some scared rustic who happens to be passing in the dark. Rats and the winds of heaven play hide-and-seek through the deserted rooms and corridors, and owls find sanctuary in the surrounding gardens. Their cries, varying from the exultant shriek to the mournful wail, add a weird suggestiveness to the abiding melancholy of such abandoned habitations.

There is so much talk nowadays of hauntings and ghosts, that it seems strange we should know so very little about them. I have never heard a really convincing explanation of why ghosts should haunt certain houses, and I have no explanation of my own to offer. If ghosts could be commanded, if one could be sure of witnessing certain phenomena that have been elaborately described to one, then there might be the ghost of a chance of advantageous investigation. No such opportunities seem to be afforded the investigator. He may watch for months and see nothing, yet the elusive wraith may turn up before several witnesses on the very night after he has abandoned his quest out of sheer boredom and discouragement.

---

[2] Tweedale, pp. 251-75.

Some seven years ago, whilst wintering in Torquay, I heard a great deal of gossip about a villa on the Warberries, which was reputed to be badly haunted. For the last forty to fifty years nobody, it was said, had been able to live in it for any length of time. Several people asserted that they had heard screams coming from it as they passed along the high road, and no occupant had ever been able to keep a door shut or even locked.

The house is at present being pulled down, therefore I commit no indiscretion in describing the phenomena connected with it.

"Castel a Mare" is situated in what house agents would describe as "a highly residential quarter." It is surrounded by numerous villas, inhabited by people who are all very "well to do," and who make Torquay their permanent home. The majority of these villas lie right back from the road, and are hidden in their own luxuriant gardens, but the haunted house is one of several whose back premises open straight on to the road.

No dwelling could have looked more commonplace or uninteresting. It was built in the form of a high box, three storied. It was hideous and inartistic in the extreme, but along its frontage looking towards the sea and hidden from the road, there ran a wide balcony on to which the second floor rooms opened, and from there the view over the garden was charming. When I first went to look at it, dilapidation had set in. Jackdaws and starlings were busy in the chimneys, the paint was peeling off the walls, and most of the windows were broken. Year after year those windows were mended, but they never remained intact for more than a week, and during the war there has been no attempt at renewal. Even the agents' boards, "To be let or sold" dropped one by one from their stems, as if in sheer weariness of so fruitless an announcement.

It was not long before I obtained the loan of the keys, and proceeded to "take the atmosphere." It was decidedly unhealthful, I concluded, though I neither heard nor saw anything unusual during the hour I spent alone in quietly wandering through the deserted rooms. I found no trace of tramps, and all the closed windows were thickly cobwebbed *inside,* an important fact to notice in psychic research. I fixed upon the bathroom and one other small room, as the *foci* of the trouble, and left the house with no other strong impression than that my movements had been closely watched, by some one unseen by me. It was no uncommon sight in pre-war days to see several smart motor cars drawn up at the gate. Frivolous parties of explorers in search of a thrill drove in from the surrounding neighborhood, and romped gayly through the house and out again, and I discovered that several of those visitors had distinctly felt that they were being followed about and watched.

My husband and I were naturally much interested in this haunted dwelling, so accessible, and so near to our own house. We determined that if we could make friends with the owner we would do a little investigation on our own. Numerous people, on the plea that the house might suit them as a residence, got the loan of the keys, and spent an hour or two inside the place, wandering about the house and garden, but the owner was getting tired of this rush of spurious house-hunters. He was beginning to ask for *bona fides,* so we determined honestly to state our purpose.

The proprietor was an old builder who owned several other houses. He received me very civilly, even gratefully. He would willingly give us the keys for as long a period as we required them. "Castel a Mare" brought him extreme bad luck; he longed to be rid of it, and he added that after our investigations, if my husband could give the house a clean bill of health it would be of enormous benefit to him, in enabling him to let or sell it. He did not seem very hopeful, but stated it to be his opinion that the hauntings were all nonsense, and that the screams people heard were the cries of some peacocks that lived in a property not far off. This sounded very reasonable, and I promised him that if we could honestly state that the house was perfectly unhealthful, we would permit our conclusions to be made public.

My husband and I decided that the hour one p.m. till two p.m. would be the quietest and least conspicuous time in which to investigate. Doubtless the night would have been better still, but it would have created too much excitement in the neighborhood, and callers to see "how we were bearing up" would have defeated our object. Between one and two all Torquay would be lunching, and we could easily slip in unobserved, and we would require neither lights nor warm comforts.

We started at once, my husband keeping the keys, and making himself responsible for the doors. Though the window-panes were badly broken there were no openings large enough to admit a small child, and, as I have said, the network of cobwebs within was evidence that no human being entered the house by the windows. The front door lock was in good order, and so were most of the other locks in the house. We shut ourselves in, and after a thorough examination of the premises we mounted to the first floor. Three rooms opened on to it, belonging to the principal bedroom—a smaller room and a bathroom opening out of the big bedroom. My husband closed all the doors, and we sat down on the lower steps of the bare staircase leading to the floor above. That day we drew an absolute blank, and at two o'clock we closed every door in the house, and just inside the front door we made a careless looking arrangement of twigs, dead leaves, pieces of straw and dust, which could not fail to betray the passing of human feet, should anybody possess a duplicate key to the front door and enter by that means.

The second day we found our twig and straw arrangements intact, but not a single door was shut, all were thrown defiantly wide. This seemed rather promising and we went upstairs to our seat on the steps, and carefully reclosing the doors immediately in front of us, sat down to await events.

Quite half an hour must have passed when suddenly a click made us both look up. The handle of the door, but a couple of yards distant from me, leading into the small room, was turning, and the door quietly opened wide enough to admit the passing of a human being. It was a bright sunny day, and one could see the brass knob turning round quite distinctly. We saw no form of any sort, and the door remained half open. For perhaps a couple of moments we awaited developments, then our attention was suddenly switched off the door by the sound of hurrying footsteps running along the bare boards on the corridor above us. My husband rushed up and searched each empty room, but neither saw anything nor heard anything more. Before leaving the house we shut all doors, and locked all that would lock. Such was the meager extent of our second day's investigations.

On the third day the doors were all found wide flung. No door opened before our eyes as on our former visit, but a brushing sound was heard ascending the stairs, as if from some one pressing close against the wall.

For about a fortnight nothing happened beyond what I have recounted, but I was strongly conscious that we were being watched. The most unhealthful spots were the bathroom, a servants' room entered by a staircase leading from the kitchen, and the stable, a small building immediately to the right of the house. The bathroom was in great disrepair, long strips of paper hung from the walls, and an air of profound depression pervaded it. Obviously it had once been merely a large cupboard, and it had a window admitting light from a passage behind it.

We had never once failed to find every door which we had closed thrown wide on our return, and one day we locked the bathroom, and removing the key we looked about for some spot in which to secrete it. On that floor was nothing large enough to hide even so small an object as a key, so we took it downstairs to the dining-room. In a corner lay a rag of linoleum about six inches square, under this we placed the bathroom key and left the house.

That afternoon a house agent called and asked for the loan of the keys. He told us that a brave widow, who knew the history of the house, thought it might suit her to live in. and he proposed to take her over it and point out its charms. He would return the keys to us directly afterwards. I took advantage of this occasion to say to the agent that probably the screams some people had heard proceeded from the peacocks in the neighborhood.

He shook his head and answered, "We hoped that might prove to be the case, but we have ascertained that it is not so." He seemed despondent about the place, even though what we had to tell him was as yet nothing very formidable or exciting. What we did not tell him was that we had locked up the bathroom, and hidden the key. We left him to discover that fact for himself.

He returned with the keys in about an hour, and I asked him what the widow thought of "Castel a Mare."

"She thinks something might be made of it. The cheapness attracts her," he answered.

"But it will need so much doing to it," I demurred. "What did she think of the bathroom?"

"She said it only needed cleaning and repapering. The bath itself she found in good enough condition."

So the bathroom door was open, in spite of our having locked it and hidden the key!

After the agent had gone we went to the house. Every door stood wide. The bathroom key was still in its hiding-place, and the door open. We replaced the key. The ghosts laughed to scorn such securities as locks and keys.

For a month or two we pursued our investigations, then we returned the keys to the owner. Though we had seen and heard so little it was impossible to give the house a clean bill of health, and the old builder was much cast down. A few days afterwards we received a letter from him offering us the house as a free gift. It would pay him to be rid of the ground rent, and the place was as useless to him as to any one else. We thanked him and refused the gift.

About this period I was lucky enough to get into touch with a former tenant of "Castel a Mare," and this lady most kindly gave me many details of her residence there. About thirty years ago she occupied it with her father and mother, and they were the last family to live in it for any length of time, and for many years it has remained empty.

Soon after their arrival this family discovered that there was something very much amiss with their new residence. The house, the garden, and the stable were decidedly uncanny, but it was some time before they would admit, even to themselves, that the strange happenings were of a supernatural order.

The phenomena fell under three headings: a piercing scream heard continually, at any hour and during all seasons; continuous steps running along corridors, and up and down stairs; constant lockings of doors by unseen hands.

The scream was decidedly the most unnerving of the various phenomena. The family lived in constant dread of it. Sometimes it came from the garden, sometimes from inside the house. One morning whilst they sat at breakfast, they were violently startled by this horrible sound coming from the inner hall, just outside the room in which they sat. It took but a moment to throw open the door, but, as usual, there was nothing to be seen.

On another occasion the family doctor had just arrived at the front door, and was about to ring, when he was startled by the scream coming from inside the house. This doctor still lives in the neighborhood, and is one of many people who can bear witness to the fact.

The footsteps of unseen people kept the family pretty busy. They were always running to the doors to see who was hurrying past, and up and down stairs. Very soon the drawing-room became extremely uncomfortable, and practically uninhabitable. It was always full of unseen people moving about. The lady of the house never felt herself alone, and when she found herself locked into her own room, the behavior of her astral guests seemed to her to have become intolerable. The master of the house no more escaped these attentions than did the rest of the inhabitants, and finally all keys had to be removed from all doors.

One night some guests, after getting into bed, heard some one open the door of their room and enter. Astonishment kept them silent, and in a minute or two their visitor quietly withdrew and closed the door again. They concluded that it must have been their hostess, and that thinking they were asleep she had not spoken, yet still they thought the incident very strange. The next morning they discovered that no member of the household had entered their room.

On another occasion a lady who had come to help nurse a sick sister saw, one night, a strange woman dressed in black velvet walk downstairs.

Animals fared badly at "Castel a Mare." A large dog belonging to the family was often found cowering and growling in abject fear of something visible to it, but not to the human inhabitants, and the harness horse showed such an invincible objection to its stable, that it could only be got in by backing.

Later on I was told that a member of the Psychical Society had visited "Castel a Mare," and had pronounced the garden to be more haunted than the house.

It is interesting to note how absolutely untenable badly haunted houses become. No matter how skeptical, how resolutely material the tenants may be, the phenomena wear them down to a humble surrender at last. After all, what can people do but quit a residence which is constantly showing incontrovertible evidence that it is possessed by numerous unseen entities that defy analysis?

Every one is interested in getting rid of this weird disturbance, but how to do it? The skeptic is resolute in unmasking the fraud, but finds himself balked by intangibility. He hears the scream at his door, and rushes to arrest the miscreant, but sees no one to grapple with. Domestic difficulties become acute. No warning is given, no wages asked. The servants decamp, too scared to care for anything but putting distance between themselves and the nameless dread. Visitors begin to fight shy of the house. They have heard the screams.

Month after month the master of the house, thinking of his rent, and his reputation for sanity, and what the loss of both would mean to him, clings to skepticism as his only hope and refuge. He is not going to be driven forth by any such stuff and nonsense as ghosts! Why! there are no such things! "Seen things? heard things?" Well, yes, he has, but, of course, there must be some rational explanation. A man who has fought for king and country is not going to be defeated and put to flight by a pack of silly women's stories. He will soon get to the bottom of the whole affair, then woe betide the practical joker!

When alone he racks his brains in vain. He is furious with himself for having heard the scream, and tells himself he must be "going dotty." He is puzzled, baffled, irritated, but more determined than ever to "stick it out." Who can the "joker" be who is demoralizing his household, who has even dared to lock him into his own room? He thinks of his wife and family, and of their shattered nerves; he thinks of his terrified servants, and of his dog, which can no longer be persuaded to enter the house. He feels he must look elsewhere for the disturber of his peace. But where? He keeps careful watch unknown (as he thinks) to his family. The steps approach him, pass close to him, then die away in the distance, leaving him fuming, impotent. He finds it necessary to wipe his brow, which enrages him still more. At dead of night he watches on the staircase, with all lights full on.

Silence, utter silence! Absolutely nothing to be seen or heard. He thinks of going to bed. He always said the whole thing was "tommy rot." The deathly silence is suddenly rent by a piercing scream at his very elbow, and he leaps to his feet, growling out an oath below his breath. He looks wildly round on every side of him. Nothing! Something strange is happening to his head. He passes his hand over his hair. It seems to be creeping along his scalp, and he thinks of the quills of a porcupine. "What the devil is he to do?" "Go to bed," answers inclination, "you're doing no good here. Yes! Go to bed; that's the sensible thing to do."

The next morning every one asks him if he heard "it." He acknowledges to himself that his temper is becoming vile.

The day comes when he is left alone with his family. The staff has fled and he feels rather broken.

At last he gives in, and agrees to seek another home, but it is not to the ghosts he gives in, but to the nervous fancies of a pack of silly women. He feels wonderfully light-hearted, however, now that his mind is made up, and a glow of magnanimity pervades him. "If you do a thing at all do it well and at *once*," he tells himself, and promptly hires another house in another neighborhood.

When questioned by his men friends he laughs. The man in the street might understand certain things that he could tell, but the man in the club, never! "All tommy rot, my dear chap, but my wife got nervous, and the servants! You know what they are. Scared by the scratch of a mouse. For the women's sake I thought it best to quit. You know what women are, when they once get an idea into their heads!"

The Sequel

In 1917 a friend rang me up and asked me if I would form one of a party of investigation at "Castel a Mare." The services of a medium had been secured, and a soldier on leave, who was deeply immersed in psychic research, was in high hopes of getting some genuine results.

I accepted the invitation because a certain incident had once more roused my curiosity in the haunted house.

During our investigations I had been disappointed at not hearing the much-talked-of scream, the more so after learning from the former tenants how very often they had heard it. When I did at last hear it I was walking past the house on a very hot summer morning, about eleven o'clock. I was not thinking of the house, and had just passed it on my way home, when a piercing scream arrested my attention. I wheeled round instantly; there was not a doubt as to where the scream came from, but unfortunately, though there were people on the road, there was no one near enough to bear witness. The scream appeared to come from some one in abject terror, and would have arrested the attention of any one who happened to be passing. I mean that had no haunted house stood there, had the scream proceeded from any other villa, I am sure that any passer-by would have halted wonderingly, and awaited further developments.

"Castel a Mare" lay in absolute silence, under the blazing sunshine, and in a minute or two I walked on. I could now understand what it must have meant to live in that house, in constant dread of that weird and hideous sound resounding through the rooms or garden.

This incident made me eager to join my friend's party, and on reaching the house I found a small crowd assembled.

The medium, myself, and four other women. The soldier, and an elderly and burly builder belonging to the neighborhood, who was interested in psychic research. Eight persons in all.

As there was no chair or furniture of any description in the house, we carried in a small empty box from a rubbish heap outside, and followed the medium through the rooms. She elected to remain in the large bedroom, on the first floor, out of which opened the bathroom, and she sat down on the box and leaned her back against the wall, whilst we lounged about the room and awaited events. It was a sunny summer afternoon, and the many broken panes of glass throughout the house admitted plenty of air.

After some minutes it was plain to see that the medium had fallen into a trance. Her eyes were closed, and she lay back as if in sound sleep. Time passed, nothing happened, we were all rather silent, as I had warned the party that though we were in a room at the side of the house farthest from the road, our voices could plainly be heard by passers-by, and we wanted no interference.

Just as we were all beginning to feel rather bored and tired of standing, the medium sprang to her feet with surprising agility, pouring out a volume of violent language. Her voice had taken on the deep growling tones of an infuriated man, who advanced menacingly towards those of us who were nearest to him. In harsh, threatening voice he demanded to know what right we had to intrude on his privacy.

There was a general scattering of the scared party before this unlooked-for attack, and the soldier gave it as his opinion that the medium was now controlled by the spirit of a very violent male entity. I had no doubt upon the point.

Then commenced so very unpleasant a scene that I had no doubt also of the medium's genuineness. No charlatan, dependent upon fraudulent mediumship for her daily bread, would have made herself so intensely obnoxious as did this frail little woman. I found myself saying, "Never again. This isn't good enough."

The entity that controlled her possessed superhuman strength. His voice was like the bellow of a bull, as he told us to be gone, or he would throw us out himself, and his language was shocking.

I had warned the medium on entering the house that we must be as quiet as possible, or we would have the police walking in on us. Now I expected any moment to see a policeman, or some male stranger arrive on the scene, and demand to know what was the matter.

The majority of our party were keeping at a safe distance, but suddenly the control rushed full tilt at the soldier, who had stood his ground, and attacking him with a tigerish fury drew blood at once. The big builder and I rushed forward to his aid. The rest of the party forsook us and fled, pell-mell, out of the house and into the garden. Glancing through a window, near which we fought, I saw below a row of scared faces staring up in awed wonder.

The scene being enacted was really amazing. This frail little creature threw us off like feathers, and drove us foot by foot before her, always heading us off the bathroom. We tried to stand our ground, and dodge her furious lunges, but she was too much for us. After a desperate scuffle, which lasted quite seven or eight minutes, and resulted in much torn clothing, she drove us out of the room and on to the landing. Then suddenly, without warning, the entity seemed to evacuate the body he had controlled, and the medium went down with a crash and lay at our feet, just a little crumpled disheveled heap.

For some considerable time I thought that she was dead. Her lips were blue, and I could feel no pulse. We had neither water nor brandy with which to revive her, and we decided to carry her down into the garden and see what fresh air would do. Though villas stood all round us, the foliage of the trees gave us absolute privacy, and we laid her flat on the lawn. There, after about ten minutes, she gradually regained her consciousness, and seemingly none the worse for her experiences she sat up and asked what had happened.

We did not give her the truth in its entirety, and contrived to account for the blood-stained soldier and the torn clothing, without unduly shocking and distressing her. We then dispersed; the medium walking off as if nothing whatever had occurred to deplete her strength.

Some days after this the soldier begged for another experiment with the medium. He had no doubts as to her genuineness, and he was sure that if we tried again we would get further developments. She was willing to try again, and so was the builder, but with one exception the rest of the party refused to have anything more to do with the unpleasant affair, and the one exception stipulated to remain in the garden. She very wisely remarked that if she came into the house there was no knowing what entity might not attach itself to her, and return home with her, and she was not going to risk it. Of course this real danger always had to be counted upon in such investigations, but as the men of the party desired a woman to accompany the medium, I consented, and we entered the house once more, a reduced party of four.

After the medium had remained entranced for some minutes, the same male entity again controlled her. The same violence, the same attacks began once more, but this time we were better prepared to defend ourselves. The soldier and the stalwart builder warded off the attacks, and tried conciliatory expostulations, but all to no purpose. Then the soldier, who seemed to have considerable experience in such matters, tried a system of exorcising, sternly bidding the malignant entity depart. There ensued a very curious spiritual conflict between the exorcist and the entity, in which sometimes it seemed as if one, then the other, was about to triumph.

Those wavering moments were useful in giving us breathing space from the assaults, and at length having failed, as we desired, to get into the bathroom, we drove him back against the wall at the far end of the room. Finally the exorcist triumphed, and the medium collapsed on the floor, as the strength of the control left her.

For a few moments we allowed the crumpled up little heap to remain where she lay, whilst we mopped our brows and regained our breath. The soldier had brought a flask of brandy which we proposed to administer to the unconscious medium, but quite suddenly a new development began.

She raised her head, and still crouching on the floor with closed eyes she began to cry bitterly. Wailing, and moaning, and uttering inarticulate words, she had become the picture of absolute woe.

"Another entity has got hold of her," announced the soldier. It certainly appeared to be so.

All signs of violence had gone. The medium had become a heart-broken woman.

We raised her to her feet, her condition was pitiable, but her words became more coherent.

"Poor master! On the bed. Help him! Help him!" she moaned, and pointed to one side of the room. Again and again she indicated, by clenching her hands on her throat, that death by strangulation was the culmination of some terrible tragedy that had been enacted in that room.

She wandered, in a desolate manner, about the floor, wringing her hands, the tears pouring down her cheeks, whilst she pointed to the bed, then towards the bathroom with shuddering horror.

Suddenly we were startled out of our compassionate sympathy by a piercing scream, and my thoughts flew instantly to the experiences of the former tenants, and what I myself had heard in passing on that June morning of the former year.

The medium had turned at bay, and began a frantic encounter with some entity unseen by us. Wildly she wrestled and fought, as if for her life, whilst she emitted piercing shrieks for "help." We rushed to the rescue, dragging her away from her invisible assailant, but a disembodied fighter has a considerable pull over a fighter in the flesh, who possesses something tangible that can be seized. I placed the medium behind me, with her back to the wall, but though I pressed her close she continued to fight, and I had to defend myself as well as defend her. Her assailant was undoubtedly the first terrible entity which had controlled her. At intervals she gasped out, "Terrible doctor—will kill me—he's killed master—help! help!"

Gradually she ceased to fight. The soldier was exorcising with all his force, and was gaining power; finally he triumphed, inasmuch as he banished the "terrible doctor."

The medium was, however, still under the control of the broken-hearted entity, and began again to wander about the room. We extracted from her further details. An approximate date of the tragedy. Her master's name, that he was mentally deficient when the murder took place. She was a maidservant in the house, and after witnessing the crime she appeared to have shared her master's fate, though by what means we could not determine. The doctor was a resident physician of foreign origin.

At last we induced her to enter the bathroom, which she seemed to dread, and there she fell to lamenting over the dead body of her master, which had lain hidden there when the room was used as a large cupboard. It was a very painful scene, which was ended abruptly by her falling down insensible.

She had collapsed in an awkward corner, but at last we lifted her out, and carried her downstairs to the garden. When I tried to revive her with brandy I found that her teeth were tightly clenched. I then tried artificial respiration, as I could feel no pulse. Gradually she came back to life, quietly, calmly, and in total ignorance of what had occurred. The most amazing thing was that she showed no signs whatever of exhaustion or mental fatigue. We were all dead beat, but not so the fragile-looking little medium, though externally she looked terribly disheveled and draggled.

This was the last time I set foot in the haunted house, which is now being demolished, but I still had to experience more of its odd phenomena.

The date and names the medium had given us were later on verified by means of a record of villa residents, which for many years had been kept in the town of Torquay.

There is no one left now who has any interest in verifying a tragic story supposed to have been enacted about fifty years ago. It must be left in the realms of psychic research, by which means it was dragged to light. Certain it is that no such murder came to the knowledge of those who were alive then, and live still in Torquay.

If there is any truth in the story it falls under the category of undiscovered crimes. The murderer was able somehow to hide his iniquities, and escape suspicion and punishment. I do not know if it is intended to build another house on the same site. I hope not, for it is very probable that a new residence would share the fate of the old. Bricks and mortar are no impediment to the free passage of the disembodied, and there is no reason why they should not elect to manifest for an indefinite period of time.

There can be no doubt that the scream was an actual fact. There are so many people living who heard it, and are willing to testify to the horror of it. Amongst those living people are former tenants, who for long bore the nervous strain of its constant recurrence.

There remains one other weird incident in connection with "Castel a Mare" which I will now try to describe.

In the winter of 1917 I was engaged in war work which took me out at night. Like every other coast town Torquay was plunged at sunset into deepest darkness, save when the moon defied the authorities. The road leading from the nearest tramcar to our house was not lit at all, and one had to stumble along as best one could, even electric torches being forbidden.

I was returning home one very dark, still night about a quarter past ten, and being very tired I was walking very slowly. Owing to the inky darkness I thought it best to walk in the middle of the road, in order to avoid the inequalities in the footpath at each garden entrance to the villas. At that hour there was no traffic, and not a soul about.

Suddenly my steps were arrested by a loud knocking on a window-pane, and I collected my thoughts and tried to take my bearings. The sound came from the left, where two or three villas stand close to the road. All I could distinguish was a denser blot of black against the dense surroundings, but by making certain calculations I recognized that I stood outside "Castel a Mare." The knocking on the pane lasted only a moment or two, and was insistent and peremptory. I jumped to the instant conclusion that some one was having "a lark " inside, and was trying to "get a rise " out of me. I was too tired to be bothered, and moved on again with a strong inclination towards my own warm bed, when the knocking rang out more peremptory than ever. It seemed to say "Stop! don't go on. I have something to say to you." Involuntarily I stood still again, and wished that some human being would pass along the road. I really would not have cared who it was, policeman, soldier, maidservant. I would have laid hold of them and said, "Do you hear that knocking? It comes from the haunted house."

Alas! no one did come. The night lay like an inky pall all about me, silent as the grave, save for that commanding order to stop which was rapped upon a window-pane whenever I attempted to move on.

Though the being who thus sought to detain me could not possibly distinguish who I was, or whether my gender was male or female, he could certainly hear my footsteps as I walked, and the cool inconsequence of his behavior began to nettle me. I was about to move resolutely on when I heard something else. This time something really thrilling!

Peal after peal of light laughter, accompanied by flying feet. But such laughter! Thin, high treble laughter, right away up and out of the scale, and apparently proceeding from many persons. Such flying feet! racing, pattering, rushing feet, light as those of the trained athlete. I stood enthralled with wonder, for in the pitch-black darkness of that house surely no human feet could avoid disaster. They were rushing up and down that steep, bare wooden staircase that I knew so well, and the laughter and the swift-winged feet sounded now from the ground floor, then could be clearly traced ascending, till they reached the third and last floor. Tearing along the empty corridors, they began the breakneck descent again to the bottom, a pell-mell, wild rush of demented demons chasing each other. That is what it sounded like.

I must have stood there for quite ten minutes, longing intensely for some one to share in my experiences, but Torquay had gone to bed, and I felt it was time for me to do likewise.

What could I make of the affair? Nothing! Rats? Rats don't laugh. Human beings having a rag and trying to scare the neighborhood? No human being could have run up and down that staircase in such profound darkness. It would have been a case of crawling up with a firm hand on the banister rail.

I gave up trying to think and turned resolutely away. As I did so the knocking began again upon the window-pane.

"Do stop; oh! don't go away. Stop! stop!" it seemed to call after me insistently as I quickened my footsteps and gradually outdistanced the imperious demand.

What explanation have I to offer? None! The hallucinations of a tired woman? That may do for the general public, but not for me. You see, I was the person who heard it. There are many haunted houses that are quite habitable, such as Hampton Court Palace, etc. Where the apparition keeps strictly to an anniversary, or where the phenomena are mild and inoffensive, their presence can be endured with a certain amount of equanimity. The point really lies in this. Are the ghosts who haunt a dwelling indifferent to, or hostile to, the presence of their companions in the flesh? If the situation is according to the latter, then the ghosts will certainly score. They will rid themselves of the human inhabitants by a wearing-down nerve pressure, which cannot be fought against with any chance of success. If the ghosts are shy or indifferent, wrapped up in their own concerns and containing themselves in a world of their own, then there is no reason why the incarnate and discarnate should not live peacefully together.

To-day, February 27th, 1919, I read the following in the *Morning Post:*

Haunted or disturbed properties. A lady who has deeply studied this subject and possesses unusual powers will find out the history of the trouble and undertake to remedy it. Houses with persistent bad luck can often be freed from the influence. Strictest confidence. Social references asked and offered.

What would our grandparents have thought of this means of turning an honest penny? I have no doubt the lady "possessing the unusual powers" will be employed, and in many cases she will be successful. In the majority of cases I venture to say that she will fail, simply because the majority of cases are too elusive to be dealt with by human means. How would this lady treat the "Castel a Mare" scream? How would she deal with the next story I am going to relate?

It is a simple matter to compile a book of thrilling ghost stories if direct evidence is not given, if names of persons and places are suppressed. I claim that my stories have a special interest and value, because I have tried to restrict them to such as can be attested to by living persons, closely related to me either by friendship or by family ties. In a very few instances I have been obliged for obvious reasons to suppress the names of houses and hotels. In these cases I am ready personally to supply full information to genuine students of the occult, if they are willing to approach me privately.

Appendix:
Two American Ghost Hunts

I have confined the twelve cases in this book to haunted sites within the realm of Queen Victoria. Of course, ghost hunters were researching and surveilling houses alleged to be haunted in other countries, too, but I had to struggle to find *detailed,* credible chronicles of investigations that took place in my own, the United States. I suppose this is to be expected, given that the history of the New World has afforded it far fewer centuries-old, crumbling houses and almost no castles, the preferred habitats of the discriminating ghost.

Yet my research on a book titled *Spectral Edition: Ghost Reports from U.S. Newspapers, 1864-1917* (2017) confirms that plenty of specters were being documented stateside during Victoria's reign, and a few of the articles there involve reporters assuming the role of ghost hunters as do their Welsh colleagues in Case 10. Like that case, the articles I unearthed for that earlier project tend to be short and to the point: the accounts from witnesses are concise and the reporter's own surveillance of the haunted site is summarized briefly. The two chronicles that follow, on the other hand, are taken from prominent U.S. magazines—one from the north and one from the south—and provide a fuller and richer look into ghost hunting as portrayed by the American press during the Victorian era.

A Real Ghost Story

Anonymous[1]

The following narrative was obtained by the writer directly from the family of the person designated as Friend G.[2] The house supposed to be haunted was known as Clermont Seminary, and was once occupied by Carré and Sanderson, and afterward by the late David Griscom, as a boarding-school for boys. An engraved view of it will be found in the *Portfolio* of November, 1810, together with a description from the accomplished pen of the editor, Joseph Dennie.—ED.

I have often been solicited to relate the incidents of a ghost-hunting expedition which I once undertook, and my hearers generally were pleased to say that the account was quite interesting; and now, as the occupants of the haunted house have passed away, and the house itself was destroyed by fire not long since, I see no impropriety in telling the story to a larger circle of hearers. I will not weary the reader's patience any longer, but will plunge at once *in medias res,* only premising that the substance of the following narrative is strictly true.

Many years ago, one lovely spring morning, a number of wagons, loaded with household utensils, furniture, etc., the property of a worthy Friend, whom we will call G., might have been seen slowly approaching the junction of two roads near Frankford, Pennsylvania, then and now known as Hart and Nicetown lanes. Here all was hustle and confusion, for upon this day Friend G. and his family were to take possession of the elegant mansion, with its fine lawn, handsome trees and shrubbery, which stood a few hundred yards from the junction of the two lanes.

The grounds just at this time were not in the best order imaginable, owing to the fact that the house had for some time been unoccupied. This, however, was soon remedied, and, under the energetic management of Friend G., in a few months the walks were newly laid out, the shrubbery trimmed, grass cut and everything put in perfect order. The house itself needed few repairs. It was one of those antiquated buildings erected in the good old times when lumber was to be had in abundance and almost for the asking, and

---

[1] This appeared in *Lippincott's* 3 (May, 1869) pp. 561-66.
[2] The capitalized "Friend" suggests G. was a Quaker.

workmen knew not how to do other than the best of work. The present appearance of the ruins would indicate that even more than ordinary care and pains had been taken in its construction.

The main building was large, and nearly, if not quite, square, with two wings—one to the north, the other to the east. These were large and comfortable, and, in connection with the grounds, made the place admirably adapted to the purpose for which Friend G. designed it—viz., a boarding-school for boys. The main building was appropriated for dormitories and recitation-rooms, the east wing contained the lecture-room, while the first floor of the wing to the north was used as a kitchen and dining-room; and the second was occupied by Friend G. and his wife. As we have principally to do with this northern wing, we will describe it more particularly.

Upon opening the outer door you entered the kitchen, which was quite a large room. From this a passage-way led toward the main building, terminating in the dining-room. On the left of the passage-way were the stairs leading to the room occupied by Friend G. and his wife, which was directly over the kitchen.

Having made all the necessary arrangements for the comfortable accommodation of his scholars, Friend G. had no difficulty in obtaining them, for he was known far and wide as a successful instructor of the young; and thus September found him with a full school and every prospect of a remunerative year.

About the middle of October, when school had been in session a month or more, Friend G. and his wife were awakened in the night by hearing a noise at the kitchen door. This was followed by the opening and shutting of the door with violence; a great noise in the kitchen underneath, as of two persons struggling, and using every available article in the fight; then the sound as of rushing wind in the passage-way to the dining-room; and finally a noise like that made by twirling a large waiter on the floor and leaving it to die away.[3]

In all haste Friend G., considerably alarmed, descended the stairway, expecting that his house was about being robbed by burglars who had burst open the outer kitchen door. Imagine his astonishment, on opening the door into the kitchen, to find everything in perfect order, just as he had left it on retiring for the

---

[3] In this case, "waiter" means a large tray used for carrying, say, dishes or glasses.

night, the door locked, and nothing to indicate the presence of any one in the house. He carefully examined the passage-way and the dining-room, looked behind the doors and in the closets, but failed to find anything that would explain the cause of such a disturbance. With the conviction that he had been dreaming, and that in awaking his imagination had played him false, he once more retired to rest, and slept soundly until morning. But his wife had also heard the same sounds, so that they could not have been entirely imaginary. However, as they had failed to discover the cause, they dismissed the subject from their minds.

The next night they were awakened in the same manner, about the same time. The sounds they now heard were exactly similar to those of the preceding night, and, listening but a moment, Friend G., satisfied that there could be no mistake this time, rushed down stairs while the racket was going on in the kitchen, and opened the kitchen door. He could hardly believe his senses. Everything was still and silent as the grave; no sounds but those made by himself, not a chair displaced, or one thing other than as they had left it upon retiring. Perplexed beyond expression, he went up stairs to communicate the result to his wife, when immediately the noise recommenced, seemingly just where he had interrupted it, and terminated as on the preceding night. Another investigation followed, which was as unsuccessful as that of the night before. That both himself and his wife were worried at what they had heard, but could not explain, Friend G. would readily have admitted. Every-thing likely, and some things unlikely, were talked of as being the probable cause of their disturbance, but upon cool reflection none of them could satisfy our friends. The possibility that the scholars were playing them some trick was thought of; but, as they, as well as the servants, occupied the main building, and as there was no communication between these two portions of the house when everything was fastened for the night, this idea also was abandoned.

Night after night through the remainder of the month they were annoyed in this manner, and faithfully did they endeavor to obtain some clue to such mysterious proceedings, but without success.

Plain old Friends, knowing and believing nothing but matter-of-fact affairs, they no more believed in the existence of anything supernatural than you or I; and if any one had suggested the idea to them that uneasy spirits were troubled in the shadow-land at the injustice their bodies had received while upon the earth, they would not have listened to it for a moment. No: effects were the results of causes, and the causes must be manifest; so, with all the energy of persons determined to succeed, they endeavored to discover the causes which led to such mysterious results. Every night they tried some new plan, and every night failed to discover anything to explain the mystery. In this manner October passed away, when suddenly the sounds ceased to annoy them: absorbed in their varied cares and duties, the worthy couple no longer thought of them.

Time softens what were once disagreeable and annoying things, and displays them to us in a new and sometimes not an unpleasant light; and when our friends did recur to the mysterious disturbances of the previous autumn, it was not with that feeling of uneasiness and dread which they had experienced at the time of their occurrence, although they were still in ignorance as to their origin.

The summer months glided swiftly and pleasantly away, and October, with its fading leaves touched by the first frosts of winter, again appeared. With it came again the mysterious sounds that had so puzzled and annoyed them the preceding year. Again they endeavored to ascertain the cause, and again were they unsuccessful. The supposition that the scholars had something to do with it was not to be thought of now, as most of them had not been there the previous year, and it was not likely that new pupils should have hit upon the same trick as the old ones.

The baffled searchers feared to mention what they heard to any one, well knowing that if the servants knew anything about it they would not stay, and that, most probably, it would be injurious to their school; so they strictly kept their own counsel, and hoped, like Micawber, that something would "turn up."[4]

But October again passed without leaving them any wiser. They had now tried every plan they could think of, but were just as much in ignorance as on the first night of the disturbance. What was to be done? That there was something supernatural in these mysterious sounds, this matter-of-fact couple could not for one moment believe; and yet, with all their care and penetration, they could not discover that these noises were the result of any human agency.

---

4 Wilkins Micawber, from Charles Dickens' *David Copperfield* (1850), is characterized by hopefulness, trusting that "something will turn up."

They were not frightened, as was evident from the manner in which they investigated the affair, going down in the dark together and alone, sitting up till the hour when the noises generally were heard, sometimes with, and sometimes without, a light; still, there was a something mysterious about it, which was anything but pleasant to them, and they earnestly hoped for a solution of the problem.

Four years passed away in this manner. Early in the fifth year Mrs. G. was taken ill, and a woman living in the neighborhood was employed to nurse her. Mrs. G. was so ill as to render it necessary for her to keep her bed, and, as it was quite cool, she had a fire burning in her room. One evening the nurse forgot to bring up the wood for the night until the servants had gone to bed and the house was locked up. When she discovered this, she seemed afraid to go down stairs after it. There was that coupled with her reluctance which convinced Mrs. G. that there was something more than mere fear of the dark which influenced the nurse, and she immediately desired to know what it was.

The nurse tried to evade the question, but that was not to be done when Mrs. G. asked it; so she finally said that people in the neighborhood had told her the house was haunted; and, turning to Mrs. G., she asked,

"Did you ever hear any noises here?"

"Yes," replied Mrs. G., "we have: my husband says it must be the rats; but tell me, what do people say about the house?"

This the nurse did not wish to do as Mrs. G. was an invalid, but she would listen to no objections, and finally drew from the nurse the following story. What she said corresponded so exactly with their own experiences that Mrs. G. wrote it down as soon as she was able, and we give it here in the nurse's own language:

THE NURSE'S STORY.

"Well, ma'am, it isn't much of a story, but folks around here say this house is haunted, and this is what they say about it: The house was built by a Frenchman, who lived in it a little while and then went back to France, leaving it in charge of an old servant who had come here with him. This old man was very cross and crabbed, and used to frighten the boys whom he caught about the house almost out of their wits, and the whole neighborhood disliked him. One cold, stormy night about the middle of October, a peddler came to the kitchen door and asked the old man, who was alone in the house, to let him stay over night, as there was no tavern near. Well, ma'am, the old man was very cross that day, and he refused to let the peddler in, and would not even let him sleep in the shed. The peddler was very angry, and when at last the old man tried to put him out the kitchen door, he struck him. Then they went at it, scuffling all over the kitchen: they threw the firewood at each other, and anything else that came in their way, till the peddler, finding the old man was getting the better of him, ran into the entry leading to the dining-room, and the old man followed him and snatched a knife from the sideboard and killed him. Leastways, that is how the story is told; and it is certain the peddler was seen going toward the house and was never heard of afterward; and folks do say, ma'am, that every October the peddler comes again to the door, and the old man fights him, and, at last, chases him into the dining-room and murders him. And you see, ma'am, nobody ever lives here long, because they say they hear such noises at nights that they can't sleep."

The interest with which Mrs. G. listened to the story of the nurse can easily be imagined. It corresponded so exactly with their own experience, and was so startling in its details, that, had the nurse but glanced at the countenance of her mistress, she might easily have surmised that her story was the solving of some mystery to her attentive listener. But by the time she had finished, Mrs. G. had regained her usual composed and quiet manner, and with the remark that she should never think of such foolish stories and should never repeat them, dismissed her for the night.

The coming of October was now looked forward to with an indescribable feeling of uneasiness and dread. To make further efforts to discover the origin of the sounds seemed useless, and the knowledge that there was something connected with the house which, while they did not, could not, believe was supernatural, they yet were unable to explain, began to work upon their minds to such an extent that they thought it best to break up their school and move to some other place. This they did; but although this move on their part was unaccountable to their friends, yet they did not choose to tell any one the real reason for it, partly because they wished to see whether other persons would occupy the house undisturbed, and partly because they did not wish to put in circulation a story of this character unless they could offer a satisfactory explanation with it. Their experience in the Old Academy was not made public until many years afterward, and until they had satisfied themselves that there were mysteries connected with the building which were manifested to others as well as to them; for no one from that time until the present has occupied the house for more than a year or two at a time.

I heard this story from the lips of Friend G.'s daughter, who lived in the house at the time. She is still living, and will tell you the story just as I have told it. When I first heard it, and understood also that the house was still standing uninhabited, I resolved that I would visit it, would stay all night in it, and see if these strange, mysterious sounds could be heard. How this was accomplished, and the result thereof, I shall now tell you.

I was in Philadelphia about the middle of October of last year, and having some leisure time on my hands, decided to fulfill my long-intended plan and spend a night in the "Old Academy," as it is still called in the neighborhood. I mentioned my intention one evening to some friends, when they immediately volunteered to accompany me, declaring they would like nothing better than to see or, as in this instance, to hear—a real ghost. Quite a party was made up, and finally twelve of us set out about nine o'clock in the evening for the old house. I had seen in the morning the person who was in charge of the property, and told him of our wish to spend the night there, and obtained a ready permission. I then spoke of the stories in circulation, and inquired if he had ever heard anything there which corroborated them. He said yes; that they had heard noises the night before; that he had gone down stairs quickly, but could not find any one, but that he was not afraid; and I went away quite impressed with his courage.

We approached the house about ten o'clock, and we all agreed we had never seen a more lonely and deserted-looking building. It stood, as I have said before, at the junction of two lanes. A row of tall, stately Lombardy poplars stood along one side of it, and looked very ghostly and melancholy in the pale light of the new moon. However, nothing daunted by the weird appearance of the house, with its peaked roof now silvered by the moonlight, we boldly marched up to the door and knocked. There was no answer, and we knocked and knocked again. Again no direct response, but we heard dogs barking violently; and finally, after more knocking, a window was thrown open in the upper story, and the occupant of the house, whom I had seen in the morning, thrust his head out. In answer to our demands to be let in, he besought us in frightened accents to leave. In vain I reminded him of our agreement of the morning: he evidently considered us robbers, and was determined not to admit us. We were highly indignant at this breach of contract, and concluded to force an entrance into the ground-floor of the north wing, where the spectres were supposed to reign. Again we walked around the house through the long grass, now wet with the dew, and passed the door whence the barking of the dogs had proceeded. To our astonishment, this door was ajar, and we saw the dogs quietly sleeping by the fire. I advanced a short distance into the room and asked in a loud voice if the door had been left open for us to enter. Receiving no reply, I repeated my question—again in vain; when I returned to my party outside. After remaining undecided for a short time, we at length concluded that it was better not to enter there, but to go to the north wing. We easily got in there, and taking up our quarters in the dining-room, proceeded to make ourselves as comfortable as circumstances would allow.

As the last train for the city left in a short time, a lady and gentleman of our party, who wished to return then, resolved to abandon the ghost-hunt, and therefore started for the cars. But our obstinacy—shall I say?—had been aroused by the obstacles thrown in our path, and one and all we were eager to see the dénoûment.

As the night was cool, a deputation of gentlemen, myself among the number, was sent to collect wood for a fire. It was certainly very romantic in the tangled shrubbery around this desolate old house in the moonlight; but the grass was very wet, and we were decidedly relieved when we had gathered sufficient fuel and had a roaring fire in the great chimney-place. The fire cast its genial light and warmth upon our chilled company, and awakened by its glow that cheerfulness which a wood-fire was said to have produced upon our forefathers. Talking and laughing, we sat around it, but as the time drew nigh—"The very witching time when churchyards yawn"—we grew quieter, and told ghost stories fit to make one's hair stand on end. One succeeded another, until, finally, some one said, "Now is the time: it is twelve o'clock." The fire had died down and gave but a glimmering light: our every faculty was on the utmost stretch, every ear was strained to catch the slightest sound, when suddenly we heard a noise on the porch. We looked at each other with frightened faces: still the noise increased and seemed to come nearer, and now it was like the tread of soldiers— tramp, tramp, nearer and nearer—till finally the door opened slowly. The figure of a man appeared, and in marched, one after the other, about twenty armed men. They slowly filed in, and then stood glaring at us. Our nerves had been terribly wrought upon; but now that the vague dread, more paralyzing because it was vague, was changed to a sensation rather of physical fear, the revulsion came, and we felt more able to combat our bodily than any spiritual visitants. In their train, carefully guarded on either side by two rough laborers, were the lady and gentleman who had started some time previously for the cars. They cast despairing glances at us, as if imploring us to attempt their rescue. One of the boldest of our party came forward, and addressing the man who seemed to be foremost, and who held a rusty gun, demanded the cause of this startling intrusion. He answered by telling us to leave immediately—that they had come to compel us to quit the premises. We replied that we had received permission from the man who lived there to stay that night, and that we had come to see the ghosts which were supposed to haunt the house. Then, catching sight of the man himself, who was shrinking behind the others, and seemed in a panic of fear, I called to him to come forward and verify our statement. Every one looked toward him as he advanced, trembling and shaking, his knees knocking together and with a most terrified expression of countenance. He was evidently in mortal fear of us, and denied he had given us any permission to stay there. But, after some further conversation with the leader, we managed to persuade him we were not a band of robbers, as they had supposed, but a party of ghost-seekers. They were finally persuaded to refrain from marching us, ladies and all, ignominiously back to the station; and after further protest we were allowed to spend the night in the haunted room. But, alas! when these rude disturbers of our peace had departed after liberating their captives, the ghostly dwellers, frightened by their clamor, refused to gladden our sight or hearing, and we passed the night quite comfortably, but not at all romantically. The next morning we returned to the city in the early train, making ourselves merry over our night's mishaps.

I had some further conversation with the leader of the invaders, in which he described the manner of their alarm. The man who lived in the "Old Academy " was his son-in-law, lately married, and, as he expressed it, "hadn't much wit, anyhow." The couple had been terribly alarmed by our coming, and, incited by his wife, the man had run to his father-in-law's and aroused him with the report that a band of robbers had taken possession of his domicile. The farmer and his sons had armed in haste with scythes, axes and every weapon they could find, and, arousing the neighbors, had marched upon us. The farmer said, moreover, that one or two of us had run a great chance of being shot while gathering wood, as they were concealed in the shrubbery all about, and only refrained from shooting, fearing that the noise would give warning of their approach to the supposed robbers within. A cold shudder ran through me as I thought our frolic might have had a tragical termination.

Since our memorable visit I have always kept myself informed of the welfare of the "Old Academy," though never again revisiting it; and it was with quite a feeling of pain that I heard lately of its demolition without any farther revelation of its mysteries.

✣

A Night in a Haunted House

Anonymous[5]

Within a stone's throw of the line of the Richmond and Petersburg rail-road, and no more than half a mile from James river, stand the blackened and roofless walls of a large brick building. Its position on a naked and barren hill renders it visible in some directions for several miles; and from various parts of Richmond, especially from the southern windows of the Capitol, it still forms a conspicuous object in the distant landscape. If the reader is not a resident of that vicinity, but has passed along the rail-road between Richmond and Petersburg, before the fire occurred by which the wood work of the building was a few months since destroyed, he may have been struck by the lone and desolate appearance of the house, and been led to make some inquiry respecting it: and if his question was asked of one in any degree familiar with neighborhood traditions, he was informed, among other particulars, that the place had long had the reputation of being haunted.

Indeed, its situation alone might well raise evil surmises in minds of a superstitious turn. No other house stood near it; no pale

---

5 This appeared in the *Southern Literary Messenger* 21.6 (June, 1855) pp. 374-80.

or hedge enclosed it; no tree or shrub or flower grew in its vicinity; nothing but the bare and sterile heath, over which a few consumptive cows and lean broken-down horses turned out to die, wandered about in quest of such subsistence as the place afforded. Its unsheltered site exposed it to every wind that blows, especially to the north wind, which, sweeping across the river from the hills on the Richmond side, raved and roared about the old mansion in such a way as to put timorous misgivings into the heart of any chance tenant who happened to occupy it. If he was right who said that superstition

"Can yells of demons in the zephyr hear,"

then certainly superstition might have heard a whole legion of demons yelling in the winds that howled round the old haunted house.

It was built by a man of wealth and standing in the days of our grandfathers. Why he selected so singular a site, I have never been able to learn. But the old gentleman was a sort of humorist in his way, and no doubt had his own reasons for the choice. Perhaps he was ambitious to cover the barren hill with groves and gardens, and make the desert heath blossom like the rose. If such was his plan, however, the fates were against it; for whether the strange sights and sounds that gave the house its evil reputation made it an unpleasant residence to him, or whatever else was the cause, it is certain he abandoned it before any sort of out-of-door improvement had been made.

After his departure, the place fell from time to time to various tenants, who were attracted by the low rate of rent. None, however, remained long; for it was remarked that misfortune seemed to brood over the house; that sickness and death were alarmingly frequent within its walls; and that whether its stately halls and pannelled chambers were haunted by preternatural visitants or not, they certainly were singularly often the scenes of the heaviest afflictions that human life is heir to.

It is now many years since I paid the old house a visit. My curiosity was excited by the current tales in regard to it; for I always had rather a taste for superstitious marvels. I found it a large and stately building, finished within in the old aristocratic style of Virginia; though its fine mahogany pannelling had been soiled and defaced in many places by the carelessness of tenants, who had of late always been persons in humble life. At the time of my visit, it had been but a few weeks abandoned, and several pieces of furniture of small value were still left in some of the rooms. In one of the principal chambers I observed an old black-walnut cup-board, which may have been used as a wardrobe, a stick-backed chair without the top-board, and a black hair sofa, on which lay a single ragged cushion covered with the same material. On seeing the old sofa the thought occurred to me that as the weather was warm and no covering required, it might be made a tolerable couch for the night, if I had courage enough to despise the popular stories about the place, and defy the powers of evil that were supposed to hold their revels there. The thought I confess was a little startling; but I considered myself quite a philosopher for my years (then about 19) and was vain enough to think such idle superstitions as shook the souls of the weak and credulous were far below that serene region in which my thoughts were accustomed to soar.

In short, I resolved to pass the night in the haunted house, and thus put to proof my courage and philosophy. Accordingly I returned to Richmond; and after nightfall, having wrapped up a candle in a newspaper, and put a book and match-box in one coat pocket, and a loaded pistol in the other, set forth without communicating my purpose to any one. It may raise a smile to think I should arm myself against ghosts with a pocket pistol, and I might have been puzzled to give a reason for the precaution; but I felt that my courage could somehow be firmer, and less liable to surprise by any sudden assault, if I had such a staunch and trusty supporter at hand in case of need.

It was a clear, moonlight night in midsummer, and the walk, though long, was not unpleasant. The lonely old building looked particularly grim by moonlight, and I felt an uneasy misgiving as I approached it. But I had gone too far to think of retreating. An old white horse that in the moon's uncertain light had a pale and ghostly appearance, stood a few rods from the front porch. I walked up to him in order to be quite sure that he was a veritable thing of earth; for I had no wish to be assailed by a doubt from this quarter in the midst of such a mental conflict as I might have to pass through before the night should be over. He made no movement to avoid me, but gazed mournfully at me with his large hollow eyes, as I patted his shoulder and addressed him in some kind sympathizing words. He seemed, I thought, to be worn out with years and privation, and evidently not destined to a much longer sojourn in this world of sorrow. He turned his head and looked wistfully after me when I left him; but I could do nothing to lighten his grief, and therefore endeavoured to dismiss his case from my thoughts.

The front door was open, just as I had left it in the morning. I paused on the threshold an instant, and then bracing my nerves with a long, deep breath, entered and stood a few feet within the hall. All seemed deserted, and still as a churchyard at midnight. The moon shining through the casements shewed me the staircase leading to the room I had selected, and I commenced ascending. Every step resounded through the great empty house with a prolonged reverberation that was almost appalling. But I kept steadily on, partly groping and partly guided by the moonlight, till I stood safe in my destined apartment. I lost no time in lighting the candle by means of a match, and then looked carefully round to see that no lurking thing of evil lay hidden in any of the recesses. All was empty and still, and no enemy near. I next cast about for some sort of candlestick; and finding no better substitute, trimmed to a sharp point one of the sticks of the broken chair, and impaling the candle firmly upon it, placed it conveniently near the end of the sofa. I then reclined upon the sofa: propping up my head with the cushion, which I first carefully covered with my handkerchief, as I much misdoubted the heads that had been pillowed there before mine. Finally, I drew the book from my pocket; and resolving to give imagination the least possible leisure for idle vagacies, tried to immerse all my thoughts in reading.

The volume I had brought was Pliny's Epistles. I had some recollection of a story told by him about a haunted house, in which a sage old Greek had ventured to pass the night; and fancying a resemblance between him and myself in more points than one, I had a curiosity to learn the issue of his adventure.[6] The letter I was in search of was soon found; but I quickly began to suspect that the choice of that story for my evening's entertainment was not very judicious, and that the disparity between the force of will and reason shown by the old philosopher, and that I could call up at need, was somewhat broader than I had imagined. The story is

---

[6] The writer is referring to Pliny the Younger's letter about Athenodorus, the granddaddy of ghost hunters. This legendary figure's adventure in a haunted house is discussed in this book's Introduction.

indeed a striking one, and impressively told. I shuddered as I read, lest a spectre like that described, of the old man, squalid and emaciated, with his long neglected beard, and clanking his iron fetters as he walked, should visit me in my lonely room. Several times I almost started at what seemed the sound of human footsteps in the adjoining apartment. I listened attentively, and thought the noises, though strangely loud for such a cause, were produced by the multitude of rats with which the old house abounded. They scampered about in every direction, squeaking and gibbering in such a way as to deepen the vague feeling of terror which, in spite of all my philosophy, I found was fast creeping over me. They seemed not to have abandoned the house since its human occupants left it: perhaps the long waste of naked common that must have been traversed before reaching any other habitation deterred them from migrating. But to judge from the commotion among them, famine had begun its work, and was inciting a predatory cannibal war among themselves. The sounds of fierce struggling, and the shrieks of pain, sometimes so startling and loud as to make me doubt the real nature of the combatants, appeared to indicate when a death grapple had commenced; and deepened the effect which night and solitude, and the ghost story I had been reading, had already produced on my imagination.

I had, however, in my own esteem, quite too much manhood to be seriously disconcerted by a horde of rats, numerous and savage as they might be; so, calling in my straggling thoughts and rebuking my wandering attention, I again turned to the courtly old Roman, resolving to keep imagination under a steady control, as became a philosopher. But this wise resolution was destined to a speedy trial. Suddenly there issued from the next room the most demoniac yell I ever heard, which made me bound quite up from the sofa on which I was lying. Again the frightful sound arose; but accompanied this time with certain sputtering noises and lengthened wailing cadences, which I had heard too often to find a difficulty in recognizing. "They are only cats, after all," I mentally exclaimed; "but, bless my soul! how much like devils in conflict their voices sound." Taking the candle from its stick, I advanced to the next room, though with some trepidation; for old tales of the alliance of cats with the infernal powers officiously forced themselves upon my memory at the instant. On entering the room, immediately two of these animals, one grey and white, the other as black as a demon, rushed out of the opposite door, and down the stair case. A minute after, I heard their voices in a second conflict far off in the direction of the river.

Returning to my room, I readjusted the candle and lay down again. It was now nearly one o'clock, and the fresh night breeze blowing through the open window had melted the spermaceti so rapidly that only two or three inches remained. Thinking it more prudent to reserve this portion for any emergency which might require a light, I extinguished the candle, and tried to compose myself to sleep. This was the less difficult, as the long walk had fatigued me considerably. How long I slept I cannot tell, but probably only a short time, when I was waked by a heavy pressure on the chest. The moonlight was sufficient to show me the cause of the disturbance. The large black cat I had chased out of the adjoining room had returned; and seated on my breast, was gazing intently into my face with his great glassy eyes. I gave him a smart blow with my clenched hand, on which he bounded away and disappeared. I then rose, and determined to exclude for the rest of the night all such intruders, bolted the door; after which I returned to the sofa and lay down again, musing on the occurrences of the evening. The old black cat's visit appeared a little singular. There were some nursery tales about cats destroying infants by sucking their breath; a charge which is physically absurd, but which might have arisen from occurrences like that of which I had been made the subject. The instinct seemed strange, and its object not easily guessed; but might in some way be connected with the mysterious fascination the human form seems often to exercise over the inferior animals, when not counteracted by fear.

It was quite evident, that nothing strange or unnatural had happened to me during the evening. Still, if my imagination could be excited by such trivial causes, then certainly I was not the man to undertake such philosophic knight-errantry as attacking popular superstitions and expelling ghosts from haunted houses. If any thing should occur during the night of such a nature as to baffle all my attempts to explain it, it was impossible to say how far my nervous system might be deranged, or my reason disordered, by phantoms of my own creation. On the whole, it might be better to abandon the enterprise, and late as it was, return to Richmond to pass the night. But then, on the other hand, I was ashamed to confess even to myself that I was afraid of my own imagination, as children fear the dark, and as to ghosts, my reason, I flattered myself, was so well fortified against them, that even if one should actually appear wrapped in its winding sheet, and gliding through the room in the stealthy noiseless way which seems the approved mode among them, I should still have sense enough to despise the spectre as a mere dreaming fancy, or some other illusion quite as unreal. I concluded therefore to stay the night out, come what might; for I was determined not to yield to apprehensions which even a schoolboy ought to be ashamed of.

Feeling more secure with the door bolted, I soon sunk to sleep again; during which I had a dream that took its complexion in some degree from my present situation. I found myself in an old deserted castle, which seemed to belong to days of feudal antiquity. It was surrounded and in part overshadowed by a dark grove of gigantic oaks, that added gloom and awe to the solitude of the place. The wind which moaned sullenly through the trees dashed the shutters against the sides of the building, and made the old broken doors creak, and the walls shake, as it swept through the long empty halls. Impelled by curiosity, I wandered about from one apartment to another, till I came to a square aperture cut out of the floor, from which was seen the upper portion of a ladder communicating with the darkness below. I descended a few steps, and then, resting on one of the rounds of the ladder, gazed intently into the vaulted recess that opened before me. Something like a human figure indistinctly seen in the dim obscurity of the place arrested my attention. Shading my brow to exclude the light from above, I looked again; and my eye becoming accustomed to the darkness, I was enabled to discern an object from which I recoiled in horror. It was the body of a man suspended by a rope, and so near me that if he had been alive, I might have felt his breath upon my face. His strained staring eye-balls, his clenched and grinning teeth, and his distorted features, livid and swollen with the blood forced back from the heart by the cord around his neck, were frightful indications if his last agony. I hastily ascended the ladder on which I stood, and was hurrying away from the place, when my dream was suddenly dispersed, and I started awake and trembling at some dreadful sound. Something I had heard acted to alarm me, I could not mistake in that; but what it was, I was at an utter loss to conjecture. The cats in the next room occurred to me; but I was fully convinced that in this case they were not the cause of the disturbance. I listened attentively; but all was still, except the commotion among the rats, which still continued, though much abated, and the sighing and whistling of the wind, that had risen while I slept. I was beginning to doubt whether it was not all a mere dreaming illusion, when a sound, which I at once recognized as what had made me start in terror from sleep, burst upon the silence and reechoed through the house. It seemed a hollow, maniac laughter, choked and throttled by sudden strangulation. A second time it resounded from the next room, and a moment after appeared to float upon the air without the building. I was now terribly frightened. All my philosophy vanished in an instant, for such unearthly sounds could scarcely be imagined to proceed from a thing of this world. I lay trembling with terror, and covered with a cold sweat; but what was my horror when, a few minutes after, the hideous sounds were heard in the very room I occupied. Starting half erect from the sofa, I saw by the light of the setting moon, which now shone broadly in at the western window, what seemed an enormous spectral head, with horns and great glaring eyes, peering from above the old cupboard in the corner. With a suppressed shriek I fell back upon the sofa; on which the phantom spread its wings, and gliding out of the nearest window, again sent forth a peal of fiendish laughter, as if in derision. It was an owl, the great horned owl of Virginia.

I was now too much agitated to sleep again. These repeated alarms had disordered my imagination so far that it had become a prey to all sorts of fancies; and the reason which by daylight derided superstitious tales failed me at my utmost need. The casual remarks of some grave and reverend men of former days in favor of the reappearance of the dead, and of the interposition of preternatural agencies in human affairs, were now brought to my recollection with a vivid distinctness and almost a convincing force. Dr. Johnson declares it is impossible to account for the belief in ghosts among nearly all nations except by supposing the reality of their appearance. Wesley and Davies, both pious and able divines, entertained similar opinions, and Addison, in a number of the *Spectator* written expressly to combat popular superstitions, did not venture to disavow all belief in the visits of phantoms from the world of spirits.[7] If then such men had to bow their minds to the weight of evidence, was not my contrary belief so dogmatically held, a vain presumption? It is true, nothing had occurred during the night which might not be easily explained on natural principles. Cats and owls are apt to haunt deserted buildings, especially when peopled with rats as this house was. But still, the concurrence of so many startling incidents was singular; and might have been designed by some preternatural power to punish that proud conceit of my own reason which had led me into the present undertaking. There might have been more reality in the Nemesis of the ancient belief than I suspected—possibly old Herodotus had some reason in ascribing so much of human casualty to that jealousy of the gods which punished pride, rather than to merely natural causes.[8] And who could tell what more I might have to pass through during the night, as the proper punishment of my presumption?

It is surprising what an effect thoughts of this kind, which came thronging into my brain, had upon my excited imagination. The arguments by which ordinarily I might have repelled them, either refused to come at my bidding, or seemed to have lost all force. In this state I remained a considerable time, my mind tossed to and fro, in the contest between fear and reason, and my disturbed fancy

---

[7] The tradition of attributing this claim, made by one of Johnson's fictional characters, to Johnson himself is discussed in the Introduction. John Wesley (1703-1791), a key figure in the Methodist Church, claimed his father's house was haunted. Andrew Jackson Davis (1826-1910), aka the Poughkeepsie Seer, was a self-proclaimed prophet whose books and lectures paved a path for the surge of Spiritualism beginning in the mid-1800s. Joseph Addison (1672-1719) co-founded *The Spectator,* a publication featuring Addison's essays on a variety of topics. The anonymous writer here might be confusing Addison's essay combatting superstitions, which suggests replacing them with faith in God, with a later essay in which he admits to siding less with historians who deem "the appearances of spirits fabulous and groundless" and more with living people who claim to have encountered a ghost and "whom I cannot distrust in other matters of fact." See *Spectator* 7 (March 8, 1711) pp. 35-39 and 110 (July 6, 1711) p. 128.

[8] In ancient Greek religion, Nemesis punishes those guilty of hubris (or arrogance). In Herodotus's *Histories* (c. 440 BCE), Crœsus, King of Lydia, asks wise Solon to name the happiest of men, hoping the answer will be the king himself, given his great wealth. However, Solon lists others, angering Crœsus. Solon explains that "the divine Nemesis is always jealous of man's happiness, and delights in confounding him in his greatest prosperity. . . . I cannot judge of the happiness of your life until I hear how your life has terminated" (J. Talboy Wheeler, *The Life and Travels of Herodotus* [Vol. 2, Longman, Brown, Green, and Longmans, 1855] p. 255). In other words, Crœsus might find his fortune reversed as a punishment for his hubris.

incessantly conjuring up fresh sources of alarm. Meanwhile the question of returning to Richmond was again suggested. But the moon was now set, and a cloud which had for some time been gathering had overcast the sky and rendered the night intensely dark. I thought I should probably be unable to find my way back to the city before daylight. Then I should have a difficulty in rousing the toll keeper on the bridge, and a still greater difficulty in gaining access to my own room at such an hour. But what I most dreaded was, lest some of the household should be led to make enquiries which would disclose where and how I had passed the night, and the ignominious result of my enterprise. Such a discovery with the ridicule it would call forth, was too much to be borne; and the fear of that had as much effect as any thing else in determining me to spend the entire night in the haunted house, and confront my fate, whatever it might be. I therefore lay quiet on the sofa, composing my thoughts as well as I could, but not daring to dispel the darkness by lighting my short end of candle, lest it should burn out before day, and leave me without the possibility of a light, whatever emergency might call for one. There could not, I thought, be more than an hour or two of darkness remaining, and that time I hoped to pass without farther disturbance. But in this I was destined to a signal disappointment.

The house had now become comparatively quiet. The rats no longer ranged about with the same restless energy, or fought with the same fury, as before. Except an occasional squeak, or a slight scrambling noise, they were now silent and still. The darkness, it seemed, was too thick and impenetrable, to allow even them, imps of the night as they were, to roam about with freedom. The pattering of the rain, which had begun to fall, was almost the only sound audible. I was beginning to feel the soothing influence of this continued quiet, and my imaginations were gradually assuming a less excited cast.

But an indistinct noise of what sounded like irregular tottering footsteps at length reached my ear. I listened with a beating heart and an undefined dread, fearing the sounds were the precursor of something terrible. Nor did my apprehension deceive me. A noise as of violent struggling ensued, followed by a dreadful groan which seemed to roll upon my ear out of the pitchy darkness in which my room was shrouded. And such a groan, so long, deep and agonizing, surely never fell on mortal ears before. It was such as might have come from one of the lost spirits of Dante's Inferno—so much of hopeless convulsive anguish seemed poured out in the sound. Then followed a heavy stamping and struggling, as of hoofs on the floor, and again and again those awful groans resounded through the house. At length the sounds grew fainter, appearing to come far and farther away from the depths below; as if the condemned spirit my terrified imagination supposed it to be, had been seized by his jailor demon, and borne struggling downward to the dark prison from which he had escaped. All this time I lay half-mad with terror. Indeed I think I must have been for a time in a high delirium; for I lost all distinct consciousness of my situation, and fancied myself begirt by such horrible phantoms, as only an insane imagination could have presented. Devils grinned in my face, and yelled blasphemies in my ear: sheeted ghosts glided by gazing at me with their dead rayless eyes; and cold clammy corpses laid their lifeless faces against mine, and sought to fold me in their embraces. How my reason escaped an utter wreck I can scarcely conceive; but surely no one ever approached nearer the gulf of raving madness, without falling into it, than I then did.

At last I began to recover consciousness, and found that the day was perceptibly dawning. My courage in some degree revived; and I ventured to hope I might after all survive that dreadful night. Still, my limbs were twitching convulsively with nervous excitement, and I feared to move, or look around, lest some frightful spectre should blast my view. I remained therefore, lying on the sofa, trembling and anxious, till it grew light enough to distinguish surrounding objects clearly. I then summoned courage to look around my room, almost expecting some strange and terrible sight would meet my glance. Everything, however, appeared just as I had left it when the candle was extinguished the night before. At length I rose and opened the door, glancing fearfully into the next room as I passed through the passage. But nothing was to be seen that could help to explain the mystery. I then descended the stairs, and reaching the front-door, was about to sally forth, too glad to escape from such a pandemonium; when I was startled and shocked to find the old white horse of the night before lying dead on the porch steps, with his head and forefeet resting on the flooring of the porch, which in some places was smeared with blood and foam. I gazed at him a moment, with a feeling of pity, not unmoved with terror, and then forcing my way with some difficulty (for his body left but a narrow passage) I hurried from the fatal house.

My mind was still so much disturbed by the deep agitations it had recently suffered, that for a time I never thought of connecting the frightful sounds of the previous night with the death of the poor old horse. But while walking across Mayo's bridge on my way to the city, the truth flashed upon me at once. He had been seized with one of those painful disorders to which that species of animal is subject—perhaps intestinal worms gnawing his vitals and causing intolerable anguish. In his distress he remembered having seen me enter the haunted house; and with that instinct which drives domestic animals to seek relief from men, he endeavoured to make his way up the porch stair-case he had seen me ascend. But his strength failed, and he sunk on the steps; and the dreadful sounds which had driven me almost to madness were the groans and convulsions of his dying agony. How I came to think the noise proceeded from my own room, I cannot well explain. Perhaps terror, combined with the startling loudness of the reverberation through the old empty house in the dead of night, may have suffered to produce the illusion.

I returned to the city, not a little humbled and crest-fallen, and reached my place of abode before the family had risen. The night's adventures, I kept a secret from every one: for I had no mind to encounter the ridicule which my ambitious design and ignoble failures merited: but they taught me such a lesson that I have never since then ventured to play the philosophic hero, or indulged the conceit of a mission to attack and exterminate popular super-stitions:

—Sum paulo infirmior, unus
Multorum—[9]

has been my modest self-estimate since the events of that memorable night.

If the reader is disposed to sneer at the timidity displayed under the circumstances I have recounted, permit me to suggest that he can scarcely anticipate how he would himself act in a like situation, unless his strength of nerve has been fairly proved by

---

[9] A line from the ninth poem in Horace's *Satires,* this Latin phrase means "I am something weaker, one of the multitude." In other words, the ghost hunter has been humbled, and he's now on the same level as most people.

some similar trial. In ordinary conjunctures my courage, I flatter myself, may compare with that of other men. But the imagination, when fully roused, is an agent of fearful power; and my own experience recommends it as a safe and wise maxim, never to subject it, without necessity, to dangerous experiments, in which it may escape beyond the control of the judgment, and lay reason prostrate in the dust.

About the Editor

With a doctorate degree in English, Tim Prasil has taught at the university level, specializing in American literature from the 1800s and early 1900s and in popular genres, such as ghost stories and science fiction. He researches the histories of quirky genres of fiction with the goal of compiling the entertaining yet informative anthologies that make up the Phantom Traditions Library, published by his independent imprint: Brom Bones Books.

Prasil also writes fiction about a ghost hunter named Vera Van Slyke. She appears in two novels: *Guilt Is a Ghost* and *Help for the Haunted*. Interested readers can start with either novel. *The Lost Limericks of Edgar Allan Poe* is a collection of 100 limericks inspired by the great author's work, life, and spirit. All three works are also available from Brom Bones Books.

The same publisher offers *Spectral Edition: Ghost Reports in U.S. Newspapers, 1864-1917*, in which Prasil presents the best of his extensive collection of actual articles about haunted houses and graveyards, haunted roads and rivers, even haunted people.

One more thing: "Tim Prasil" rhymes with *grim fossil*. Flattering, ain't it?

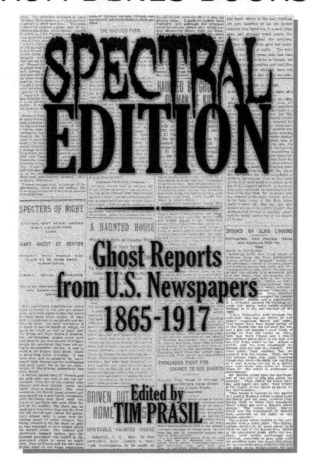

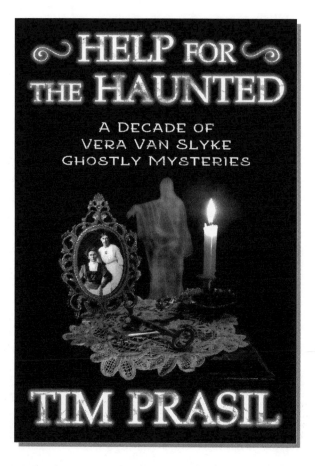

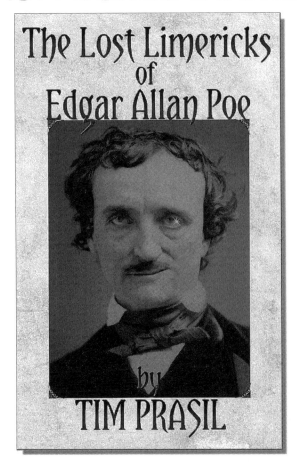

Made in the USA
Middletown, DE
01 April 2021

36688649R00130